议论其实并不难

高中英语议论文写作教学研究

孙饴 著

上海教育出版社
SHANGHAI EDUCATIONAL
PUBLISHING HOUSE

嘉定区第五届名师名校长培养工程成果书系
编委会

主　编：田晓余　管文洁

副主编：许敏杰　王巍清　李　娟　许晓芳

编　委：王冰清　李珊珊　颜晓莉　钱丽君

顾　问：凤光宇

总　序

嘉定区教育系统"名师名校长"培养工程至今已经圆满走过了五届。多年来，依托培养工程，持续发挥区域名师名校长的引领、辐射和示范作用，致力培养一批师德高尚、教学与管理特色鲜明，在全区乃至全市有影响力的优秀人才，为建设高素质专业化创新型教师队伍，推进教育高位均衡发展提供有力保障。

一流的教育需要一流的人才。"双名工程"牢牢把握"人才是第一资源、创新是第一动力"的要义，将"成才"放在首位，一批具有教育情怀、仁爱之心、专业追求的工作室主持人以其人格魅力和教育智慧给学员以精神滋养，成为带动全区教师与校长成长成才的第一资源。与此同时，"双名工程"强调"成事"并重，通过打造基于共同愿景的学习共同体，激励教师与校长立足教育实践场域开展研习，创新解决教学和管理难题。由此，"成才"与"成事"相辅相成，理论与实践紧密结合，形成了螺旋式上升发展，为更好建设"名师名校长"培养工程提供了诸多宝贵经验。

一是遵循人才成长规律。"双名工程"分设特级教师与特级校长工作室、学科带头人学科高地和学科基地共 96 个。根据实际，以不同的目标和内容，分层培养优秀骨干教师、学科新星和青年教师，更加注重系统设计、分层培养，并聚合国内外最优质资源，统整多方力量，协力支持项目的高质量运行。既创新了高端教育人才的培养模式，又形成了系统的、相互衔接的后备教育人才储备与培养体系。

二是创新提升核心素养。学科核心素养是育人价值的核心体现，有助于学生形成正确的价值观、必备品格和关键能力，是新时代教育改革的要

1

求。"双名工程"注重激发教师和校长的创新积极性，将培育学生核心素养作为课堂教学改革的重中之重。工作中，由浅入深地分解学科核心素养的内容和层次，提高认知；由表及里地改革教学方法，培养学科能力和核心素养；由此及彼地开展跨学科主题活动和项目化学习，创新培养学生学习方式。这种协同教学机制有助于教师综合素养的提升，同时也为学生提供了更全面的学习支持。

三是搭建人才展示平台。教育是动态生成的，为此，我们构建了更开放、更宽广的平台。"双名工程"坚持从实践中来、反思实践、服务实践的理念，形成了特有的、开放的学科文化交流圈，如教学和管理论坛、教学公开课、学术研讨会、区际交流会、发表论文、出版专著等，促进教师与校长在更高层面思考和解决问题，有力地推动专业进步，也提高了嘉定教育的影响力。

四是形成培养评价体系。培养工程借鉴了"教学研评一体"观点，从教师教学和校长管理出发，把学习作为过程，突出学以致用，再回到出发点评价教师与校长的变革，由此融合为一体。"教学研评一体"既重过程性评价，又重结果性评价，既有评价量表，又有评价描述，较好地解决了培养评价难题，保证了培养工程的顺利进行，具有创新意义。

第五届"双名工程"历时三年，硕果累累，各团队将实践上升为理论，梳理和提炼了一批优质成果，此次成果书系由上海教育出版社集结出版，可喜可贺。今天，当我们在为一件事做总结的时候，也就意味着又一件事的开始。衷心希望，成果书系能够发挥积极作用，给予教师与校长更多前瞻性的启示；更加希望，新一届培养工程继续砥砺前行，传承发展，为嘉定教育高质量发展再献力量！

上海市嘉定区教育局局长

管文洁

2024 年 2 月

序

今年是我在教研员岗位上的第 20 年。20 年来，我与许多拥有 20 年左右教龄的老师们建立了深厚的友谊，孙饴老师就是其中一位，我们共同见证了彼此的成长。虽然不常见面，但我们以文会友，相互学习，在教学改革的关键时刻总能提出相同的问题，并且相互促进，努力寻找更好的解决方案。今天，孙饴老师把自己的一部分研究成果以严谨的笔触记录下来，这不仅是一份教研教学的成长档案，也是我们上海英语教研人担当和贡献的体现。

议论其实并不简单。据理说事、据事说理贯穿于我们的日常交流，但在议论文写作中，我们还需要关注其交际背景、交际对象、交际目标、交际效果，这也体现了作者的语言能力、文化理解、逻辑思维、知识储备等方面的基础和积累。孙饴老师的这本书根据高中生的特点，依据图尔敏论证模型，呈现了议论文写作及其教学的思想方法和实践案例，为我们提供了宝贵的启示。

教研其实也不简单。我回忆了与孙饴老师交流的一些细节，她与我们许多优秀的教研员一样，有着共同的气质。教研员要有课堂的灵感，熟悉教材，了解学生，持续积累，反复修正，灵活应变。教研员要有思考的质感，面对教育教学理论应具备阅读理解、分析判断、概括提炼、联系对照的能力，尤其要善于把教育教学理论转化为教学行为，自然地体现在学生的学习活动中。教研员要有教研的触感，来自一线，服务一线，具有敏锐的教学感受力、师生共情力。

一本书并非只是给出一个已知的答案，或提供一种可行的方案。教研员著书和分享的价值在于启发大家，促生更多的优秀经验，引领探索，寻找多元的方案和路径，沉淀反思，积蓄强大的教研能量。感谢嘉定区"双名工程计划"成果，为全市英语教研作出示范；感谢孙饴老师的精心设计，为英语教师及其他相关群体提供宝贵的学习资源；感谢我年轻的朋友，是他们推动我坚持学习，不断积累知识，不断更新能力。

上海市教师教育学院（上海市教委教研室）高中英语教研员

汤青

前　言

一、这本书是写给谁的

本书的目标读者群体是国内从事"英语作为外语教学"（TEFL，Teaching English as a Foreign Language）的高中英语教师。本书旨在为高中英语教师提供一整套议论文写作教学的解决方案，包括英语议论文写作相关知识、议论文写作课程的序列开发案例以及议论文写作教学的相关原则。

除此之外，任何对高中英语议论文写作感兴趣的读者也都是本书的受众群体，包括但不限于从事中文议论文写作教学的老师、逻辑学初学者、教学研究者、写作爱好者、大学生、中学生等，相信本书能够为以上人群提供有用的素材和信息。

同时，本书为国内高中生自学英语议论文写作提供了学习素材和资源，学生可以不依赖于教师而独立使用本书。书中专门设立了思考题环节，可供学生阅读后进行自我检测。学生也可以对照书中实践篇的案例，在案例的活动指令指导下，独立开展英语议论文写作，并进行自评。在此过程中，如果遇到困难，可再求助教师。

二、这本书的结构是怎样的

本书主要分为上篇理论篇和下篇实践篇，以下是两部分的概览。

理论篇的导言介绍了高中英语议论文写作教学的必要性，并结合《普通高中英语课程标准》分析了高中英语议论文写作的课程要求，以及如今高中英语议论文写作教学中师生普遍面临的问题和困惑。

第一章讨论了议论文写作的相关概念和特点，探索了议论的过程性和产品性，分析了议论中的三大修辞要素、事实和观点之间的关系，以及议论文和说明文的区别等。同时，介绍了英语议论文写作的实用思维工具——图尔敏论证模型，并分析了模型中各论证要素之间的关系及注意要点。除此之外，本章还介绍了议论文的三大类型——事实型、价值型、政策型，以及它们之间的螺旋上升关系。

第二章至第五章分别取自国内高中英语教材中的语篇实例，介绍了事实型议论文、价值型议论文、政策型议论文以及驳论文的特点，并将前三章提到的英语议论文写作相关知识及工具应用到这四类议论文的分析、写作和评价中，帮助读者更好地理解英语议论文写作相关知识。

实践篇展现了高中英语议论文写作教学课程实施的完整过程，由 15 个高中英语议论文写作教学案例组成，按照事实型、价值型、政策型议论文和驳论文的进阶序列排列，与理论篇交相呼应。15 个教学案例由浅入深、层层推进、环环相扣，每个案例都具有承上启下的作用。

并且，每个案例都以具体的任务型写作话题为载体，循序渐进地渗透理论篇所介绍的议论文写作相关知识。以图尔敏论证模型六要素相关知识的教学为例，它并不是通过某一个写作话题来完成，而是根据不同话题的特点渐进式展开，直到写作话题 7 才真正完成。

表 1　图尔敏论证模型六要素写作话题安排

写作话题	话题	图尔敏论证模型要素
写作话题 1	案件报告	三大基本要素：主张（claim）、根据（grounds）、保证（warrants）
写作话题 2	虚假广告	隐性保证和显性保证 补充要素：反驳条件（conditions of rebuttal）
写作话题 3	数字艺术	事实型议论中，保证即定义
写作话题 5	择业述评	价值型议论中，保证即价值标准 补充要素：限定（qualifiers）
写作话题 7	人选推荐	补充要素：支撑（backing） 保证和支撑的关系

同样地,其他高中英语议论文写作相关知识也在15个教学案例中有层次地、循序渐进地展开,以确保学生在学习过程中能够深入理解相关知识和概念。每个案例都整合了教案、学案、活动资源和参考答案,记录了完整的课堂教学过程,方便教研组或教师在备课时进行参考。

结语介绍了笔者如何充分利用本土教材资源进行高中英语议论文写作项目的设计和实施,并探讨了教学过程中所遵循的原则。

三、如何使用这本书

对教师读者来说,建议按照本书顺序,先理解理论篇中有关英语议论文写作的理论知识,完成思考题后进入实践篇的阅读,等到熟悉了实践篇中的教学案例后,再阅读结语,加深对15个案例整体设计思路的理解。当然,如果教师迫切想要开展相关的教学实践,也可以在阅读完理论篇的第一章"议论文写作概览"后直接阅读实践篇的教学案例,等到进行相关教学实践后,再阅读理论篇的第二章到第五章,由实践带动理论提升。

对学生读者来说,如果对理论研究要求不高,可以直接从实践篇开始阅读。遇到不懂之处再回到理论篇,查找相应章节进行学习。

对学校教研组和备课组来说,可以先阅读结语,从该部分梳理出的高中英语教材议论文语篇编排,探讨如何有效开展议论文写作校本教学设计。在组里老师对该话题有了一定的思考和思维碰撞之后,再带着任务阅读上篇和下篇,以期为校本写作教学设计增加更多灵感。

无论哪类读者,建议大家都要完成理论篇中每一章所设置的思考题。这些思考题由笔者精心设置,旨在通过具体案例帮助读者深入理解英语议论文写作的相关知识和概念。

期待本书能够给爱好写作及写作教学的您带来阅读的享受,并给您的工作带来一定启发。如果遇到任何问题,欢迎联系笔者交流!

目 录

上篇 理论篇

上篇

理论篇

导言

一、议论文写作的重要性和必要性

（一）学科课程内容的组成部分

写作能力是高中英语学生语言能力中的重要一环。《普通高中英语课程标准（2017 年版 2020 年修订）》（以下简称《课标》）指出，语言技能包括听、说、读、看、写等方面的技能。听、读、看是理解性技能，说和写是表达性技能。理解性技能和表达性技能在语言学习过程中相辅相成、相互促进。学生应通过大量的专项和综合性语言实践活动，发展语言技能，为真实语言交际打基础。

高中英语议论文读写是《课标》对高中生英语学习内容的基本要求之一。《课标》"课程内容—语言知识"板块要求选择性必修阶段的学生应该掌握"议论文语篇的主要写作目的及其主要语篇结构特征和论证方法"。《课标》"课程内容—语言技能"板块也从理解性技能和表达性技能两方面对议论文读写教学作出了明确规定，要求学生能够"识别语篇中的内容要点和相应的支撑论据"以及"以口头或书面形式传递信息、论证观点、表达情感"等（见表 0-1）。同时，高中英语议论文写作也是高中英语学科诊断性评价中的重要环节，是检验学生高中英语输出性语言技能和思维能力的关键项目。

表 0-1 《课标》中与议论文读写相关的能力要求

语言技能	具体要求
理解性技能	能根据语篇中的事实进行逻辑推理。 能辨别并推论语篇中隐含的观点。 能识别语篇中的内容要点和相应的支撑论据。 能解析语篇结构的合理性和语篇主要观点与事实之间的逻辑关系。 能根据不同的环境条件，客观分析各种信息之间的内在关联和差异。

（续表）

语言技能	具体要求
表达性技能	能基于所读和所看内容,进行推断、比较、分析和概括。 能以口头或书面形式传递信息、论证观点、表达情感。 能准确、熟练和得体地陈述事件,传递信息,表达个人观点和情感,体现意图、态度和价值取向。 能以解决问题为目的,整合语言知识和语言技能的学习与发展。

（二）思维品质提升的必然要求

在人工智能发展日新月异的当今,教育教学的目标不可能仅仅停留在单纯地教会学生掌握知识或技能上。层出不穷的人工智能软件和应用程序已经学会写作,能在短时间内创作出优美的诗歌,甚至写出商业分析报告和学术论文。那么,我们的写作教学还有意义吗? 如果有,意义究竟在哪里呢? 笔者认为,写作教学最重要的价值就在于对学生思维品质的塑造。思维品质指的是人的思维在逻辑性、批判性、创新性等方面所表现出的能力和水平,而写作过程本身就是思维和认知的建构过程,议论文写作尤为如此。学生只有在思维品质上得到足够的锻炼,获得独立思考和判断的能力,才能开展独具风格的个人写作,在未来和人工智能的较量中立于不败之地。

思维品质也是学生英语学科核心素养的重要组成部分,思维品质体现英语学科核心素养的心智特征,这就意味着思维品质是对高中阶段所有学生的普适性要求。对照《课标》对学生思维品质的要求,很多都与议论文读写直接相关(见表0-2)。

以上对学生思维品质的要求也正与布鲁姆教育目标分类学中的高阶思维部分相对应,包括分析、评价和创造。高阶思维能力超越了简单的记忆和信息检索能力,关注的是学生较高认知水平层次上的能力发展,而议论文写作正是形成原因、证明信念、得出结论的过程。[①] 在这个过程中,作者必须梳理整合各种信息,并对信息的价值进行分析和判断,从而得出自己的结论,可见议论文写作中渗透着高阶思维品质的培养。

[①] Nordquist R. What Does Argumentation Mean?［R/OL］.（2018-04-30）［2022-04-21］https://www.thoughtco.com/what-is-argumentation-1689133.

表 0-2 《课标》中思维品质水平与议论文读写相关的要求

思维品质水平	与议论文读写相关的要求
一级	1. 客观分析各种信息之间的关联和差异，发现产生差异的基本原因，从中推断出它们之间形成的简单逻辑关系。 2. 根据所获得的信息，提取共同特征，形成新的简单概念。 3. 针对所获取的信息，提出自己的看法，并通过简单的求证手段，判断信息的真实性，形成自己的看法。
二级	1. 通过比较，识别各种信息之间的主次关系。 2. 客观分析各种信息之间的内在关联和差异，发现产生差异的各种原因，从中推断出它们之间形成的逻辑关系。 3. 根据所获得的多种信息，归纳共同要素，建构新的概念。 4. 针对所获取的各种观点，提出批判性的问题，辨析、判断观点和思想的价值，并形成自己的观点。
三级	1. 根据不同的环境条件，综合分析各种信息之间的内在关联和存在的各种矛盾，梳理产生这些矛盾的原因，从中推断出它们之间形成的各种逻辑关系。 2. 根据所获得的综合信息，归纳、概括内在形成的规律，建构新的概念。 3. 针对各种观点和思想的假设前提，提出合理的质疑，通过辨析、判断其价值，作出正确的评价，以此形成自己独立的思想。

高中英语议论文写作教学为学生思维品质的培养创造了情境和机会，搭建了交流思想的平台，同时助力了学生英语语言能力的发展和学习策略的培养。因此，学习高中英语议论文写作不仅是学生学科思维品质提升的需要，更是核心素养发展的必然要求。

（三）学生生涯发展的内在需求

议论文写作技能是学生步入大学乃至社会后的一项重要交际能力。在高等教育阶段，学生将广泛接触并阅读大量英文学术论文，并需要撰写相关论文、分析报告。通过高中阶段英语议论文的写作思维训练，学生能更好地了解中西方思维模式的差异，树立正确的世界观和价值观。这样，在高等教育学习中，他们就能更高效地开展学术交流，同时更好地传播中国技术与文化，推动中外文化相互理解和交流，增强文化自信。

此外，在当今国际化的背景下，学生在未来的职场中必然会接触到使用英语进行现象分析、事物选择、措施决策、行为评价及个人行为准则阐述等场景。如果在高中阶段就打下良好的议论文读写基础，将对学生在职场上分析和解决问题能力的提升大有裨益。另外，在日常交流中，如果拥有一套较为系统的思维方式，也更容易让他人接受并信服自己的观点，从而说服他人据此行事。

除了对未来学业和事业的帮助之外，议论文还有一个非常重要的精神价值——促进人的内省。事实上，议论文的构思过程就是学生积极监控和调节自身认知活动的过程，这本身就可以大大促进学生元认知能力的发展。比如，在接触到一个议论文写作话题后，学生可能需要通过网络和图书馆等渠道获得大量原始信息，并有意识地关注和积累相关信息和报道。再如，在写作过程中，如果遇到逻辑不通的表述，学生需要主动分析原因并尝试解决问题，或及时向同学和教师求助，以调整自己的英文表达。这些都是学生对自身认知过程及结果进行有效监控的策略，也就是元认知策略的体现。可以说，议论文写作"牵一发而动全身"，一个写作项目可以促进学生多元智力的发展，是学生生涯发展的内在需求。

二、当前高中英语议论文写作教与学存在的问题

前文分析了高中英语议论文写作教学的重要性和必要性，但在日常教学中，高中英语议论文写作似乎并未得到应有的重视。教师和学生仍然没有摸索出英语议论文写作的门道，觉得写作是英语学习中"性价比较低"（投入时间多但见效不大）的技能板块，从而不愿意投入过多精力，这意味着教师和学生在英语议论文写作方面普遍存在困惑。

（一）高中英语议论文写作教与学的现状

1. 教师层面

议论文写作是高中英语写作教学和高考的重点，但在日常教学中，受学生英语语言能力、教材和教学课时等多种因素影响，许多高中的议论文写作教学往往到高三才真正开始。而且，有些教师并未养成定期（如每周一次或每月两次）开设写作专项课的习惯，而是将议论文写作教学穿插在备考教学中，过于随意，缺乏连贯性和整体性。

从教学内容看，高中英语议论文写作教学主要偏向以考试为导向的语

言教学和结构教学，内容教学缺失。比如，教师经常向学生展示高考范文中的好词好句，并要求他们背诵，或根据高考考题将作文细分为图表类、漫画类、推荐信类等，帮助学生进行结构上的梳理和训练。然而，对于如何进行完整、透彻的说理，教师几乎没有提供任何系统的指导。

从教学模式看，如今高中教师普遍采用"展示性教学法"，通过发放讲义、教师讲解的形式授课，而师生之间就写作内容开展深入、系统的交流相对较少。

在学生习作的评价方面，从笔者自身和身边高三教师的经历来看，大部分教师倾向于指出学生习作中的语法错误，有些教师虽然会提到作文中心不明确、说理不透彻等问题，但往往泛泛而谈，并未提出具体的修改建议，通常寄希望于学生读完范文自己领会。但事实是，许多学生听到教师的分析和评价后，依然不知道怎样从内容上进行修改，不知道如何做到中心明确、说理透彻。从目前的教学来看，多数教师对学生习作的评价仍停留在指出问题层面，无法有效解决问题。

2. 学生层面

和教师一样，学生在写作时也存在诸多困惑。很多学生按照教师的要求背诵了不少英语单词和短语，但仍写不出逻辑连贯、说理透彻的文章。在与学生的交谈中，笔者了解到他们的困惑其实并不在语言上。学生反映自己遇到"分析原因""给出建议"等看似简单的议论文指令时常常"不知从何处下笔"，并且在"如何有效展开一个说理段落"方面得不到足够的教师指导，或者说可操作性不强。除此之外，笔者发现学生的写作动机也很"现实"，常常是为了应付高考，极少有学生发自内心地对英语议论文写作的说理过程表现出浓厚兴趣，不少学生对写作还存在畏难情绪。

以上这些现象反映出高中英语议论文写作教学的盲区，即在高中英语教学过程中较少或从未开展过系统的英语议论文写作思维训练，学生很少有机会培养自身的解释、分析、推论、评估等能力，也就是说，他们缺乏高阶思维能力的锻炼。同时，学生的写作动机不足，常常是为了写作而写作，而非在真实情境下出于内心的表达需求来写作。

思考：

1. 你在议论文写作教学中曾经遇到过哪些问题？这些问题的根源在哪里？

2. 你自己尝试过英语议论文写作吗？你觉得英语议论文写作难在什么地方？

2. 你的学生愿意写议论文吗？你认为他们为什么缺乏动力？

（二）高中英语议论文写作教学中的典型问题

1. 教师自身缺乏英语议论文写作的理论知识

写作常常被定义为一种能力，议论文写作也是如此。因此，有些教师将学生习作的好坏归因于能力的差异，还有一些教师则将责任推给语文老师，认为语文老师肯定教过议论文怎么写，学生可以自然地将方法迁移到英语写作中。当然，也有相当一部分教师确实教授了一些议论文写作知识，即议论文主题句（topic sentence）和支撑句（supporting details）之间的关系，但通常情况下也仅限于此。

写作的确是一种能力，但能力培养应建立在一定的知识体系基础之上，目前学生关于议论文写作的知识体系非常有限，这与英语教师自身缺乏议论文写作的理论知识有关。实际上，西方学界对逻辑学有着2000多年的研究历史，已形成了较为完善的论证理论和模型，而高中英语教师普遍缺乏对这一领域的研究和关注。

2. 教师重语言训练胜过思维训练

大部分英语教师的写作教学以语言教学为主，常常让学生大量背诵范文、圈画好词好句，殊不知语言只是思维的外显和表达形式。如果华丽的语言背后没有清晰的逻辑思维作为支撑，一篇优秀的议论文是不可能诞生的。此外，如果写作教学一直以语言训练为最终目的，学生难以有机会去进行理性和清晰的思考，这就背离了写作的真正目的，写作的乐趣也将随之消失。

然而，许多教师认为思维是不可见的，也是不可能统一的，因此从来不涉足思维教学；有些教师在某种程度上认识到思维的重要性，但因为前人鲜有探索，因此对思维教学也是浅尝辄止。其实，东西方思维的差异导致很多学生无法完全将语文课上学到的议论文写作思维迁移到英语学习中。议论文写作是西方直线型思维的典型代表，这种思维模式遵循一定的原则和模式，而高中英语教师在这方面的探索普遍较少。

思维指导的缺失也间接影响了学生对写作的热情。不少学生在写完初稿后不愿再进一步修改，原因在于教师的评价总是停留在"写得不如范文清楚，多看看范文"或"多模仿几个漂亮句子"，而较少具体指出学生习作在内容和思维上如何提升，导致学生的作文难以实现质的飞跃。

要解决以上问题，英语教师必须提升自身的议论文写作本体知识及专业素养，解决学生在议论文写作思维上的根本问题和实际困难，进而实施系统的、有层次的、循序渐进的高中英语议论文写作课程，帮助学生真正学会开展英语议论文写作。

第一章 议论文写作概览

第一节 什么是议论文写作

何为议论？议论是形成原因（form reasons）、证明信念（justify beliefs）、得出结论（draw conclusions）的过程，其写作目的是以所写内容影响他人的想法和行动（influencing the thoughts and/or actions of others）。[①]关于议论，学界一直没有统一的定义，以上是笔者目前找到的相对完整的定义，该定义包含议论的过程和目的。从中可以看出，"议论"二字听起来宏大，其实离我们的生活并不远。

一、生活中的议论

生活中处处都是议论的影子。很多时候，议论是由人们的实际需求催生的。比如，你想养一只宠物，但你妈妈不同意，这时你需要说一段话来说服她，这段话就是议论，你的目的是改变妈妈的想法，进而改变她的行动，达成你的实际需求。当然，还有一些时候，人们并不因实际需求而展开议论。比如，我们时常会和家人或朋友讨论"外星人真的存在吗？""宇宙是由于大爆炸产生的吗？""人类是否由猿猴进化而来？"等问题。事实上，我们对以上问题的答案并没有什么实际需求，这些问题的答案也不会立刻影响我们的生活。既然如此，人们为什么还要讨论这类话题呢？这就是议论的另一个目的，即探求真理或真相。因此，议论不仅仅是为了影响他人的想法和行动，还是一个追求真理的过程。当然，这个过程最终也会影响他

[①] Nordquist R. What Does Argumentation Mean?［R/OL］.（2018-04-30）［2022-04-21］https://www.thoughtco.com/what-is-argumentation-1689133.

人的想法和行动，就如哥白尼提出"日心说"最终改变世界一样，整个过程是相当漫长的。由此可见，议论的影响可能是短期的（能产生即时效果或回应），也可能是长期的（对人类文明有深远影响）。

那么，生活中任何有争议的问题是否都可以转化为议论文的论题呢？试想一下，如果你说从 A 城市到 B 城市的高速公路过路费是 25 元，而你朋友说是 40 元，你会和你朋友议论吗？如果会，那可能叫作争论或争吵，而不是议论。因为常识告诉我们，这个问题不具备可辩驳性，这是一个有且只有一个标准答案的问题，而且这个标准答案是可以得到验证的，只需查询高速公路收费的相关网站，或亲自从 A 城市到 B 城市开车走一趟即可。因此，这样的绝对事实不可能成为议论文的论题。

生活中，我们还会遇到一些有关个人喜好的表述，比如"我喜欢吃臭豆腐"，那么这个表述可以成为议论文的论题吗？有人可能会说，我可以用理由支撑这个表述，比如"臭豆腐总是让我想起家乡的味道"等。但这个看似合理的说理过程并不能称作议论，只能称作个人喜好。首先，"我喜欢吃臭豆腐"这个表述只能由"我"作出，这是个人口味问题，有时甚至不需要理由，所以不可能遭到他人的驳斥。其次，"臭豆腐总是让我想起家乡的味道"这条理由本身也很私人化，他人无法驳斥，因为他人不是"我"，无法拥有"我"的感受。因此，这种纯粹的个人喜好不能成为议论文的论题，不具备可辩驳性。[①]

从以上分析中，我们可以看到，不是所有表述都可以作为议论文的论题。首先，有标准答案的绝对事实不能成为议论文的论题；其次，无法提出相反意见的个人喜好类表述也不能成为议论文的论题。可见，议论文的论题必须是可辩驳的（arguable/debatable）。那么，可辩驳性是否就是议论的唯一特点呢？

二、议论的特点

Fahnestock 和 Secor（1990）认为，每个论题都应该包含以下四个元素：可辩驳的主张、支撑主张的理由、需要劝说的对象、展开议论的紧迫性。[②]这

---

① Fahnestock J, Secor M. A Rhetoric of Argument［M］. 2nd ed. New York, NY: McGraw-Hill, 1990.

② 同上

四个元素将议论划分为两个维度——过程和产品，前两个元素将议论看成一个过程，后两个元素将议论看成一个产品。

（一）过程和产品

1. 将议论看成一种过程

首先，议论需要有一个主张（claim），而且这个主张必须是可辩驳的，用英文说也就是 an arguable/debatable claim。上文提到，如果这个主张是某种可验证的事实或人们普遍接受的真理（比如"地球是圆的"），那么它就不能作为一个合适的议论文主张，因为作者并不需要去证明这件事情，也无法再以此"影响他人的想法和行动"。因此，提出一个可辩驳的主张（a debatable claim）是议论文写作的第一步。

其次，作者要以理性的方式去证明这个主张，并说服潜在的反方，这个"提供理由—得出结论"的过程就是论证的过程。如果只有主张而没有理性的说理过程，就只能称作争吵、仗势欺人或讲蛮理，不能称作议论。

2. 将议论看成一种产品

可见，议论涉及一个从提出主张到证明主张的过程（process），是一个和读者不断交流、厘清想法的活动。然而，如果只看说理过程，可能会出现这样的现象：一篇议论文读起来逻辑通顺、论证严密，但只是作者的一厢情愿，读者并不想读，或者觉得这个论题和自己没关系。这时，议论文的另一个性质——产品（product）就凸显出来了。

一个产品如果要卖得好（引起读者的兴趣），就要考虑发行方（作者的身份、性格和声望）、受众方（读者的状态、性质）以及发行的渠道或环境（文章发表的载体等）。如果不关注以上这些，一篇议论文就无法真正影响和说服他人，也就难以达到最初的写作目的。因此，议论文写作既要关注论证的过程，即前文提到的严谨追求真理的过程，又要关注论证各方之间的关系，比如作者自身的身份和立场、读者的水平和需求、发表刊物的受众和特征等。

因此，从产品的属性来说，议论的形式不仅限于文字，很可能以其他方式存在，比如一个户外广告、一幅海报、一张照片、一幅讽刺漫画，都可能包含议论的成分。以广告为例：广告劝说你购买某种产品，这就是主张；广告中一定有吸引你购买的元素，这就是理由，这也就是议论的过程性；广告有目标顾客，这就是需要劝说的对象；广告也要满足发行方和受众方的需

11

求，这就是展开议论的紧迫性，是议论的产品性。从这些角度观察，会发现我们身边处处有议论的影子。

（二）三大修辞要素

正因为议论文是过程也是产品，最终需要面向市场，所以需要考虑论点本身的可信性、论证逻辑以及读者的接受程度等。古希腊学者亚里士多德早在 2000 多年前就分析了有效说服听众的方式，得出了三种说服性诉求，称之为 logos、ethos 和 pathos，也就是理性诉求、人格诉求和情感诉求。

logos（希腊语中的"文字"）关注写作本身的质量，即论点本身的内在一致性和清晰性，以及理由和支撑内容是否具备逻辑。logos 对读者的影响被称为理性诉求或逻辑诉求。

ethos（希腊语中的"品格"）关注作者本人的品性，也就是作者的可信度。在某些情况下，这也取决于作者立场、专业知识方面的声誉以及他对读者的了解等。ethos 对读者的影响被称为人格诉求或可信度诉求。

pathos（希腊语中的"共情"）关注目标受众的价值观和信仰，与情感诉求有关。它能唤起读者的同理心，当抽象的逻辑话语变成一个有形的、直接的故事时，就产生了一种共情，从而激发读者的想象力和情感，让他们更深刻地理解论点的意义。pathos 对读者的影响被称为情感诉求。

三者聚焦的角度不同，理性诉求聚焦于议论中的信息本身是否具有逻辑性，人格诉求聚焦于作者本人是否值得读者信赖，而情感诉求聚焦于读者的情感是否能被调动。[①]

表 1-1　亚里士多德的修辞三要素

三大诉求	聚焦	自设问
理性诉求 （logos）	信息	怎样才能使我的论证逻辑内在一致？ 怎样才能找到有效的证据来支撑我的论点？
人格诉求 （ethos）	作者	怎样才能展示我对这个话题的熟悉度？ 怎样才能提升我话语的可信度？

---

① Lunsford A, Ruszkiewicz J. Everything's an Argument［M］. 7th ed. Boston, MA: Bedford/St Martin's, 2016.

（续表）

三大诉求	聚焦	自设问
情感诉求 （pathos）	读者	怎样才能使读者更好地接受我的观点？ 怎样才能吸引读者的兴趣，激发读者的情感？

当然，并不是每一篇议论文都要具备这三大要素，但如果能够兼具，就不失为一篇质量上乘的议论文。每篇议论文都有自己的特点，有的胜在"思路清晰"，有的胜在"德高望重"，有的胜在"情真意切"。同样的一个主张，以不同的诉求方式来写，可能产生完全不同的效果，比如以下的"思考"，你能识别出这三个语段分别是以哪种诉求方式写的吗？你最喜欢哪种方式？你最擅长哪种方式？你觉得哪种方式对你来说最具说服力？

思考：

　　请阅读以下三个语段，分析三大修辞要素，你认为它们分别以哪种诉求为主？

1. We should not keep pets at home because they carry diseases. Nobody wants family members to catch diseases.

2. Have you ever got watery eyes for apparently no reason? Have you suddenly felt itchy and got an allergic rash? One way to prevent such suffering is to stop keeping pets at home.

3. As a doctor, I want people who care about their personal hygiene and health to seriously consider the necessity of keeping a pet at home. You cannot imagine what kind of diseases a pet can bring to your house.

第二节　议论文与说明文的区别

一、事实和观点

学会区分事实（fact）和观点（opinion）是议论文阅读和写作中的重要

能力，人们普遍认为讲事实的就是说明文，写观点的就是议论文，但仔细剖析会发现二者并不容易区分。

如果我们读到的是一些接近真理的表述，比如"地球是圆的""猫是哺乳动物""夏天之后是秋天"等，我们很容易就能判定这些表述为事实。但如果我们读到这样一句话——"他在一所好学校教书"，这句话是事实还是观点呢？尽管听起来像是一个事实，但这句话也可以是一个观点，因为"好学校"是一个主观色彩非常强的短语。"好学校"到底是指这所学校办学质量优异，还是研究氛围浓厚？是指管理水平卓越，还是同事关系融洽？如果要把这句话变成事实，我们必须用足够的证据来支撑"好学校"这个说法。这些证据越接近公理和常识，我们就越可以说这句话是事实。相反，如果没有足够的证据来支撑"好学校"这个说法，那就只能说这句话是说话人本身的一种主观判断，只是一个观点。

另外，即便有些说法看似是事实，也会受到作者本人观点的影响。在一些媒体报道中，某些所谓的"事实"并非记者描述的那么真实，细究之下，我们可能会发现事件背后隐藏着经过处理的图片、断章取义的采访、不加思考的断言，只要没有可靠证据的支撑，这些所谓的"事实"就只能称作观点。此外，在一些科学研究中，研究人员会选择性地发布一些数据，告知大众一些所谓的科学研究"事实"或"真相"（比如"每天喝一杯咖啡的人比不喝咖啡的人患心脑血管疾病的几率小"），但实际上这些"事实"背后可能暗含着研究人员本人的主观看法和价值体系，甚至牵扯到某些集团的利益需求。

因此，除非是绝对事实（前文提到，绝对事实必须要有且只有一个标准答案，并且该答案可以得到验证），在其他情况下，事实和观点并非总是界限分明。高中生接触到的语篇难度较大，探讨的话题也多与现实生活紧密相关，教师应该引导学生具体问题具体分析，帮助他们理解事实和观点之间的转换和交织，体悟生活和语言的复杂性和多维性。

二、议论文和说明文的界限

既然事实和观点的界限并不那么清楚，那么议论文和说明文的界限又在哪里呢？身边的教师和学生经常会有这样的困惑。从形式看，议论文和说明文的段落构成方式非常相近，通常都会出现主题句和支撑句，教材中也很常见。以《高中英语》（沪外教版）选择性必修第二册第 2 单元的一个语段为例：

Languages differ in how they express colours. Some languages have lots of words for colours, while some have only a couple of words—"light" and "dark." For example, in English, there is a word for blue, but in Russian, there isn't just one word. Instead, Russian speakers have to tell the difference between light blue, "goluboy," and dark blue, "siniy." When we test people's ability to recognise the differences between these colours, we find that Russian speakers are faster.

我们可以看到，在该语段中，主题句是 Languages differ in how they express colours，随后语段以大量的证据（例子和解释）佐证主题句的内容。那么这样的语段能不能称作议论语段呢？这就又要回到议论文的定义了。

首先，议论文定义中最关键的一点就是"可辩驳的主张"，如果这个主张是举世公认的真理、客观存在的事实或人们熟知的常识，它就不具备被他人挑战的可能。该语段中的主张 "Languages differ in how they express colours" 虽然不是举世公认的真理，却是客观存在的事实。因此，该主张的可辩驳程度并不强，整个段落的目的更偏向于说明和解释。

其次，一个语段是说明性质还是议论性质取决于作者和读者之间的关系，以及他们交流的目的。如果作者和读者之间是传播知识的关系，读者的目的仅仅是希望通过阅读获取新的信息，那么这个语段就是说明性质的。上文教材中的语段改编自 Lera Boroditsky 在 2017 年的一个讲座，该讲座的主要目的是向观众传播知识，因此这个语段可以视为说明性质。但如果读者的目的是通过阅读权衡不同观点、作出某种决定，该语段就是议论性质的。

由此可见，在不同目的下，同一个主张的性质可能会发生变化。比如，"某城市的某公园很有名"这一主张如果写在该城市的旅游宣传册上，向游客介绍值得游玩的景点，其目的仅仅是传播知识，更偏向于一个事实，也就是说明性质；但如果这句话出自一个市场调查员之口，想向公司汇报该公园是否适合作为产品推广的地点，这个主张的性质就发生了变化，公司很有可能质疑这个主张（这个公园真的很有名吗？有名到什么程度？公园的名气和产品的档次匹配吗？），因为它很可能会影响公司的决策，公司需要权衡多方观点来决定是否将这个公园作为该产品市场推广的最佳地点，这样一来，这个主张更偏向于一个观点，也就是议论性质。

思考：

　　以下英文命题中，哪些更偏向于议论文命题，哪些更偏向于说明文命题？

1. Typhoons often occur in the northwestern Pacific Ocean.

2. To have a balanced life is the best way to avoid stress.

3. Stonehenge is made of enormous blocks of stone.

4. The sea level is rising very slowly from year to year.

5. There are both advantages and disadvantages in using e-dictionaries.

6. Using e-dictionaries brings more advantages than disadvantages.

7. Smoking in public places should be banned.

8. Playing computer games causes his failure in the exam.

第三节　有效的议论文思维模型

　　前一节提到，议论文需要一个可辩驳的主张以及支撑该主张的理由，同时，议论文需要考虑三大修辞要素，其中首要的就是理性诉求，也就是有逻辑的表达。但逻辑是一个抽象概念，是不是有了主张和理由就是有逻辑的表达呢？学生的议论文写作需达到怎样的标准才算中心明确、逻辑连贯、条理清晰、说理透彻呢？有没有可操作、可检测的度量标准？英国哲学家史蒂芬·图尔敏（Stephen Toulmin）给出了答案。20 世纪 50 年代，图尔敏提出了一套论证模型，这是一种能够很好地处理实质论证的方法，其影响力使图尔敏成为现代论证理论的开创者。[1]

---

[1] Toulmin S E. The Uses of Argument [M]. Updated Edition. Cambridge: Cambridge University Press, 2003.

该模型的重要性在于打破了"形式逻辑"对论证的各种约束，由于形式逻辑过于注重数理推演，对于分析和评估公民在日常生活中遇到的各种问题无法发挥有效作用，这一局限性使得人们开始呼吁一种新的逻辑用于分析论证。[①] 图尔敏论证模型恰好能满足人们的需要，该模型属于"非形式逻辑"，起初主要用于修辞学和交际领域，后逐渐成为用于分析和评估社会热点的论证工具。

一、图尔敏论证模型

图尔敏的论证模型由主张（claim）、根据（grounds）、保证（warrants）、支撑（backing）、限定（qualifiers）和反驳条件（conditions of rebuttal）六个要素组成。其中，前三个要素属于基本要素（在语文教学中常称为论点、论据和论证），在每个论证过程中一般都会出现，后三个要素是补充要素。

（一）主张

主张，英文为 claim，也可以翻译为"断言"。图尔敏这样描述：假定我们作出一个断定，我们应当保证该断定必然包含某种主张。如果这个主张受到挑战且是一个好的或者合理的主张，我们必须要使之成立。[②] 主张的特点是具有争议性，会受到挑战，而说话者必须在主张受到挑战的情况下为其辩护。主张可能有多种类型，最常见的是事实型主张（claim of fact）（比如"沙漠化是干旱导致的"）、价值型主张（claim of value）（比如"看电视对孩子有害""我认为小明最适合当班长"），还有政策型主张（claim of policy）（比如"应该禁止公共场合吸烟"）。

（二）根据

有了主张之后，必须考虑用何种理由支撑这一主张，这就是根据（grounds）。图尔敏先前在《论证的使用》（*The Uses of Argument*）一书中将这一要素称作"予料"（data），后在《推理导论》[③] 一书中将"予料"改为"根据"。因为主张的类型多样，"予料"一词不足以支撑不同的主张；"根据"

---

① 张晓娜. 图尔敏论证模型研究［D］. 北京：中国政法大学，2013.

② Toulmin S E. The Uses of Argument［M］. Updated Edition. Cambridge: Cambridge University Press, 2003.

③ Toulmin S, Rieke R D, Janik A. An Introduction to Reasoning［M］. New York, NY: MacMillan Publishing Company, 1984.

则可以包括口头证言、实验观察、统计数据、历史报告以及先前已经建立的主张。

（三）保证

图尔敏指出，即使给出根据，依旧会出现被进一步追问的情况。在《论证的使用》中，图尔敏举了一个例子，假使有人提出一个主张"哈利是英国人"，所给的根据是"哈利出生在百慕大群岛"，质疑者会进一步追问："为什么你会得到这样的结论呢？"这时说话人就要进一步给出"因为法律规定，在百慕大群岛出生的人就是英国人"的理由，这就是保证（warrants），确保从根据到主张的推理是合理的。保证其实就是隐藏在主张和根据关系背后的一种假设。图尔敏指出，如果没有人质疑主张和根据之间的关系，保证就无须明示。

（四）支援

支援（backing）是对保证的支援性陈述。继续上文图尔敏提到的例子，可能有人会进一步质疑保证："为什么出生在百慕大群岛的人就是英国人呢？"针对这一质疑，说话者需要作出一个强有力的支援——"因为英国的法律对殖民地出生者的国籍有明文规定"。这种用来强化保证的权威性的支持性陈述即支援。

（五）限定

图尔敏认为，由于根据和保证种类不同，它们证明主张的力量强度也不同。在某些论证中，可以必然得出主张，而在另一些论证中，有些主张的成立需要某些条件，或存在某些例外，所以就需要一些限定（qualifiers）来修正主张，从而达到使人信服的目的。

（六）反驳条件

在很多书中，反驳条件（conditions of rebuttal）又称作相反意见（counter-arguments）或保留意见（reservations）。反驳条件在论证中起"阻碍"作用，通常是对根据或保证提出相反意见，使从根据到主张的推理不顺利或不合理。之所以叫作反驳条件，就是因为它可以为后续的反驳（rebuttal）树立靶子。如果加以合理运用，反驳可以起到加固立论的作用。

图尔敏论证模型不仅为高中生英语议论文写作提供了基本的思维路径，也是学生进行独立写作的"脚手架"，为学生的写作提供了一个合理的、有效的框架模式。

二、图尔敏论证模型的操作

图尔敏在论辩理论上的贡献是举世公认的,该论证模型的六个要素相互支撑,互为依托。而在日常写作中,学生所习惯的论证方式往往止步于主张和根据,忽略了其他要素。要将图尔敏论证模型更好地应用于英语议论文教学中,必须帮助学生进一步理解该模型是如何应用于实际议论的。以下是一个具体案例[①]:

某人提出一个主张"小张的房间着火了",给出的根据是"小张的房间里冒出烟",但这条根据一定站得住脚吗?不一定,其实这条根据里存在一个隐藏的假设,也就是"烟是火的主要标志",这就是保证,有了这条保证,这条根据才能证明主张的合理性。当然,这条保证接近于常识,所以常常被人们忽略。接下来,如果有人进一步质疑"烟为什么是火的主要标志",就需要支援,即"科学知识告诉我们,加热的空气推升水蒸气和燃料中的细小微粒,会产生烟"。但这时有人会质疑"烟不一定代表火,也可能是化学实验中某些物质发生了化学反应",这一反驳导致主张变得不确定,因此这个主张必须添加一个限定才能站得住脚,我们可以添加限定"有可能",对主张的肯定程度进行修正,也就是"小张的房间有可能着火了"。这样,这个论证过程就完整了。

可见,一篇令人信服的议论文必须有可辩驳的主张、可靠的根据以及

---

① Karbach J. Using Toulmin's Model of Argumentation [J]. Journal of Teaching Writing, 1987, 6 (1): 81–91.

强有力的保证。在保证不足的情况下,还需支援。如果这些还不能完全支撑主张,或者主张仍然容易遭受他人的反驳,就需要用一些限定来限制主张的强度和适用范围。当然,如果作者能很好地回应反驳条件,立论就更经得起考验。

在日常议论文阅读教学中,教师可以指导学生尝试用图尔敏论证模型来分析一个议论语句或议论语段的论证结构。通过引导学生反复观察和学习他人的论证,厘清里面的逻辑关系,教师能够更好地帮助学生开展议论文论证写作。

> 思考:
>
> 你能用图尔敏论证模型分析以下论点吗?
>
> We should not keep pets at home because they carry diseases.

三、保证和根据的应用

(一)保证

前文提到,在图尔敏论证模型中,主张、根据、保证是三个基本要素,是任何议论文都必须包含的。这三个要素中最难掌握的就是保证。保证的目的是确保根据和主张之间的证明关系,它决定了根据是否牢靠,以及某一论证关系背后的假设是否合理。保证之所以难以掌握,是因为它很多时候是隐性的[①]。以下面的对话为例,你能找到这两人对话逻辑背后的隐性保证吗?

A: Smoking is harmful because it causes lung cancer.

B: So what? What's the big deal?

A: Are you insane? Cancer causes suffering and death.

B: Don't be alarmist. Suffering and death are part of human life.

从该对话可以看出,A 首先提出一个主张"吸烟是有害的",给出的根据是"因为吸烟会导致肺癌",但 B 马上反驳"那又怎么样"。实际上,从这

---

① Toulmin S E. The Uses of Argument[M]. Updated Edition. Cambridge: Cambridge University Press, 2003.

个反驳就可以看出，两位说话者背后的假设不一样，A 的假设是"癌症是很痛苦的，是一件不好的事情"，但 B 并不赞同这一假设，说"痛苦和死亡是人生的一部分"。由此可见，A 和 B 再继续争辩下去就没有意义了，因为两人的基本假设不同。这个基本假设就是图尔敏论证模型中的隐性保证。作为读者，我们要学会思考每一个论证背后的保证，这是帮助我们科学运用图尔敏论证模型的关键。

思考：

你能说出以下议论中的隐性保证吗？

1. UFO does exist because the science program on TV yesterday said so.

2. Cats make good pets because they are gentle.

3. Women should stay at home because they take care of babies better.

4. Students shouldn't wear school uniforms because they restrict students' individuality.

5. We should not elect Alice as monitor because she is too shy.

学会找到隐性保证非常重要，这既可以帮助我们更好地理解论证关系，也可以启发我们更好地找到对方论证中的漏洞，提出自己的看法和见解。

（二）根据

根据可以说是论证中最重要的一环。针对一个主张，我们往往需要给出多条根据来证明其合理性，那么是否每条根据都能达到预期的证明效果呢？并不尽然。在下面的例子中，假设你是学生，想提出一个主张，即说服校长给同学们换一种校服，你会使用以下哪条根据呢？

① The style of our school uniform should be changed <u>because the uniform we have now is out of fashion and most students don't like it</u>.

② The style of our school uniform should be changed <u>because a refreshing look of the students can improve the image of the school</u>.

显然，学生往往喜欢用第一条根据，因为它更贴近学生们的心声。但在论证时，我们的目的不是说服自己，而是说服读者。那么，哪一条论证更贴近读者（也就是校长）的需求呢？这里就要再次提到上文所说的保证。

一条根据要令人信服，背后必须有一个能支撑该根据的保证。一个保证越能为读者所接受，这个保证支撑下的根据就越能打动读者，并影响其思想和行动。

我们用图尔敏论证模型来分析一下这两则议论背后的逻辑思路。

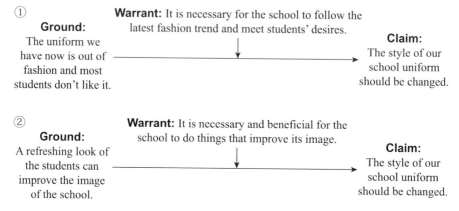

① **Ground:** The uniform we have now is out of fashion and most students don't like it. **Warrant:** It is necessary for the school to follow the latest fashion trend and meet students' desires. **Claim:** The style of our school uniform should be changed.

② **Ground:** A refreshing look of the students can improve the image of the school. **Warrant:** It is necessary and beneficial for the school to do things that improve its image. **Claim:** The style of our school uniform should be changed.

从以上分析可以看出，两则议论的主张完全一致，都是要求学校换一种校服款式，但达到的效果完全不同。为什么会造成这样的差别呢？其原因就在于根据背后的假设不同。很明显，第二条根据背后的假设"学校有必要做对其形象有利的事情"更符合读者（也就是校长）的需求，相比之下，第一个假设"学校有必要迎合时尚潮流和学生的喜好"容易被校长否定。

因此，我们在思考根据的时候，必须将读者或听众的需求考虑进去，如果只照顾自己的喜好，可能最终很难实现主张。这就再次回到了上一节提到的"议论"概念。议论既是一个过程也是一个产品：从过程的角度来说，以上两段有关校服的议论都包含完整的过程，有主张、根据和保证，具备议论三大诉求中的理性诉求；但从产品的角度来看，仅有理性诉求是不够的，我们必须要考虑"买家"，也就是读者或听众的需求，考虑三大诉求中的情感诉求。

图尔敏论证模型是一个很好的框架，能够帮助我们理清论证的结构和思路，但并不能决定论证的质量。因此，必须深刻理解议论的产品性质，并从三大诉求的角度去考虑，这样才能提出更切合读者价值观的理由，从而更好地实现议论的目的。

四、反驳条件的预设

前文重点解释了如何使用图尔敏论证模型让我们的立论更富有逻辑性，同时我们要对保证有充分的认识，它是隐藏在主张和根据之间的重要假设。如果我们想要使根据更容易为读者所接受，就要考虑每一条根据背后的假设。如果假设能够贴近读者的需求，立论就更能站得住脚。但除了立论本身，在撰写每一条论证的过程中，我们还要考虑可能遇到的反驳条件，即相反观点或质疑。只有对可能遭遇的攻击做好准备，我们才能更好地予以反驳，使论证更丰满。

为了更好地驳斥相反意见，首先要明白相反意见是如何产生的。我们再次回到前文的图尔敏论证模型应用案例，该论证的逻辑关系已非常明确：主张是"小张的房间着火了"，根据是"小张的房间里冒出烟"，保证是"烟是火的主要标志"。如果很多人都看到小张的房间里冒出烟，那这条根据就是事实，不容置疑。这样一来，对方很可能会将目光聚焦于保证——"烟是火的主要标志"。针对这条保证，对方可能会提出相反意见，即"火确实能产生烟，但化学反应也可能会产生烟，所以小张的房间不一定着火了，小张可能是在做化学实验"。这时，我方需要对这样的相反意见予以反驳，比如"小张是中文系的学生，对化学实验一窍不通，房间里也没有任何化学药品"。

从以上分析可以看出，相反意见的提出通常有两种途径：一是针对根据，二是针对保证。我们仍以之前校服的论证为例，你能提出相反意见吗？

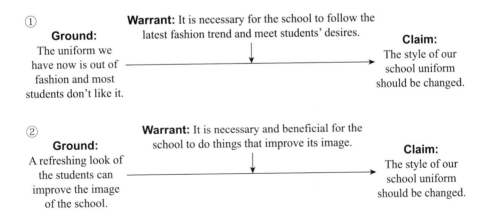

① **Ground:**
The uniform we have now is out of fashion and most students don't like it.

Warrant: It is necessary for the school to follow the latest fashion trend and meet students' desires.

Claim:
The style of our school uniform should be changed.

② **Ground:**
A refreshing look of the students can improve the image of the school.

Warrant: It is necessary and beneficial for the school to do things that improve its image.

Claim:
The style of our school uniform should be changed.

显然，第一条论证容易遭到他人反对。首先，这条根据过于主观，对方很容易提出相反意见，完全可以说"现在的校服并没有过时"，甚至如果真的开展民意调查,不喜欢校服的学生人数能否过半都很难说。其次,对方还可以攻击保证,也就是"学校不应一味迎合学生的时尚喜好,而应加以正确引导,校园作为立德树人的一方净土,应该保持纯洁性与高尚性"等。以上两条反对意见都很有道理,作者也很难反驳。

相比之下,第二条论证不太容易遭到反对。首先,"新款校服能提振学生的精神面貌,从而提升学校形象"这一根据较难被对方攻击。所谓"人靠衣装",穿着在一定程度上确实可以提升人的精神面貌,这属于常识范畴。其次,"学校有必要做对其形象有利的事情"这一保证也符合常理,很难反对。因此第二条论证更站得住脚。

以上例子说明,对相反意见的预设非常重要,可以帮助作者更好地选取根据。比如,对于第一条有关校服的论证,如果作者事先预测到如此强有力的质疑,就可以尽量避免使用该条根据。预设相反意见还有另一个作用,即作者可对相反意见进行驳斥,使自身的论点看上去更可信。比如,对于第一条论证,如果预设了可能遭遇的质疑,作者就可以设计一个调查问卷,以数据证明"超过一半的学生确实不喜欢如今的校服款式",或者以本地其他学校的校服款式作为对比来说明"校服确实过时了"。在对于保证的质疑方面,作者可以先同意对方的观点,即承认"学校确实不应一味迎合学生的喜好",然后从另一个角度切入,说明换校服的好处更大,如"好的穿着可以给人带来自信,如果能适当更换校服款式,满足学生的喜好,对学生自信心的提升是任何事物都代替不了的"。

总之,在运用图尔敏论证模型辅助议论文写作时,作者一定要重视反驳条件,也就是要学会预设相反意见。如前文所述,相反意见的提出有两种方式:一种是质疑根据,另一种是质疑保证。对相反意见的驳斥也有两种方式:一是简要总结相反意见,然后直接利用相关证据予以驳斥;二是先承认相反意见的合理性,再从一个新的角度来反驳对方,也就是说,虽然对方的观点有可取之处,但相比之下,己方的主张能够带来更大的益处,或者己方的主张更为重要。

当然,作者不需要每次都列出所有的相反意见,尤其当读者已对主张产生一定信任时。如果列出过多连读者都没想到的相反意见,读者反而会质疑主张的力度,认为作者对自己的主张没有信心,也就是削弱了议论中的人格诉求,这容易使作者失去可信度。不过,如果作者非常熟悉读者,知道读者本身持有怀疑的态度，就可以适当列出可能的相反意见，尽可能打消读者的疑虑。

第四节　议论文包含哪些类型

一、三种类型的议论

西方学者对议论文的写作类型有着清晰的归类，而高中英语教师普遍缺乏对这方面的研究和关注，对议论文写作中的思维培养无从下手，导致无法系统性地开展写作教学。西方学界对议论文论题的讨论始于古希腊时期，亚里士多德曾在《修辞术》中提出庭辩性（forensic）、表现性（epideictic）、审议性（deliberative）三种言说，分别用于面向过去、面向现在和面向未来的论辩。后西方学界将亚里士多德的理论进一步发展为事实型（fact）、价值型（value）、政策型（policy）三种论题，分别对应他提出的三种言说，即对已发生事情的证明、对当下事情的价值判断和对未来所采取的政策推演[①]。

事实型、价值型、政策型是层层递进的关系：在人们作出价值型主张之前，必须要有一些事实型主张作为基础，比如"张三是最合适的学生会主席人选"这一价值型主张必须建立在"张三是一个有责任心的人"这样的事实型主张之上。若没有事实型主张作基础，价值型主张就无从谈起。并且，价值型论题还可以进一步衍生出价值标准的写作，例如在证明"张三是最合适的学生会主席人选"时，一定会涉及每个人对学生会主席这一职位的判断标准，即"什么样的人适合当学生会主席"，张三只有符合这一标准，才能担任学生会主席，这就是价值标准。

而政策型主张需要建立在价值型主张的基础上，比如"我们必须禁止公共场所吸烟"这一政策型主张必须建立在"吸烟有害公众健康"这一价值型主张之上。这三种类型的论题相互支撑，为议论文写作教学提供了一个

---

① Lunsford A, Ruszkiewicz J. Everything's an Argument［M］. 7th ed. Boston, MA: Bedford/St Martin's, 2016.

基本且科学的框架。

思考：

　　你能判断以下主张的类型吗？

1. This company has a glass ceiling for women.

2. Our school should make it a rule not to bring cellphones to campus.

3. Opening universities to the public does more harm than good.

4. Eating too much chocolate may lead to drug addiction.

5. Ali's death wasn't a case of suicide.

6. Bullfighting is inhumane.

7. Human cloning is not morally right.

8. Bike-sharing should be promoted.

二、不同议论类型之间的关系

　　值得注意的是，这三个议论类型层层递进，前一个类型的主张往往成为后一个类型的根据。如前文所说，"张三是最合适的学生会主席人选"这一价值型主张需要"张三是一个有责任心的人"来作为根据，而"张三是一个有责任心的人"就是一个事实型主张，这个事实型主张又需要进一步的根据来证明，比如"凡是张三承诺的事情，他一定会按时完成，深受同学信任"。因此，不同类型的议论文之间往往又是嵌套或包含关系。

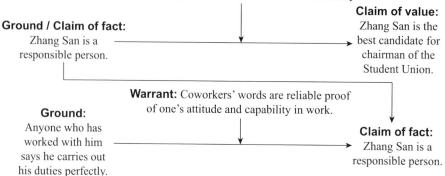

用图尔敏论证模型梳理清楚论证思路后，我们可以形成一个价值型议论段落：

Zhang San is the best candidate for the position of chairman of the Student Union. As we all know, a chairman has many important duties to deal with, like working with students to resolve problems, informing school administration of ideas from the student body, so the position calls for someone who can take these duties seriously. As it happens, Zhang San is just the responsible person you are looking for. His sense of responsibility has been vouched for by his coworkers. If you ask anyone who has worked with him in the Student Union, they will tell you Zhang San always carries out his duties perfectly.

接下来，我们对段落里的每一句话进行分析。

表 1-2 价值型议论段落分析

An Argument of Value		
Zhang San is the best candidate for the position of chairman of the Student Union.	A claim of value	
As we all know, a chairman has many important duties to deal with, like working with students to resolve problems, informing school administration of ideas from the student body（backing）, so the position calls for someone who can take these duties seriously.（warrant）	Warrant + Backing	
As it happens, Zhang San is just the responsible person you are looking for.	Ground for the claim of value & A claim of fact	
	His sense of responsibility has been vouched for by his coworkers.	Warrant
	If you ask anyone who has worked with him in the Student Union, they will tell you Zhang San always carries out his duties perfectly.	Ground

从以上分析可以清楚地看到，价值型主张的根据同时也是一个需要证明的事实型主张。因此，搞清楚三种议论类型之间的关系有助于帮助我们理清思路，抽丝剥茧，找到议论文写作的核心框架。

当然，有的时候，事实型议论文的根据还需要进一步证明，比如以上语段中的根据（Anyone who has worked with him says he carries out his duties perfectly）。我们可能需要引述一位或多位与张三在学生会里合作过的同学的话来证明这条根据的准确性，证明根据的理由可以称作证据（evidence）。

在接下来的几章中，笔者将分别介绍如何分析事实型议论文、价值型议论文和政策型议论文，以及如何开展和评价这几类议论文写作。

本章小结

本章介绍了议论文写作的相关概念和理论框架。议论有别于争吵和辩论，是一个理性证明观点的过程，其目的是影响他人的想法和行动。作者不仅要关注论证信息本身，还要关注议论的三大修辞要素：理性诉求、情感诉求和人格诉求。

议论和说明的界限也是困扰师生的一大问题，虽然论证和解释的过程在形式上看似接近，但二者存在本质的区别。议论的一个重要特点就是具有一个可辩驳的主张。

图尔敏论证模型是有效的议论文写作思维模型，该模型由六大要素（主张、根据、保证、支撑、限定、反驳条件）组成，突破了传统数理逻辑的限制，是广泛应用于现代社会生活的论证分析方法。议论文可以分为三大基本类型：事实型、价值型和政策型。根据图尔敏论证模型的分析，可以发现三种议论类型之间是层层递进、相互嵌套的关系。图尔敏论证模型的灵活应用，可以帮助读者更好地理解、分析所接触到的议论文，也可以帮助作者更好地建构三类议论文写作的逻辑框架。

第二章 如何写好事实型议论文

前文介绍了高中英语议论文写作的重要性和必要性、议论文写作的概念和特征，以及议论文写作中重要的逻辑分析工具——图尔敏论证模型。那么，在日常教学中，教师应如何运用以上知识和工具来规划议论文写作教学呢？从本章开始，笔者将从事实型议论、价值型议论和政策型议论出发，分别探讨如何基于这三种议论类型进行高中英语议论文写作教学的设计和实施。

第一节 什么是事实型议论

事实型议论指的是对事件真伪的判定，比如什么是存在的，什么是不存在的，什么是发生了的，什么是没有发生的，哪条陈述是真实的，哪条是不真实的，等等。有些事实问题很容易回答，比如"中国第一颗卫星是什么时候发射的？""昨晚八点的电视节目是什么？""今天下午的会议何时举行？""王教授的电子邮箱是什么？"，我们可以通过查看一些参考书、找到相关权威网站或询问知道答案的人来得到准确且唯一的答案，也就是第一章提到的绝对事实。这类问题无法构成事实型议论文的论题，因为它们无法满足议论文第一个基本要素，也就是可辩驳的主张。这些问题的答案都是唯一的"标准答案"，不存在可辩驳性。

哪些问题能够成为事实型议论文的论题呢？事实型议论文的论题虽然也有答案，但答案有很强的不确定性，甚至可能永远也找不到。比如"某一公司是否存在性别歧视？""这场事故是意外还是人为？""某一言论是否构成诽谤？""一天喝三杯咖啡是否能促进心血管健康？"，这些问题虽然可以回答，但我们可能无法在短时间内（或者在现有资源范围内）找到确切答案。也就是说，这类具有争议性的、答案不确定的事实问题都可以成为事实型议论文的论题。这些论题具备可辩驳的主张这一要素，而作者的工作就是要在有限的资源范围内尽可能说服读者相信你的答案是最大程度接近事实的。

第二节　如何分析事实型议论文

在日常阅读中，我们经常会碰到一些带有议论性质的语段或语篇。这时，我们就可以运用前文所述的议论文相关知识来分析这些议论语段或语篇，识别出这些议论背后的理性诉求、情感诉求和人格诉求，找出其中涉及的议论技巧和策略，理解和总结作者想要表达的要义。

鉴于议论带有产品性，我们可以把作者和读者的相关信息从人格诉求和情感诉求中单独剥离出来，作为一个议论的前提去思考。也就是说，在观察产品交易前，我们首先要考虑买家和卖家之间的身份关系和交易目的等信息。在一个真实的写作交际情境下，目标读者的身份及作者与目标读者之间的关系尤为重要，这决定了作者在写作时采用怎样的语气与读者交流，用词是偏正式还是非正式的，等等。了解了这些信息后，我们才能更好地理解和分析写作内容。

结合上述内容，我们可以用以下表格来分析事实型议论文。

表 2-1　事实型议论文分析工具

Aspects 方面	Guiding questions 自设问
The author and the writing purpose 作者和写作目的	• Who is the author? 作者是谁？ • What is the author's writing purpose? 作者的写作目的是什么？
The target reader 目标读者	• Who are the target readers? 潜在的目标读者是谁？

（续表）

Aspects 方面	Guiding questions 自设问
The target reader 目标读者	• What is the relationship between the author and the readers? What tone (formal, informal or neutral) is used? 作者和读者之间是什么关系？使用了怎样的语气（正式、非正式还是中立）？ • How much do the readers know about the subject? 读者对这个话题了解多少？
Logos of the argument 理性诉求	• What is the claim of the argument? 这则议论的主张是什么？ • Is the claim supported by relevant grounds and warrants? 这个主张是否有相关的根据和保证来支撑？ • Does the argument consider possible conditions of rebuttal? 这则议论是否考虑到了可能的反驳条件？ • How does the argument respond to the conditions of rebuttal? 这则议论是如何回应这些反驳条件的？
Pathos of the argument 情感诉求	• Are the grounds based on readers' needs? 这些根据是否基于读者需求？ • What techniques (applying descriptions, narrative, examples, word choices) does the author use to arouse the readers' emotions and imagination? 作者使用了哪些手段（使用描写、叙述、举例、用词等）来唤起读者的情感和想象力？ • How does the author reveal his understanding of the readers? 作者如何展现出他对读者的理解？
Ethos of the argument 人格诉求	• How does the author project himself as a trustworthy person who is familiar with the subject being discussed? 作者如何把自己展现为一个值得读者信任、熟悉该话题的人？ • Is the author able to recognize the opposing views and how does he respond to them? 作者能否意识到相反观点？作者是如何回应相反观点的？

　　当然，以上这些方面和问题不一定每则议论都会涉及，但它们可以帮助我们拓宽思路，找到分析议论文的角度和途径，从而更全面地理解作者的想法，提升审辩式思维。

31

分析案例1

高中英语教材中不乏事实型议论的语段，以《高中英语》（沪教版）必修第一册第4单元的一个语段为例：

> Domestic chores were a challenge too. In the 1940s, these chores were like a full-time job. While Michael went out to work, Lyn and her daughter spent most of their time preparing meals, doing the dishes and cleaning the floor. Things that Lyn did easily before, now became terribly difficult. She missed her washing machine most of all. "We had to boil the clothes and when the weather wasn't good, it was impossible to dry anything," said Lyn.

针对以上语段，我们可以作出如下分析。

表 2-2　分析案例 1 议论语段分析

方面	自设问
作者和写作目的	• 该语段的作者是报道一个历史现实类真人秀节目（让一个现代家庭尝试生活在 20 世纪 40 年代的英国）的记者。 • 该语段的写作目的是向读者证明 20 世纪 40 年代的家务活对现代家庭来说是一个挑战。
目标读者	• 目标读者是（可能看过或没看过该节目的）大众，因此语气较为正式。 • 大多数读者都没有参与过这个真人秀节目，因此无法体会真人秀参与者的真实感受。
理性诉求	• 主张：家务活（对真人秀参与者来说）是一个挑战。 • 根据：爸爸出去上班后，妈妈和孩子们大多数时间都在烧饭、整理内务，没有现代化的家用电器。 • 保证：该议论中的保证是隐性的（因为较为接近常识），即"习惯了各种电器做家务的现代人，突然回到手工家务的时代，必定会经受体力和精神的双重考验，因此是有挑战性的"。

（续表）

方面	自设问
情感诉求	• 作者在陈述根据时采用了大量的细节描写和人物对话等记叙手法，以启发读者的想象力，调动读者的情感，比如列举妈妈和孩子们每天要做的具体家务活（preparing meals, doing the dishes and cleaning the floor），还用到了人物的直接引语 "we had to boil the clothes and ..." • 作者在陈述根据时充分考虑到现代读者可能不熟悉 20 世纪 40 年代家务活的强度，因此特地使用 "a full-time job"（全职工作）来归纳。
人格诉求	• 该语段人格诉求体现不明显，但从全文大量的直接引用来看，作者对该节目及参与者做过全面的调查和了解，所以在读者看来，作者的话是可信的。

通过以上分析可以发现，该语段逻辑较为清晰，也具备情感诉求和人格诉求，是各方面元素都较为齐备的事实型议论语段。为了调动读者的情感，使论据更令人信服，该语段还运用了描写和叙述手段。在这里，我们会发现，议论、描写、记叙并不是割裂开来的，议论文中也常常会使用描写和叙述来提升证据的可信度，拉近作者和读者之间的距离。

思考：

请以表 2-1 为工具分析以下事实型议论语段。

The Carterets are the victim of global warming. High tides often flood across the villages and wash away people's homes. Salt water from the sea is overflowing into vegetable gardens and destroying fruit trees. It's polluting the fresh water supply too. Islanders are struggling to survive on coconut milk and fish, and children are suffering from malnutrition. ... John and his fellow islanders are facing great challenges, and they know that life on the island is coming to an end.

——选自《高中英语》（沪教版）选择性必修第一册第 2 单元

分析案例 2

学会分析事实型议论文不仅能帮助我们理解议论语篇和语段,还能帮助我们发现某些议论语段中的不足之处,并及时改进。以《高中英语》(沪教版)必修第二册第 2 单元的一个议论语段为例,你能通过分析发现它的不足之处吗?

> Still, others argue that school uniforms can save parents money because they are cheaper than fashionable clothes. Besides, wearing school uniforms will help to reduce pressure in students' daily lives: if students all wear the same uniform, they won't be judged by the clothes they wear. Most importantly, school uniforms express a group identity and a sense of belonging, which encourages students to take pride in their school.

通过分析可以发现,这个语段存在多处不足,具体见表 2-3。

表 2-3　分析案例 2 议论语段分析

方面	自设问
作者和写作目的	• 作者身份尚不清楚,但写作目的是证明穿校服的优势。
目标读者	• 读者身份尚不清楚,因此不能针对目标读者的特点进行证明和反驳。
理性诉求	• 该语段涉及三个主张: 主张一:校服可以省钱(根据:校服比时装便宜)。 主张二:穿校服可以减轻学生的压力(根据:如果每个学生都穿校服,就不会因为服装被他人评头论足)。 主张三:校服表达了身份感和归属感(根据:校服鼓励学生以学校为荣)。
情感诉求	无
人格诉求	无

这个语段主要存在以下三个问题：

第一，从该语段提供的信息来看，目标读者不明。我们不知道目标读者对校服可能有哪些情感和假设，读者群体原本是否支持校服，以及他们的消费能力如何。这造成作者在写作时无法很好地抓住读者的注意力。

第二，一个段落内的主张过多，根据不够。每个主张和根据之间的逻辑关系解释也不够明显，需要更多的保证来支撑。目前，该语段陈述了三个事实型主张，而每个主张只有一句话作为根据，远远起不到支撑的作用，还需要读者自行脑补很多逻辑链条。尤其对第二个主张"穿校服可以减轻学生的压力"解释得不够清楚。总体来说，论证过程显得有些单薄。

第三，缺乏情感诉求和人格诉求，这与目标读者不够清晰有一定关系。作者在写作时心中没有想要说服的对象，因此整个议论缺乏张力，读者的情感和想象力没有被调动起来，也很难真正认识到校服的重要性。

如果要针对该语段提出建议，首先，作者应该在写作时明确目标读者的定位，了解目标读者对校服的态度，以此为依据来表达自己的观点。其次，作者可以适当增加保证，填补从根据到主张的空白，比如针对第二个主张，作者可以进一步说明"青少年是易敏感人群，容易对自己的外表（比如容貌、服饰等）不自信，一旦因为服装收到同学的负面评价，很可能会产生焦虑、压力等负面情绪"。此外，作者可以适当增加情感诉求，比如以身边同学的例子来说明校服确实可以减轻学生的压力。最后，作者可以在人格诉求上想办法，比如写作时加上自己的身份，"作为一名高中生，我深知处于青少年阶段的我们会因为穿着而相互攀比"等，使根据更令人信服。

从以上两个案例可以看到，学会分析事实型议论不仅能帮助我们更好地理解他人的观点，还能帮助我们指出他人议论中的不足。

第三节　如何开展事实型议论文写作

在开展事实型议论之前，我们首先要确定一个有争议性的论题，然后针对这个论题，鼓励学生开展头脑风暴、图式思考或自由写作，将有关该论题的想法都写下来，从而确定自己对该论题的主张。接下来，我们可以鼓励学生问自己一些问题，比如"为什么我认为这件事是真的？""我如何知道这件事是真的？"，这些问题的答案就是证明主张的理由。当然，如果身边有网络资源，也可以查询相关网站，看看别人对这个问题持什么看法。随后，我们要从众多理由中筛选出若干条最合适的，作为写作提纲的核心组成部分。同时，我们要考虑读者的观点和需求，用一些写作手法提升议论中的情感诉求和人格诉求。最后，如果可能的话，我们还需要将目标读者可能持有的反对意见考虑进去，为强有力地回应这些质疑做好充分准备，从而更好地打消读者的疑惑，使议论更有张力。

接下来，笔者将以一个事实型主张为例，解释如何开展事实型议论文写作。

A Claim of Fact: *Women are discriminated against in the job market.*

步骤一：头脑风暴，拓展思路

针对这个话题，我们首先可以开展头脑风暴或自由写作，把能想到的理由都记下来。

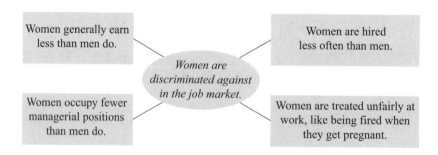

步骤二：借助图尔敏论证模型厘清基本的逻辑关系

在想出以上这些理由后，我们可以利用图尔敏论证模型这一逻辑工具来分析它们的合理性。下面以"Women generally earn less than men do"和"Women occupy fewer managerial positions than men do"为例，列一下其中的逻辑关系。

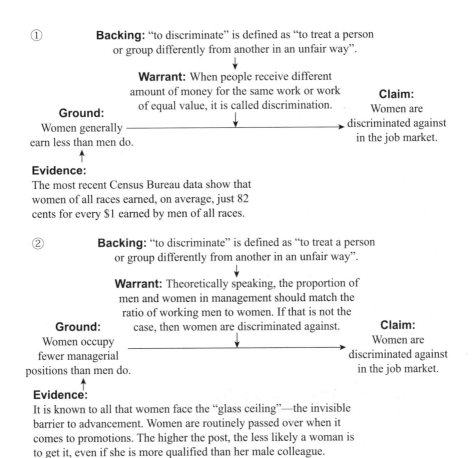

① **Backing:** "to discriminate" is defined as "to treat a person or group differently from another in an unfair way".

Warrant: When people receive different amount of money for the same work or work of equal value, it is called discrimination.

Ground: Women generally earn less than men do.

Claim: Women are discriminated against in the job market.

Evidence:
The most recent Census Bureau data show that women of all races earned, on average, just 82 cents for every $1 earned by men of all races.

② **Backing:** "to discriminate" is defined as "to treat a person or group differently from another in an unfair way".

Warrant: Theoretically speaking, the proportion of men and women in management should match the ratio of working men to women. If that is not the case, then women are discriminated against.

Ground: Women occupy fewer managerial positions than men do.

Claim: Women are discriminated against in the job market.

Evidence:
It is known to all that women face the "glass ceiling"—the invisible barrier to advancement. Women are routinely passed over when it comes to promotions. The higher the post, the less likely a woman is to get it, even if she is more qualified than her male colleague.

　　从以上分析可以看出，在这则议论中，保证和支撑较为接近常识，主要说明了"女性比男性工资低"和"身处管理岗位的女性数量比男性少"能否构成"女性在职场上受到歧视"。保证和支撑的作用就是在解释什么是歧视。简单来说，歧视就是"两者或两个团体在其他条件基本等同的情况下得到了不同的对待"。由此可见，借助图尔敏论证模型，作者可以进一步想清楚根据和主张之间还缺哪一环。在这个论题中，如果我们将"什么是歧视"这个隐性保证解释清楚，读者就能更好地理解其中的逻辑关系。

步骤三：确定目标读者和读者需求

　　该论题没有给出明确的交际情境，因此不清楚写作对象，我们可以暂时假定该语篇的读者是(可能了解或不了解女性职场生存状态的)普通大众。既然写作对象是普通大众，那么语气和用词应该是偏正式的。但不论是否了解"女性在职场上受到歧视"这一现象，也不论是否对该现象具有同理心，读者肯定都希望能从该议论中获得更多有价值的信息。因此，作者需要尽可能向读者展现女性在职场上的真实遭遇，以便更好地说服读者接受自己的观点。

步骤四：考虑情感诉求和人格诉求

根据上一步对读者需求的分析，作者在写作时有必要提升议论中的情感诉求和人格诉求，以增加议论的可信度。比如，作者可以简单叙述身边的职场女性(母亲、阿姨、女教师等)的遭遇，以此来说明女性在同等岗位上的收入不如男性。作者也可以通过描写手段，刻画女性在争取领导岗位过程中的困难，以此来证明女性在晋升中面临的困境。作者还可以提升人格诉求，比如提出自己作为女性的身份，讲述自身的遭遇或陈述自己对该话题的深入研究等，使读者更愿意相信和接受自己的观点。

步骤五：自我质疑，假设读者反应

在积累写作素材、厘清三大诉求后，我们还要开展合理的自我质疑，思考一下根据和保证有没有漏洞，比如读者是否会质疑例子的真实性和普适性，读者是否会质疑歧视的概念和定义，等等，如果可能性较大，我们要考虑对这些反对意见作出回应。根据前文所述，回应一般有两种方式：一是简单总结对方的反对意见，然后找出其中的漏洞加以驳斥；二是承认对方反对意见的合理性，然后找到新的角度加以驳斥。

步骤六：组织语篇布局

经过以上步骤后，我们有了足够的写作素材和清晰的写作思路，但在正式写作前，我们还需要梳理一下语篇布局。对于该论题，我们可以采用以下任意一种布局方式。

表 2-4　布局 1

步骤	要点
引入论题和主张	1. Arouse the readers' interest by introducing the issue of gender discrimination at work and show why the issue is worth discussing. 2. Introduce the claim that "women are discriminated against in the job market".
给出根据 1+ 保证 1	1. State the first reason（women generally earn less than men do）and give evidence. 2. State the warrant to show why earning less means being discriminated against.
给出根据 2+ 保证 2	1. State the second reason（not enough women are promoted to managerial positions）and give evidence. 2. State the warrant to show why fewer women being promoted means being discriminated against.
结语	1. Sum up the argument. 2. Remind the readers of the importance of the issue.

表 2-5　布局 2

步骤	要点
引入论题和主张	1. Arouse the readers' interest by introducing the issue of gender discrimination at work and show why the issue is worth discussing. 2. Introduce the claim that "women are discriminated against in the job market".
提出保证和支撑	State the warrant and backing（Gender discrimination means that an employee or a job applicant is treated differently or less favorably because of their gender identity, which results in equally qualified employees receiving different treatments at work. And women are exactly the object of such discrimination.）

（续表）

步骤	要点
给出根据 1	1. State the first reason (women generally earn less than men do) and show how the reason matches the warrant. 2. Give evidence.
给出根据 2	1. State the second reason (not enough women are promoted to managerial positions) and show how the reason matches the warrant. 2. Give evidence.
提出反驳	1. Summarize the possible objections. 2. Respond to the objections either through rebuttal or concessions.
结语	1. Sum up the argument. 2. Remind the readers of the importance of the issue.

以上两种布局方式各有特点。第一种在引入作者观点（即主张）后直接给出根据，然后徐徐道出根据和主张之间的关系，像打开画卷一样慢慢向读者展示论证的过程，最后对整篇议论作出小结，并再次强调该论题的重要性，这是一种较为常见的事实型议论文布局方式。

第二种和第一种略有不同。作者在陈述主张后，首先对主张中涉及的保证（也就是"什么算性别歧视"）下定义，使读者对接下来的理由产生期待。随后，作者只需将根据和保证进行匹配，即陈述女性在工作中受到了哪些不公平的对待，并且这些对待可与保证中陈述的性别歧视的定义相匹配，这样就形成了较为完整的逻辑闭环。最后，作者还可以针对读者可能提出的相反意见进行驳斥，使自己的立论更站得住脚。可见，第二种布局方式的论证效果更胜一筹。

步骤七：根据提纲产出语篇

下面我们就可以进入写作的最后一个步骤，选取以上任意一种布局，添加过渡语，撰写完整的语篇。

从以上分析可以发现，事实型议论文中的保证常涉及相关概念的定义。前文曾提到一些事实型议论文的典型论题，比如"某一公司是否存在性别歧视？""这场事故是意外还是人为？""某一言论是否构成诽谤？"等。要想较好地证明这些论题，作者必须熟悉相关概念的定义，有了强有力的定义作为保证和支撑，论证过程就会顺利很多。

第四节　如何评价事实型议论文

完成一篇事实型议论文后，作者要有自我评价的意识。我们可以借助评价清单（checklist），从内容、语言、结构三方面对习作进行评价。评价清单可用于检测习作中是否包含了前文提到的议论文应有的论证要素，并检查这些要素是否起到了应有的作用。除此之外，评价清单还可作为修订和改进习作的依据，帮助我们养成反思自身思维过程的习惯。

前文提到，在事实型议论中，我们首先要清楚自己的写作目的和写作对象，了解读者可能对该话题持有怎样的看法和意见，再以此为依据进行写作。因此，我们在自评习作时，要先检查习作是否体现了读者意识，比如查看习作中是否提到了读者可能的观点。接下来要检查习作的逻辑思路是否清晰，这是检查中最重要的一个环节，比如整篇议论文的主张是否明确，主张和根据之间的关系是否解释得通，根据是否得到了进一步解释，保证是否需要进一步证明，习作是如何回应不同观点的。最后，我们需要检查习作是否采用了相关写作手段来提升情感诉求和人格诉求。

除了内容以外，我们还要对习作的结构和语言作出基本的自评。以下评价清单可供参考。

表 2-6　事实型议论文评价清单样例

Aspects		Guiding questions	√ / ×
Organization	Introduction and conclusion	• Does the writing have an opening and closing statement? • Does the ending leave the readers with a powerful thought?	
	Transitions	• Does the writing use transitions to get from one paragraph to the next?	

（续表）

Aspects		Guiding questions	√/×
Organization	Paragraph unity	• Does the writing include only one topic in each paragraph?	
Content	Reader awareness	• Does the writing include an understanding of the readers' opinions on the subject?	
	Logos	• Does the writing have one clear claim or multiple claims? • Do the grounds and warrants support the claim? • Does the warrant match the ground? • Are the grounds supported by evidence? • Does the writing respond to alternative views in a logical way?	
	Pathos	• Are the grounds based on readers' needs? • Does the writing use some techniques to tap the readers' imagination and emotions?	
	Ethos	• Does the writing show that the author is credible and knowledgeable about the subject?	
Language	Word choice and sentence variety	• Does the author use precise words and appropriate vocabulary for the subject? • Are sentences varied in length and structure?	
	Cohesion and coherence	• Does the writing use proper pronouns and clauses to create cohesion (especially to clarify the relationships among claims, grounds and warrants)?	
	Tone	• Is the tone (including style and voice) appropriate for the purpose and the readers?	
	Convention/ CUPS	• Are there errors in capitalization, usage, punctuation, and spelling (CUPS)? If so, do these errors interfere with others' understanding of the writing?	

上表内容可用于事实型议论文写作后的评价参考。当然，并非每次习作完成后都要检查表格中列出的所有问题，教师可以根据课程进度、学生的语言水平和学习需求选取部分角度和问题，辅助学生进行自我评价和同伴评价。此外，教师要考虑学生自我评价和同伴评价的有效性。比如，学生一般能够较为明显地看出自身习作结构上的不足；但在内容和语言方面，鉴于高中生认知能力和语言能力有限，仅靠学生自己或同龄人的观察，并不一定能准确识别出问题所在。因此，教师在写作评价中的作用是不可替代的，更多时候，学生仍然需要依靠教师的帮助，并且学生也更渴望和信赖来自教师的直接反馈。但需要注意的是，评价清单主要用于发现和指出问题，不能完全解决问题，当学生无法自己解决问题时，教师需要调动自身的知识储备、写作经历和教学智慧，给予学生具体的、可执行的修改建议。

📖 本章小结

本章介绍了事实型议论的概念，并根据前文提到的议论文相关知识，提供了事实型议论文的分析工具，从读者、作者、写作目的和三大诉求等方面列出相应的辅助问题，帮助本书读者从多角度分析一篇事实型议论文的观点。

本章还介绍了开展事实型议论文写作的七大步骤，从收集想法、组织想法到撰写提纲、谋篇布局，都给出了具体的操作方法和建议，并配以相应案例。最后，本章提供了事实型议论文评价清单样例，从结构、内容和语言三方面给出评价角度的建议，并提醒英语教师，除了学生自评和互评，还要重视教师评价。

第三章 如何写好价值型议论文

上一章介绍了事实型议论文的特点、分析方法及写作思路，本章将进入第二种议论类型——价值型议论文写作的探讨。

第一节 什么是价值型议论

价值型议论在日常生活中很常见。总体来说，它指的是对事物价值的评判，比如某件事是否是好的、是否是正确的、是否是道德的、是否是正义的。常见的价值型议论的论题有"吃狗肉是不人道的""这个牌子的车不好""这个行为是勇敢的"等，可以看到以上几个论题都使用带有价值判断的形容词充当表语；还有一类价值型论题则是形容词加名词的形式，比如"小张是个好演员""他是学生会主席的最佳人选""这是一辆质量上乘的卡车"等。价值型议论不仅涉及对单个事物或单个现象的判断，有时还体现在选择类论题上，比如"选择学 A 专业还是 B 专业""选择 A 礼物还是 B 礼物"等，每一个选择背后体现的就是价值标准的判断。

在价值型论题的论证中，最重要的就是价值标准。价值标准可能在某些情况下较为统一，但更多时候，价值标准因人而异或因情况而异。作者如果要有逻辑地进行一篇价值型议论文的写作，首先需要对价值标准作出解释。这个解释的过程就是价值型议论的重要一环。有些价值型议论的价值标准比较明确，比如"吃狗肉是不人道的"（Eating dog meat is inhumane），大部分读者对"不人道"（inhumane）这个概念都有一个较为基本的、普遍的理解。但还有一类价值型议论的价值标准就不够明确，比如"读大学是有价值的"（Going to college is of value），这个价值具体体现在哪方面呢？是经济价值（大学毕业生比非大学毕业生的收入高）、社会价值（在大学里可以结交到很多朋友）还是学术价值（大学可以拓宽专业眼界，提升思维能力）？对于这种价值标准较为宽泛的论题，作者需要进一步明确价值标准的定位，聚焦想要论证的要点。

第二节　如何分析价值型议论文

上一章，笔者介绍了事实型议论文的分析方法，首先要找到写作目的、作者及目标读者的需求，其次要分析三大修辞要素。对于每一方面，笔者都给出了具体的自设问题，方便本书读者以这些问题为提示，学会分析一篇事实型议论文是否具备了应有的要素，从而更好地汲取优秀事实型议论文的特点和精华。

和事实型议论文一样，价值型议论文也需要考虑作者和读者的背景及写作目的，但价值型议论文对理性诉求的要求更高。在一篇事实型议论文中，我们只需借助图尔敏论证模型分析清楚主张、根据和保证（尤其是隐性保证，即主张和根据之间的桥梁）三大基本要素，但对一篇价值型议论文来说，它的根据可能是一个新的事实型主张（详见第一章第四节），且这个事实型主张需要得到进一步论证。不仅如此，价值型议论文的保证也更难解释清楚，因为这涉及较为复杂的道德标准或评价标准，往往需要合理的、强有力的支撑。

分析案例1

以《高中英语》（牛津上海版）高二第一学期第 2 单元的一个语篇为例，该语篇是一个叫 Mandy Zhang 的学生写的对家教中心的评价。

Helpful

I have been studying at a tutorial centre for two years. The fees are very reasonable, and my command of English has improved greatly since I started.

My tutors are all qualified teachers. They are sincere and kind. I have been helped a lot by them.

One of my teachers was British. At first, I could not say anything to her. However, later I learnt how to communicate in English with a westerner.

I think that the tutorial centre has given me a lot of confidence in using English.

MANDY ZHANG

这个语篇分为四段，看似结构松散，但如果用图尔敏论证模型来分析，我们就会发现其中的合理性。

Backing: "being helpful" is defined in dictionaries as "something that helps in some way, like making a situation better or more pleasant".

Warrant: When a product or service is excellent in quality and reasonable in price, it can be called helpful.

Ground / Claim of fact:
The fees are reasonable, and my command of English has improved greatly.

Claim of value:
The tutorial centre is helpful.

Ground 1+Warrant 1:
The tutors are all qualified teachers. With their help, I learnt how to communicate in English with a westerner. (Grounds) Being able to communicate with a native speaker is a sure sign of improvement in one's language speaking abilities. (Warrant)

Ground 2+Warrant 2:
My confidence in using English has been improved. (Grounds) Learners' attitude improvement towards a subject contributes to one's overall skills. (Warrant)

从以上分析可以看出，该语篇的论证过程较为严谨。

首先，价值型主张是"家教中心是有帮助的（helpful）"，给出的根据是"家教中心价格合理，而且我的英语水平得到了很大提升"，这让读者很快就能察觉到作者隐含的评价标准，也就是"物美价廉的东西就是有帮助的"，这个标准就是价值型议论中的保证，它保证了根据的合理性。但从价值型议论的角度来说，保证本身还需要得到支撑，这里我们可以借助权威（也就是字典）来进一步证明什么是"有帮助的"（helpful）。

我们从图中可以看到,该价值型议论的根据本身也是一个需要证明的事实型主张。实际上,作者用了三个段落来证明"我的英语水平得到了很大提升",第一个理由是"我学会了和英语国家的人交流",第二个理由是"我说英语的信心提升了"。通过上图的分析可知,这两个理由完全能证明一个学习者的英语水平得到了提升。

如果说这则议论的逻辑还有什么缺憾,那就是作者在进一步证明根据时,只证明了"物美",而没有证明"价廉"。如果能够将"价廉"的证明补上,再对保证进行适当说明,议论就能更完整。以下是笔者根据图尔敏论证模型的分析对该语篇进行的扩写。

I have been studying at a tutorial centre for two years. The fees are very reasonable, and my command of English has improved greatly since I started.

My tutors are all qualified teachers. They are sincere and kind. I have been helped a lot by them. One of them was British. At first, I couldn't say anything to her. However, later I learnt how to communicate in English with a westerner. I could never imagine myself communicating with a native speaker in English, which is a sure sign of improvement of my English ability.

Besides, my confidence in using English has increased. I used to stammer when I was talking to others in English, but now I don't feel nervous any more. With my relaxed manner, I am positively sure that my English level will continue to improve.

What's more, the fees that the tutorial centre charges me are strictly within the price guidelines set by the government, which is very reasonable. With all the help I have got from the tutors there, I am pleased to say that the lessons are worth every penny. So I believe the tutorial centre is absolutely helpful to me.

借助图尔敏论证模型,我们可以发现价值型议论文的层次非常丰富。教师平日要指导学生多阅读并学会分析优秀的价值型议论文,帮助学生理

清思路，提升分析能力，并将清晰的逻辑应用于自己的习作中。

除此之外，指导学生使用图尔敏论证模型分析价值型议论文，还可以帮助学生找到价值型议论文中的逻辑谬误，也就是不合理的价值标准，比如下面这个案例。

分析案例 2

以《高中英语》（牛津上海版）高一第二学期第6单元主阅读语篇中的一段为例，该语段是价值型议论文，论题是"儿童拍广告是好还是坏？"，语段以读者来信的形式呈现。

> **Bad for children**
> With reference to your 'Little Spenders are Big Spenders' article, children should not be used as actors in TV commercials. It is illegal for them to work in factories, so why are they allowed to make commercials? Regarding the high salaries, it is bad for children to have too much money.
>
> ——Li Yue

从语段内容来看，作者是不支持儿童出演广告的，标题就是"对儿童有害"（Bad for children）。其根据有两条：一是既然儿童在工厂做工是违法的，拍广告也一样；二是孩子赚太多钱不好。我们先借助图尔敏论证模型分析第一条根据。

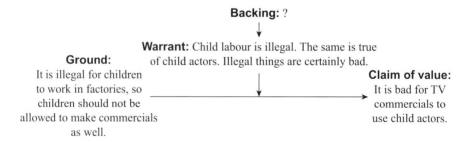

从左页图可以看出，该语段的主张是"电视广告中使用儿童演员是有害的"，根据是"工厂雇用童工是违法的，所以电视广告也不应该使用儿童演员"，潜在的隐性保证就是"儿童演员和童工一样，都是违法的，违法的事情肯定是有害的"。但这个保证并不牢靠，肯定会有人质疑："儿童演员怎么能和童工一样呢？"因此，该保证的支撑较难写下去。支撑是用来进一步解释保证的，但法律常识告诉我们，邀请儿童拍广告和工厂里使用儿童作为劳动力并不完全一样，看似都是儿童在工作，但权利保障不同。比如，根据我国有关法律规定，文艺、体育和特种工艺单位经审批可以招用未满16周岁的未成年人，但必须保障其各种权利；而童工不一样，其各种权利（包括接受义务教育的权利、人身安全等）都不能得到保障。因此，这个保证无法得到支撑。当保证不合理时，也就意味着这条根据站不住脚，不适合用来证明主张。相比之下，第二条根据（也就是"孩子赚太多钱"）更合理，因为这条根据背后的价值标准是"过早让孩子赚大钱可能使孩子形成错误的价值观，违背儿童成长规律，是不好的"，这条保证符合常理，能解释得通。

从这个例子可以看出，在分析价值型议论时，教师可以鼓励学生借助图尔敏论证模型来判断作者的价值标准是否清晰。如果发现价值标准存在值得怀疑之处，就说明作者的根据没有说服力，需要更换。

思考：

你能用图尔敏论证模型分析以下这个语段中存在的问题吗？

I disagree that TV commercials are bad for children. They cannot be harmful or the government would have banned them long ago.

——选自《高中英语》（牛津上海版）高一第二学期第6单元

从以上两个案例中，我们可以得出结论：价值型议论文中的保证就是价值标准。要判断一件事情或一个行为是好还是坏、是对还是错、有价值还是没价值，作者首先要厘清自己心中认定的价值标准，并将其清楚地表达出来。如果作者没有将价值标准明显地写出来，也不代表价值标准不存在，只不过变成了隐性保证。我们在分析这类价值型议论文时，就要试图推断出这个隐性保证，并衡量其合理性。

结合上述内容，我们可以用以下表格来分析价值型议论文。

表 3-1　价值型议论文分析工具

Aspects 方面	Guiding questions 自设问
The author and the writing purpose 作者和写作目的	• Who is the author? What background and beliefs does the author have? 作者是谁？作者有着怎样的背景和价值观？ • What is the author's writing purpose? 作者的写作目的是什么？
The target reader 目标读者	• Who are the target readers? 潜在的目标读者是谁？ • What is the relationship between the author and the readers? What tone（formal, informal or neutral）is used? 作者和读者之间是什么关系？使用了怎样的语气（正式、非正式还是中立）？ • How much do the readers know about the subject? 读者对这个话题了解多少？ • What assumptions, values or beliefs do the readers possibly hold? 读者可能持怎样的假设、价值观或信念？
Logos of the argument 理性诉求	• What is the claim of the argument? 这则议论的主张是什么？ • Are the value criteria reasonable? Can the criteria be further supported? 这则议论的价值标准是否合理？这些标准能否得到进一步支撑？ • Do the grounds meet the criteria? 根据是否符合这些价值标准？ • Do the grounds happen to be claims of fact that need to be further supported? 根据是否又是需要进一步证明的事实型主张？ • Does the argument consider possible conditions of rebuttal? 这则议论是否考虑到了可能的反驳条件？ • How does the argument respond to the conditions of rebuttal? 这则议论是如何回应这些反驳的？

（续表）

Aspects 方面	Guiding questions 自设问
Pathos of the argument 情感诉求	• Are the grounds based on readers' needs? 这些根据是否基于读者需求？ • What techniques（applying descriptions, narratives, examples, word choices）does the author use to arouse the readers' emotions and imagination? 作者使用了哪些手段（使用描写、叙述、举例、用词等）来唤起读者的情感和想象力？ • How does the author reveal his understanding of the readers? 作者如何展现出他对读者的理解？
Ethos of the argument 人格诉求	• How does the author project himself as a trustworthy person who is familiar with the subject being discussed? 作者如何把自己展现为一个值得读者信任、熟悉该话题的人？ • Is the author able to recognize the opposing views and how does he respond to them? 作者能否意识到相反观点？作者是如何回应相反观点的？

笔者仍以前文提到的《高中英语》（牛津上海版）高二第一学期第 2 单元的语篇为例，利用以上表格进行分析。

Helpful

I have been studying at a tutorial centre for two years. The fees are very reasonable, and my command of English has improved greatly since I started. My tutors are all qualified teachers. They are sincere and kind. I have been helped a lot by them.

One of my teachers was British. At first, I could not say anything to her. However, later I learnt how to communicate in English with a westerner.

I think that the tutorial centre has given me a lot of confidence in using English.

MANDY ZHANG

对照表 3-1 中的问题，我们可以进一步剖析这则价值型议论。

表 3-2 分析案例 1 议论语段分析

方面	自设问
作者和写作目的	• 该语篇的作者是该家教中心的一名学员。 • 作者写信给报社，对自己曾经上过课的家教中心作出评价。
目标读者	• 目标读者是刊载该信件的报纸的读者，因此语气较为正式或中立。 • 读者需要了解学员对家教中心的真实评价。
理性诉求	• 价值主张：该家教中心对学员是有帮助的。 • 价值标准：物美价廉的东西称得上是有帮助的。这条价值标准是符合常理的。 • 根据：该家教中心价格合理，而且我的英语水平得到了很大提升。该根据满足以上价值标准。 • 以上根据又是一个事实型主张，得到了进一步论证。 • 该论证没有涉及反驳。
情感诉求	• 在论证根据(也就是"我的英语水平得到了很大提升")的过程中，作者使用了详细的事例来说明自己的英语水平是如何提升的，以及提升到什么程度。亲身事例最能打动读者，唤起读者的情感和想象力。
人格诉求	• 作者开篇第一句话就提到"我在该家教中心学习了两年"，这句话充分体现了作者对家教中心的熟悉程度，从而大大提升了这篇价值型议论文的可信度。

从以上分析可以看出，一篇优秀的价值型议论文同样需要处理好三大诉求之间的关系：首先要考虑理性诉求，即主张、价值标准和根据之间的逻辑关系要清晰；其次，价值标准是一个较为主观的概念，每个人心中的价值标准各有不同，因此人格诉求尤为重要，作者最好能通过一些表述来增加自己话语的可信度，使读者更愿意相信其价值判断，比如该语篇里，作者家教中心长期学员的身份就大大提升了语篇的可信度；最后，为了让读者更好地接受自己的观点，情感诉求也不能少，适当运用描写和叙述手段可以激发读者的想象力，使他们产生共情。如果要提出一点建议，该语篇还可以适当增加相反意见，并做好反驳准备，以显示出作者对该家教中心的全面了解，进一步增加信件的可信度。

前文已详细分析了价值型议论中价值标准的重要性，事实上，对价值标准的探讨本身就是一个重要的话题。仍以家教中心的语篇为例，可以看到保证和支撑实际上探讨的就是"什么是有用的"，如果我们把保证和支撑单独拿出来，完全可以再写一篇文章，探讨"What kind of tutorial centre is a helpful one?"。这类有关价值标准的讨论就是价值标准写作，通常会涉及一些较抽象的或较复杂的价值概念的探讨。

分析案例 3

高中英语教材中就有价值标准写作的语篇案例。以《高中英语》（新世纪版）高三上学期第 5 单元的语篇为例，该语篇题为"What Is a Great Book"，整个语篇都在分析怎样的著作称得上是伟大著作。

> Great books are probably the most widely read. They are not bestsellers for a year or two. They are enduring bestsellers. Therefore, *Gone with the Wind* has had relatively fewer readers compared with the plays of Shakespeare.
>
> …

"伟大著作"这个话题非常值得探讨，该语篇为他人评价著作或推荐著作提供了价值准绳。当我们论证某本书是否能称作伟大著作时，就可以借助该语篇里的价值标准作为论证时的保证，比如"伟大著作的读者受众是最广泛的"（Great books are the most widely read）。而且，该语篇还对每一条价值标准进行了解释，也就是支撑。借助图尔敏论证模型，我们可以对语篇中的价值标准作出如下分析。

表 3-3 分析案例 3 的论证要素分析

Warrant	Backing
Great books are the most widely read and they stand the test of time.	Works of Shakespeare are enduring bestsellers, even topping *Gone with the wind*.
Great books are popular.	They address a large audience and are written for common people.

(续表)

Warrant	Backing
Great books are the most readable.	They can be read at different levels of understanding, and the reader can interpret them from different aspects. *Guliver's Travels* and *Robinson Crusoe* can delight both children and adults.
Great books are the most instructive.	They can make basic contributions to human thought and teach mankind something basic.

作为读者，如果我们赞同该语篇中作者对"伟大著作"的价值标准判断，就可以将此标准作为自己价值型议论文写作中的保证和支撑，来证明某本书称得上是伟大著作。当然，如果我们不赞同该语篇中的价值标准判断，也可以另写一篇文章阐明自己的看法。那么，当每个人都有自己的价值判断时，究竟谁的价值标准更合理呢？笔者将在下一节进行探讨。

第三节　如何开展价值型议论文写作

在开展价值型议论文写作之前，我们首先要问自己一个问题——我能否将论题中的价值标准解释清楚？以《高中英语》（沪外教版）必修第二册第 2 单元 Reading A 语篇的话题为例，该语篇讨论的是"动物园是残忍的还是有爱的？"（Zoos: Cruel or Caring?）

如果我们认为动物园是残忍的，我们首先要问自己怎样的行为通常被称为"残忍"。有人可能会说，残忍的东西就是不好的东西。那么，什么样的东西是不好的呢？好和坏的标准又该如何判断呢？对于这样的价值标准判断，逻辑学提出两种主要的推理方法——后果法（argument from consequences）和原则法（argument from principles）。如果对价值标准的判断符合后果法或原则法，则可以认为这个价值标准判断基本合理。

后果法又称为实用主义议论法。简单来说，后果法的推理过程如下：如果某一事物或行为可能产生一个实际意义上的良好结果或实现一个好的目标，这一事物或行为就是正确的或可行的。但是，后果法也有其缺点：首先，后果都是假设出来的，不具备可验证性；其次，后果很可能只是短期的，长期后果很难预测[①]。

原则法的推理则依赖于世间存有的普遍原则。简单来说，原则法的推理过程如下：如果某一事物或行为符合某一公认的原则或规定，这一事物或行为就是正确的或可行的；反之，如果违背了某一原则或规定，则是错误的或不可行的[②]。

根据以上两种方法，我们来尝试分析"对动物来说什么是残忍"。首先，根据后果法，我们可以思考一下动物被长时间关在动物园里会产生什么后果。动物生存空间狭窄，可能导致其情绪抑郁；动物长期被喂养，可能导致其失去基本的捕猎能力；动物可能遭到饲养员的虐待，没有反抗的能力；动物可能被迫表演节目，导致自己受伤。以上这些后果都是动物在动物园里可能遭遇的情况，是对鲜活生命的糟蹋，可以称得上"残忍"。

其次，根据原则法，动物园违背了哪些动物生存的天性或原则呢？我们可以想到，动物园束缚了动物自由的天性，剥夺了动物捕猎的本能，强行将动物与它们的族群分离。动物园的动物和人类一样都是生命，都有被尊重的权利，但以上这些违背了"任何生命应该得到尊重"的基本原则。因此，根据原则法，动物园是残忍的。

因此，在价值型议论文写作之前，教师可以鼓励学生从后果法和原则法两个角度去思考。这两种方法可以帮助我们在价值型议论中开展有方向的思考，列出更多合理的理由来证明我们的价值判断。

除此之外，有时我们还需要在两种价值标准间作出选择。仍然以"动物园是残忍的还是有爱的？"这一论题为例。根据上文介绍的后果法和原则法，我们同样可以论证"动物园是有爱的"，比如动物园带来的后果之一也有可能是保护稀有动物、防止某个物种灭绝等。那么，在两者皆有道理的情况下，作者就需要进行对比。比如，"残忍"实际上指的是"动物的生存状态残忍"，"有爱"指的是"动物园能够保护稀有动物"，我们就可以

---

① Walton D. Informal Logic: A Pragmatic Approach [M]. 2nd ed. New York, NY: Cambridge University Press, 2008.

② Stoner I, Swartwood J. Doing Practical Ethics [M]. Oxford: Oxford University Press, 2021.

思考"动物在动物园里的生存状态和某些动物作为一个物种的稀缺性，以上两者中哪个更为重要？"。梳理到此处，我们会发现，其实两者不具备可比性，前者指动物园里所有动物，而后者指的是少数稀有动物。这时，作者还可以进一步明确主张，添加图尔敏论证模型中的一大要素——限定（qualifier）（详见第一章第三节），也就是在原有主张的基础上加上"对大多数动物来说"，即"对大多数动物来说，动物园是残忍的"。这样的主张更实际，也更不容易遭到反驳。当然，如果需要的话，也可以对相反观点进行适当反驳，我们可以先概括一下对方的观点，也就是"动物园确实能够保护稀有物种不灭绝"，然后进行反驳，即"不能因为要保护少数稀有物种，就将多数动物囚禁在动物园中"，甚至可以提出建议——"对于稀有动物，可以专门建立稀有动物保护区，而不是以动物园的形式将所有动物关在一起"。

为了更加清楚地展现思考过程，笔者将以上述价值型论题"To most animals, zoos are cruel"为例，通过详细步骤，完整地说明价值型议论文的写作过程。

步骤一：头脑风暴，拓展思路

首先，根据该价值型论题的主张"对大多数动物来说，动物园是残忍的"，我们需要尽可能多地提供根据。可以从后果和原则两方面入手，比如将动物在动物园里的遭遇写下来，并思考把动物关在动物园里违背了哪些公认的原则或准则。

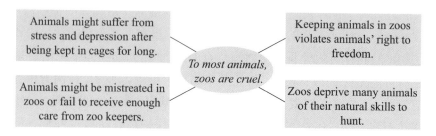

步骤二：借助图尔敏论证模型检查逻辑关系

接下来，我们需要将以上理由放在图尔敏论证模型的框架下，验证其逻辑关系是否清晰合理。这里，笔者选取其中两个理由进行验证。

① **Backing:** If something leads to extremely damaging consequences, it is considered undesirable or cruel.

↓

Warrant: It is considered cruel if animals suffer from mistreatment in zoos.

Ground 1 / Claim of fact:
Animals might be mistreated in zoos or fail to receive enough care from zoo keepers.

→

Claim of value and Qualifier:
To most animals, zoos are cruel.

Ground: It is reported that many animals died in zoos from causes ranging from malnourishment, hypothermia, and lack of veterinary care to outright neglect.
Warrant: If the symptoms are not easily found in animals in the wild, then they result from mistreatment in the zoo.

② **Backing:** If something violates certain basic principles essential for the well-being of a living thing, it is considered undesirable or cruel.

↓

Warrant: It is considered cruel if a living thing is forced to lose its natural disposition.

Ground 2 / Claim of fact:
Many animals are deprived of the opportunity to develop their natural skills, like hunting.

→

Claim of value and Qualifier:
To most animals, zoos are cruel.

Ground: Studies show captive animals can show deficiencies in hunting, social interactions, breeding and nesting, and locomotory skills, compared with wild animals.
Warrant: If an animal in the wild can develop the necessary surviving skills, then it is the environment in the zoo that causes its loss of abilities.

经过验证，我们发现这两个理由逻辑清晰，价值标准符合常理，能够证明主张。当然，如前文所述，这个主张是有限定的，也就是"对大多数动物来说"，这样能使我们的立论更合理，不容易被驳斥。

步骤三：确定目标读者和读者需求
该论题没有给出明确的交际情境，因此不清楚写作对象，但是我们可以预想到，价值型议论文的读者无非分为两类：一类站在正向，一类站在反向。因此，作者在构思时要尽量摸清读者的立场，做好说服反向读者的准备。

步骤四：理解相反观点，及时作出回应
根据上一步骤的分析，肯定存在持有相反观点的读者。因此，作者

一定要充分理解相反观点，予以恰当的反驳。比如，相反观点可能有"动物园为学校的孩子提供教育资源""动物园起到了保护濒危动物的作用"等。针对以上观点，作者可以找到其中的逻辑漏洞并进行回击，比如"动物园为学校的孩子提供教育资源"并不代表"动物园是不残忍的"，指出两者没有逻辑联系。作者也可以承认对方观点的合理性，然后从新的角度加以驳斥，比如"动物园的确为孩子提供了教育资源，但并不能以牺牲动物的健康为代价，否则这种教育方式是有问题的""有关动物的教育资源不一定要从动物园中获取，采用虚拟现实技术，学生同样有身临其境之感"。

步骤五：考虑情感诉求和人格诉求

价值型议论对情感诉求和人格诉求的要求较高，因为改变他人的价值准绳本身就是一件较难的事情。因此，在写作时，除了使自己的逻辑尽量清晰之外，作者还需要借助情感诉求和人格诉求来提升价值型议论文的可信度和论证效果。比如，作者可以上网搜索一些关于动物园中动物生存状态的研究，引用相关数据，或具体描写动物的不良状况，通过这些情感诉求来引起读者对动物遭遇的重视。人格诉求方面，作者要在写作中充分展示自己对这个话题的了解，比如查阅了权威资料，咨询了相关人士，或亲眼见过动物园一些动物的遭遇等，增加话语的可信度。

步骤六：组织语篇布局

一个清晰的布局可以帮助读者更好地理清作者的写作思路，英文写作强调线性思维，清楚的布局尤其重要。和事实型议论一样，价值型议论的布局方式大致分为以下两种。

表3-4　布局1

步骤	要点
引入论题和主张	1. Arouse the readers' attention by introducing the issue of animals' situation in zoos. 2. Introduce the claim with the qualifier that "zoos are cruel to most animals".

（续表）

步骤	要点
给出根据 1+ 价值标准 1	1. State the first ground（which is also a claim of fact）and give supporting details to the claim of fact. 2. State the warrant and backing, explaining clearly the value criteria（possibly from the consequence-based angle）.
给出根据 2+ 价值标准 2	1. State the second ground（which is also a claim of fact）and give supporting details to the claim of fact. 2. State the warrant and backing, explaining clearly the value criteria（possibly from the principle-based angle）.
提出反驳	1. Summarize the possible objections. 2. Respond to the objections either through rebuttal or concessions.
结语	1. Sum up the argument. 2. Remind the readers of the firm attitude you take towards this issue.

表 3-5 布局 2

步骤	要点
引入论题和主张	1. Arouse the readers' attention by introducing the issue of animals' situation in zoos. 2. Introduce the claim with the qualifier that "zoos are cruel to most animals".
提出心目中价值标准的定义	State the warrant and backing, i.e. the value criteria in your mind（both the argument from consequences and the argument from principles）.
给出根据 1	1. State the first ground（which is also a claim of fact）and show how the ground matches the value criteria. 2. Give supporting details to the claim of fact.
给出根据 2	1. State the second ground（which is also a claim of fact）and show how the ground matches the value criteria. 2. Give supporting details to the claim of fact.

（续表）

步骤	要点
提出反驳	1. Summarize the possible objections. 2. Respond to the objections either through rebuttal or concessions.
结语	1. Sum up the argument. 2. Remind the readers of the firm attitude you take towards this issue.

　　以上两种布局方式的主要差异在于何时引出价值标准。第一种在表明主张后直接给出第一条根据，价值标准（也就是 warrant 和 backing）紧随其后作为补充说明，让读者明白第一条根据的合理性。接下来，作者以同样的方式陈述第二条根据。这种布局可以将不同根据的价值标准分开陈述，使读者在阅读不同根据时分别理解这两种价值标准，价值标准遵循的可能是后果法，也可能是原则法。

　　第二种布局方式则将关于价值标准的陈述提前，在引入主张后先给出价值标准。以这则议论为例，就是让读者先明白"残忍"的定义，什么样的情况对动物来说是残忍的，然后分别列出根据和它们的支撑细节，并展现出这几条根据是如何匹配价值标准的。

　　作者可根据自己的需要和表达习惯选择任意一种布局方式。需要注意的是，不论选择哪一种，都要做好驳斥相反意见的准备，并且在最后一段要重新陈述自己的观点，让读者感受到作者对论题的坚定态度。

步骤七：根据提纲产出语篇

　　下面我们就可以进入写作的最后一个步骤，选取以上任意一种布局，添加过渡语，撰写完整的价值型议论文。

第四节　如何评价价值型议论文

　　在写完一篇价值型议论文后，我们同样需要借助评价清单，从内容、语言和结构三方面对习作展开相应的评价。从内容看，我们首先要检查价值标准，比如作者是否明确写出价值标准，价值标准是否合理（是否符合后果法或原则法），价值标准是否夹带作者个人偏好，等等。其次，我们要检查所给出的根据是否符合这一价值标准。最后，在价值型议论中，所给出的根据通常又是一个事实型议论，所以我们需要检查根据是否得到了进一步证明。除此之外，价值型议论文中还有一个很重要的元素，就是限定。价值型议论文中，通常需要限定价值标准所针对的对象，也就是具体说清楚究竟对哪一方有价值（比如第三节提到的"对大多数动物来说，动物园是残忍的"），以提升主张的可信度。因此，限定也是检查的重点。

　　如果以上逻辑都正确，接下来要检查写作目的是否清晰，同时观察习作是否考虑到情感诉求和人格诉求，比如所给理由是否贴近读者需求，能否回应读者对这个论题的关切，是否采用适当的手段调动读者的感情和想象力。以下评价清单可供参考。

表 3-6　价值型议论文评价清单样例

Aspects		Guiding questions	√ / ×
Organization	Introduction and conclusion	• Does the writing have an opening and closing statement? • Does the ending leave the readers with a powerful thought?	
	Transitions	• Does the writing use transitions to get from one paragraph to the next?	
	Paragraph unity	• Does the writing include only one topic in each paragraph?	
Content	Reader awareness	• Does the writing include an understanding of the readers' values or beliefs?	
	Logos	• Is the claim limited by a proper qualifier? • Does the writing have clear value criteria? • Do the grounds match the value criteria? • Are the grounds further supported? • Does the writing respond to alternative views in a logical way?	

（续表）

Aspects		Guiding questions	√/×
Content	*Pathos*	• Are the grounds based on readers' needs? • Does the writing use some techniques to tap the readers' imagination and emotions?	
	Ethos	• Does the writing show that the author is credible and trustworthy?	
Language	Word choice and sentence variety	• Does the author use precise words and appropriate vocabulary for the subject? • Are sentences varied in length and structure?	
	Cohesion and coherence	• Does the writing use words, phrases, or clauses to create cohesion and clarify the relationships among claims, grounds and warrants?	
	Tone	• Is the tone（including style and voice）appropriate for the purpose and the readers?	
	Convention/ CUPS	• Are there errors in capitalization, usage, punctuation, and spelling（CUPS）? If so, do these errors interfere with others' understanding of the writing?	

由于不涉及具体的写作话题，以上评价清单是较为笼统的，教师在使用时可根据具体话题进行相应的细化。也可以在写作的过程中，与学生相互协商，共同生成评价清单。

师生共同生成评价清单有很多好处：一方面，学生可以在教师分步骤写作指导下进行反思，发现自己在写作中可能出现的问题以及需要注意的地方；另一方面，教师可以将评价贯穿过程性写作过程，而不仅仅在最后一个环节出现，让学生体会到"评价即学习"（assessment as learning）。

📖 本章小结

本章介绍了价值型议论的概念，并从价值型议论文的分析、写作步骤和评价三个方面给出了具体的操作方法和建议，每部分都配上了相应案例或说明加以解释。

价值型议论文中的价值标准尤其值得注意。从图尔敏论证模型来看，价值型议论文中的保证即价值标准，价值标准往往还需要通过支撑进行论证。如果论证过程中出现障碍，说明根据不成立，可能产生逻辑谬误。有关好和坏的价值标准有着较深的哲学内涵，通常可以用后果法和原则法来判断，即带来良好结果或符合公认原则的事情通常被认为是好的，反之则是坏的。

本章分七个步骤详细介绍了价值型议论文写作的教学方法，并给出了参考的评价清单。建议教师可以在分步骤写作教学过程中和学生共同探讨并生成评价清单，使评价真正参与学习过程。

第四章　如何写好政策型议论文

根据第一章的介绍，议论主要包括事实型、价值型和政策型。之所以将政策型议论放在最后，是因为三种议论类型之间是层层递进的关系，政策型议论通常要建立在价值型和事实型议论的基础上。下面将进入第三种类型——政策型议论文写作的探讨。

第一节　什么是政策型议论

政策型议论涉及应该采取的行动，比如"公共场合应该禁止吸烟""小区应该搭建一个儿童游乐园"或"人类应该为子孙后代保护地球"。对以上话题稍作分析可以发现，政策型议论的话题都建立在价值判断的基础上。比如，"公共场合应该禁止吸烟"建立在"吸烟有害健康"的基础上，"小区应该搭建一个儿童游乐园"建立在"儿童游乐园有利于小区居民"的基础上，"保护地球"建立在"对后代有益"的基础上，可见政策型议论几乎离不开价值主张。

政策型议论的目的通常是号召他人行动起来，因此，和事实型、价值型议论略有不同，政策型议论通常始于一个作者或读者关心的问题。正是因为这个问题的存在，我们需要制定相应的政策来应对它，还需要号召他人采纳这项政策。所以，政策型议论不会在写作开篇就提出主张（making claims），而是需要一个"预备"阶段，即向读者阐明一个亟待解决的问题。这一"预备"步骤是政策型议论文中不可或缺的，它向读者阐明了议论开展的必要性，也为议论开展提供了前提条件。

有了亟待解决的问题后，政策型议论文写作才能真正开始。针对问题，作者通常会抛出一个解决方案，即政策，并在后文予以支撑，劝说读者采纳这个政策。在这个过程中，作者可以问自己一系列问题，比如"为什么要采纳这个政策？""为什么这个政策有可取之处？""这个政策是否能解决问题？""这个政策是否可行？""为什么这个政策比现有的政策要好？"。这些问题的答案就是该政策得以被支撑的关键。

　　根据作者身份和写作对象的不同，政策型议论大体分为以下两种：该不该做和怎么做。如果作者和写作对象的身份或经验悬殊（比如作为学生给市环境部门写一封信，提出提高空气质量的建议），或者写作、交流的对象不是政策执行者，只是一个普通读者（比如与同学一起探讨全世界应该如何抵御全球变暖），该政策型议论只能算是一封宏观的建议信，给出较为笼统的呼吁和号召（比如倡导绿色出行、减少尾气排放等）。但如果作者十分了解政策执行的细节，是政策的直接受益方（比如作为学生给学校的秋游计划提建议），甚至本身就是政策的执行者（比如作为环保社的一员为环保社清除校园垃圾提建议），该政策型议论就不仅仅是号召众人行动起来，而是涉及一个具体的策划书，可能会细化到时间、地点、工作人员的安排、费用等。

　　除此之外，政策型议论文通常还涉及政策之间的比较，要证明一个政策值得采纳，就必须和现有政策或其他可选政策进行对比。因此，在有些政策型议论文的写作中，还会用到比较和对比的写作手法。

第二节　如何分析政策型议论文

　　教师首先要自己学会分析政策型议论文，才能更好地带领学生阅读政策型议论文。根据上文分析，政策型议论文通常包含三部分：首先是问题的描述，其次是政策的提出，最后是对政策的解释。因此，在分析政策型议论文时，我们要先找到问题，即作者提出的政策针对的是什么问题。

分析案例1

　　通常来说，在政策型议论文中，作者会直接交代想要解决的问题。以《高中英语》（外研社版）选择性必修第二册第 6 单元的阅读语篇 Plan B:

Life on Mars? 中的一个节选为例：

In the 1960s and 1970s, the greatest fear was that the human race, and possibly all advanced life forms on the planet, could be wiped out by nuclear missiles, just at the push of a button. Today, however, environmental problems have taken over as the greatest risk to life on Earth. Scientists are thinking of ways to lower this risk, such as replacing coal and oil with forms of renewable energy. But they are also preparing for the worst: what can we do if the terrifying scenes in films such as *The Day After Tomorrow* happen in real life? What is our Plan B for Earth?

One option is to explore other planets to see if we could live on them. The most likely choice is Mars, which is relatively close to Earth and has an environment less hostile than that of other planets. Mars has fascinated people since ancient times, and today our interest in Martian exploration is greater than ever before. Films such as *The Martian* enjoy worldwide popularity. More governments and organizations are making efforts to educate the public on the Red Planet, for example, the Mars Desert Research Station in the Utah desert of the US and the Mars Village in North-west China's Qinghai Province.

　　该语篇节选第一段就呈现了地球所面临的问题——从 20 世纪六七十年代人类担忧的核武器问题到现在的环保问题，这些问题迫使人们不得不作好最坏的打算。作者之所以这样写，就是在强调问题的重要性和紧迫性，促使读者去思考可能的解决方案，政策也就呼之欲出。接着，作者在第二段开头给出了解决方案——"探索其他星球，看是否适合人类居住"（to explore other planets to see if we could live on them）。

　　第二段剩下的内容起什么作用呢？仔细阅读和思考后，我们会发现这些内容其实就是对该解决方案作出解释：一方面，从情感上拉近读者和该方案的距离（比如长期以来人类对火星的兴趣）；另一方面，详述方案的可行性（火星和地球的距离较近且环境较为友好，以及公众做好了相关心理准备）。

可见，该语篇节选是典型的政策型议论文。同样地，我们可以用图尔敏论证模型来梳理一下逻辑关系。

① **Warrant:** If the earth is no longer fit to live one day, human beings will have to do something for their survival—looking for other planets to live on.

Ground 1 / Claim of fact:
The earth might be destroyed one day.

Claim of policy:
Human beings should explore Mars to see if we could live on it.

Ground: Problems like nuclear missiles and environmental risks are threatening the earth.
Warrant: There is a limit to what mother nature can sustain. If nothing is done to solve the problems, Earth's destruction may be on the way.

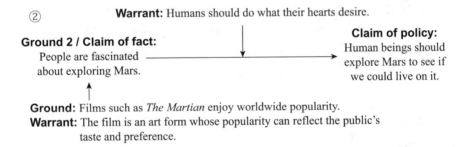

② **Warrant:** Humans should do what their hearts desire.

Ground 2 / Claim of fact:
People are fascinated about exploring Mars.

Claim of policy:
Human beings should explore Mars to see if we could live on it.

Ground: Films such as *The Martian* enjoy worldwide popularity.
Warrant: The film is an art form whose popularity can reflect the public's taste and preference.

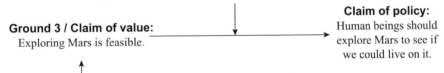

③ **Warrant:** Feasibility is an important factor in carrying out a policy.

Ground 3 / Claim of value:
Exploring Mars is feasible.

Claim of policy:
Human beings should explore Mars to see if we could live on it.

Ground: Mars is close to Earth and has a less hostile environment.
Efforts have been made to educate the public about Mars.
Warrant: Feasible means achievable. The conditions on Mars make it possible for humans to explore and educating the public about Mars prepares people to accept the plan of exploring Mars.

从上述分析来看，该语篇节选只有一个大的政策型主张，即"人类应该探索火星"，该主张由三条根据来支撑，第一条根据是"地球有一天可能会毁灭"，第二条根据是"人们对火星探索一直很着迷"，第三条根据是"探索火星是可行的"，每一条根据同时又是一个事实型或价值型主张。这再次印证了第一章提出的"政策型议论通常建立在价值型议论和事实型议论基础上"的观点。具体结构如下所示：

政策型主张：人类应该探索火星，看是否适合人类居住。

　根据1：地球有一天可能会毁灭。（事实型主张）

　　保证1：人类为了生存，不得不寻找其他星球居住。

　根据2：人类对火星探索一直很着迷。（事实型主张）

　　保证2：人们应该去做自己想做的事。

　根据3：探索火星是可行的。（价值型主张）

　　保证3：一项政策必须有可行性，才能推动读者去执行。

从以上树状结构可以看出，语篇开头提到的地球所面临的问题已经转化成了第一条根据。事实上，政策型议论文想要解决的问题本身就是提出该政策的一大原因，也就是对"为什么要提出这项政策"作出回答。因此，问题描述的位置比较灵活，既可以放在政策型议论文的开头，作为写作背景或前提，也可以放在政策型主张之后，作为第一条根据。不过，不论放在哪个位置，问题的描述都必不可少。最重要的是，作者要把问题的重要性和紧迫性解释清楚。

有读者可能会问：我在写作时如何想出这么多理由呢？前文提到，政策型议论文几乎都涉及价值主张，之所以要采纳某政策，肯定是因为该政策能带来某种好处。这就是第三章提到的后果法，某件事情如果能带来某种好处或避免某种坏处，这件事就值得去做，政策型议论也是这样。除了后果法，第三章提到的原则法同样适用于政策型议论，一项政策如果符合某原则，比如符合人的天性或事物发展的规律，这项政策就应该采纳。从这个思路出发，我们不妨分析一下该语篇的三条根据分别是从哪些角度来写的。

第一条根据"地球有一天可能会毁灭"是通过后果法得出的，该政策（人类应该探索火星）的执行可以避免地球毁灭带来的坏处，给人类带来福音。因此，这项政策应该执行。

第二条根据"人类对火星探索一直很着迷"是通过原则法得出的，探索火星是人类一直以来的愿望，有梦想就要去追逐，这符合人类的本性。因此，这项政策应该执行。

第三条根据"探索火星是可行的"是政策型议论文写作的关键，也是政策型议论文相较于价值型议论文不一样的地方，因为它不仅要考虑应然，还要考虑实然。对价值型议论文来说，作者只需论述一件事情是好是坏、是对是错，也就是应然；但政策型议论文带有操作性质，目的是号召人们行动起来，只考虑应然是不够的。如果一项政策由于某些条件的限制无法开展，说明该政策只在应然上成立，在实然上是不成立的。换句话说，该政策不能解决实际问题，那么这篇政策型议论文的效力就会大打折扣。仍以探索火星这个语篇节选为例，如果没有第三条理由，这篇政策型议论文完全可以转化为价值型议论文，即"探索火星对人类是有益的"或"探索火星是正确的"，但有了第三条理由后，这就是一篇实实在在的政策型议论文了，因为它让读者有了展开行动的勇气和动力。

由此可见，除了后果法和原则法之外，还要从实际操作层面思考政策型议论文的理由，也就是前文提到的"这个政策是否可行？""为什么这个政策比现有的政策要好？""这个政策是否有成功的先例？"等。作者只有想清楚这些问题，才能给出足够的根据来支撑政策型议论文。

从该语篇节选的分析中，我们明白了如何观察政策型议论文的逻辑架构，并得出以下结论：

（1）政策型议论文建立在价值型议论文和事实型议论文的基础上；

（2）政策型议论文必须包含要解决的问题，该问题可以放在议论文开头作为背景，也可以作为第一条理由；

（3）政策型议论文的根据最好既涉及应然，也涉及实然。

分析案例2

政策型议论文还常常涉及政策之间的比较和选择，即应该做 A 还是做 B。以《高中英语》（沪教版）选择性必修第三册第 2 单元的一个语篇为例，该语篇的论题是"埃及文物罗塞塔石碑应该放在大英博物馆还是交还埃及人民保管"。

... Imagine having an important national monument from your country kept permanently in another country. How would you feel? Would you try to get the country to return it? It's not surprising that many countries have gone on to ask for their treasures back. However, where they should be kept is a question that is still heatedly debated.

...

首先，我们来观察一下该语篇中问题的提出，也就是这句话 "Imagine having an important national monument from your country kept permanently in another country. How would you feel?"（想象一下我国的民族瑰宝被永久保存在另一个国家，你会是什么感觉？）。在这里，作者动用了大量的情感诉求来调动读者的想象力，比如 an important national monument（民族瑰宝）这一短语的使用，就隐含了作者本人的观点，该短语用到了 national 一词，意味着作者心中早已默认这些文物应归属母国。否则，作者完全可以使用不带情感色彩的短语，比如 the world heritage（世界遗产）或者 the cultural relic（文化遗迹）。除此之外，作者还使用了情感色彩很强的问句（How would you feel? Would you try to get the country to return it?），引导读者设身处地思考这一问题，调动他们的情感。可见作者描述问题时已经在暗示自己的立场。虽然直到语篇结束，作者都没有以肯定句的方式给出一个明确的政策型主张，但最后一段的 "Remember to ask yourself ..." 足以表明作者的观点，即 "这些文物应该送回埃及"。

从论证逻辑看，这篇政策型议论文列出了大英博物馆和埃及政府双方的观点。根据图尔敏论证模型，我们可总结出双方的观点。

以下是罗塞塔石碑应该由埃及保管的逻辑链条分析：

①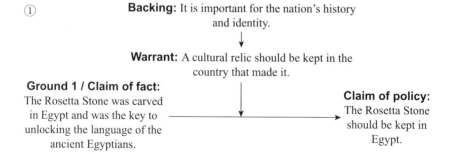

②

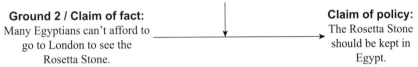

Warrant: A cultural relic should be kept at a place that brings greater benefit and convenience to the people of this culture.

Ground 2 / Claim of fact: Many Egyptians can't afford to go to London to see the Rosetta Stone.

Claim of policy: The Rosetta Stone should be kept in Egypt.

埃及政府给出的根据主要有两条。第一条根据基于原则法，即任何物件都归属于诞生地，这符合事物的天然属性，一个国家的文物对该国的历史和身份认同很重要，这是毋庸置疑的原则。第二条根据基于后果法及实际操作层面，如果罗塞塔石碑被放在英国保管，埃及人看不到自己国家的文物，这对埃及人来说是不利的。而且，很多埃及人负担不起去伦敦参观的费用，在操作层面无法实现，这就是前文提到的政策型议论文中的实然根据。

同样，作者列出了大英博物馆给出的根据，以下是罗塞塔石碑应该由大英博物馆保管的逻辑链条分析：

①

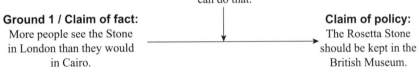

Warrant: A cultural relic should be kept at a place that can benefit a larger audience and the British Museum can do that.

Ground 1 / Claim of fact: More people see the Stone in London than they would in Cairo.

Claim of policy: The Rosetta Stone should be kept in the British Museum.

②

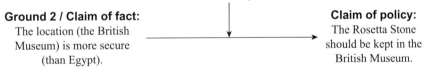

Warrant: A treasure like this may attract the attention of thieves and should be kept somewhere safer.

Ground 2 / Claim of fact: The location (the British Museum) is more secure (than Egypt).

Claim of policy: The Rosetta Stone should be kept in the British Museum.

③

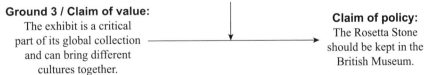

Warrant: A cultural relic should be kept where global cultural exchange can be better promoted.

Ground 3 / Claim of value: The exhibit is a critical part of its global collection and can bring different cultures together.

Claim of policy: The Rosetta Stone should be kept in the British Museum.

大英博物馆的根据来自三方面。第一条和第三条根据基于后果法，即罗塞塔石碑放在大英博物馆可以让更多游客看到，以及罗塞塔石碑是大英博物馆全球馆藏的关键组成部分，有利于促进国际文化的交流和传播。第二条根据基于原则法，即任何重要的财物都会涉及安全问题，因此将文物放在安全的地方是符合安全原则的。

在陈述完双方的理由后，作者在最后一段针对大英博物馆的第三条理由进行了反驳，认为这种促进文化融合的尝试效果并不理想，最终只会带来"无休止的国际争论"（never-ending international arguments）和"不友好的外交关系"（frosty relations with foreign countries）。

对于另外两条理由，作者没有反驳，而作为读者，我们可以尝试一下是否能够驳斥。比如第一条根据（罗塞塔石碑放在大英博物馆可以让更多观众看到），如第三章所说，我们可以先退一步，承认大英博物馆确实可以吸引更多观众，然后对保证予以驳斥，即"文物由谁保管不应该由博物馆的名气或观众人数决定，罗塞塔石碑是世界文化遗产，更是埃及人的国宝。文物首要应归属于母国，供本族人民瞻仰和研究，其次才是国际观众"；或者，我们可以先顺着这条保证的思路，引发读者反思文物的所有权是否应该由观众人数决定，比如："如果有一天埃及博物馆的名望超过了大英博物馆，英国是否愿意将自己国家的文物交给埃及博物馆保管呢？"如此一来，这条保证就没有了力度。

大英博物馆给出的第二条根据（大英博物馆更安全）就更容易驳斥了。这条根据也是一个事实型主张，需要得到进一步证明。只要稍加思考，我们就会发现这条根据本身就是值得怀疑的，因为大英博物馆不一定比埃及安全。在全球商品和贸易通畅的21世纪，难道只有大英博物馆有安全的文物保管场所吗？显然并非如此。

因此，仅从大英博物馆和埃及政府双方立论的合理性来看，埃及政府的立论更站得住脚。埃及政府给出的第一条根据基于原则法，指出任何物件都归属于诞生地，就像孩子不能忘记母亲；第二条根据从现实操作层面出发，提到许多埃及人负担不起前往英国观看自己国家文物的费用，这不利于埃及人民形成文化认同感，也给埃及人民带来了诸多不便。不论从根据还是保证来看，这两条理由都是难以驳斥的。相比之下，大英博物馆给出的理由漏洞百出，要么根据本身值得怀疑，要么保证没有力度，很容易遭到驳斥。

　　通过以上案例，我们学会了分析带有比较性质的政策型议论文。通常来说，在进行政策比较时，作者必须熟悉双方各自的理由，才能对他方政策作出更好的驳斥，从而捍卫己方的政策。此外，该语篇节选向我们展示了政策型议论文中实然理由的重要性，要证明一项政策能否顺利实施，或另一项政策为什么不能顺利实施，最好都能列出实然理由，从操作层面说服读者。

　　现在我们对政策型议论文有了更清晰的认识，以下表格可以帮助我们在阅读政策型议论文时理清思路。

表 4-1　政策型议论文分析工具

Aspects 方面	Guiding questions 自设问
The author, the target reader and the writing purpose 作者、目标读者和写作目的	• What is the author's writing purpose? Does the writer aim for a specific plan or a general suggestion? 作者的写作目的是什么？作者想写具体的策划书还是笼统的建议信？
The author, the target reader and the writing purpose 作者、目标读者和写作目的	• Who is the author? What background, belief, related experience and problem-solving skills does the author have? 作者是谁？作者有着怎样的背景、价值观、相关经验和解决问题的能力？ • Who are the target readers? What background, beliefs, related experience and problem-solving skills does the readers have? What kind of resources can the readers or policy practitioners mobilize? 潜在的目标读者是谁？读者有着怎样的背景、价值观、相关经验和解决问题的能力？读者或政策实施者能调动怎样的资源？ • What is the relationship between the author and the readers? What tone（formal, informal or neutral）is used? 作者和读者之间是什么关系？使用了怎样的语气（正式、非正式还是中立）？

（续表）

Aspects 方面	Guiding questions 自设问
Logos of the argument 理性诉求	• What is the claim of the argument of policy? 这则议论的政策型主张是什么？ • What problem is the policy aimed at solving? Is the problem important or urgent? 这个政策想要解决什么问题？这个问题重要或紧急吗？ • Do the grounds explain why the policy is desirable and feasible? 根据是否解释了为何该政策是正确且可行的（应然和实然）？ • Is the ground also a claim of fact or a claim of value that needs to be further supported? 根据是否是需要进一步证明的事实型或价值型主张？ • Are the grounds supported by reasonable warrants? 根据是否有合理的保证来支撑？ • Does the argument consider alternative policies? 这则议论是否考虑到了其他可选的政策？ • How does the argument rebut the alternative policies? 这则议论是如何反驳这些可选政策的？
Pathos of the argument 情感诉求	• What techniques does the author use to bring attention to the problem to be addressed? 作者使用了哪些手段来引起读者关注要解决的问题？ • What techniques（applying descriptions, narratives, examples, word choices）does the author use to arouse the readers' emotions and imagination? 作者使用了哪些手段（使用描写、叙述、举例、用词等）来唤起读者的情感和想象力？ • How does the author reveal his understanding of the experience, power and problem-solving skills of the readers? 作者如何展现出他对读者的经验、影响力和解决问题能力的理解？

（续表）

Aspects 方面	Guiding questions 自设问
Ethos of the argument 人格诉求	• Does the author relate himself to the problem being discussed? 作者是否将自己和讨论中的问题联系起来？ • How does the author project himself as a trustworthy person who is familiar with the subject being discussed? 作者如何把自己展现为一个值得读者信任、熟悉该话题的人？ • Is the author able to recognize alternative policies and how does he respond to them? 作者能否意识到其他可选政策？作者是如何回应这些可选政策的？

对政策型议论文来说，作者和读者之间的关系尤为重要。大多数政策型议论文中，政策执行者就是读者本人，读者很可能要根据该政策采取行动。如果读者和作者之间的关系较为亲密（比如同龄人或朋友），双方的经历和想法相仿，作者提出的政策通常较为具体，所用的语气也会更亲切一些。但如果读者和作者之间身份或经验悬殊，作者提出的政策就可能比较笼统，所用的语气也会比较正式。还有一些政策型议论文中，政策执行者并不是读者本人（比如案例一有关火星探索的议论文，这篇文章的读者并不一定会参与火星探索），这时议论文仅仅起到宏观上提升读者行动意识的作用。因此，我们在分析政策型议论文时要特别注意作者、读者和政策执行者之间的关系。

第三节　如何开展政策型议论文写作

和事实型议论文与价值型议论文不一样，政策型议论文更具现实意义。事实型议论文和价值型议论文往往只涉及判断或选择，比如判断什么发生了或没发生，判断什么是正确的或错误的，选择 A 还是 B，等等，作者只需针对某一事件或现象给出"是或不是""对或不对""选 A 还是选 B"的主张，再进行解释即可。而政策型议论文中，作者需要针对存在的问题，有创造性地提出自己的对策，即政策型主张。如果说事实型议论文或价值型议论文属于应用和评价层面，那么政策型议论文就到达了创新层面，对作者的经验、能力和创造性提出了更高要求。

要提出有价值的政策（或建议），我们必须指导学生先彻底了解需要解决的问题。教师可以鼓励学生发现身边的问题（比如班级和学校存在的问题）。一方面，这些问题是学生自己在学习生活中发现的，感同身受，肯定会较为关切；另一方面，学生有亲身经历，写作时会更加真实有趣，这比让学生讨论离他们生活较远的重大社会问题效果更好。最重要的是，通过探究身边的问题，学生能够达到真实的交际目的，获得写作带来的成就感。

接下来，笔者将通过自己设计的一个教学案例，说明如何用探究法开展政策型议论文写作教学。

步骤一：开展调查，探究问题

笔者首先在课堂上抛出写作任务，即同学们要针对班级目前存在的问题给班主任写一封建议信。接下来，笔者让学生自行组队，每组 3—4 人，讨论班级存在的问题，并将问题用英语写下来交给笔者。很快，学生就发现了许多问题，比如"很多同学存在拖延症""自习课利用效率低""上课回答问题的积极性不够"以及"许多同学存在考前焦虑问题"等。紧接着，笔者引导学生思考："这些问题是班级普遍存在的还是仅仅在你们小组里存在？""如何证明这个问题需要解决？"学生们经过讨论，一致认为需要设计调查问卷才能知晓。随后，各组着手设计调查问卷，打算在班级范围内开展简单的调查。

这时，笔者进一步提示学生：既然要开展调查，必须精心设计问卷，以便全面了解该问题，为之后提出政策做好准备。比如，针对"有同学上课犯困"，不仅可以调查上课犯困同学的比例，还可以调查该问题的原因和细节，如犯困的大致时间、前天晚上睡觉的时间等。在笔者的启发下，每个小组都设计了较为详细的针对本组问题的调查问卷，并且中英文对照。以下是笔者班级内某小组设计的调查问卷，兼具科学性和趣味性。

Questionnaire

1. 你上课会觉得困吗？ Do you feel sleepy during class?

   A. 会的，但是忍着不睡。Yes, but I always make an effort to stay awake.

   B. 我认真听讲，从不犯困。I never feel sleepy at class.

   C. 有时会困。I sometimes feel sleepy.

   D. 经常犯困，而且会睡着！ I often feel sleepy, and actually fall asleep!

2. 这样的现象一般在什么时候呢？ At what time do you usually feel sleepy?

   A. 上午或下午第一节课。The first class in the morning or afternoon.

   B. 没有特定的时间。I can't tell.

   C. 看情况，某些课上吧。It depends on the lesson.

   D. 我上课从不犯困。Never.

3. 你（或你推测上课犯困的同学们）为什么会有睡意？ Why do you think you or your classmates feel sleepy during class?

   A. 完全不知情，眼前一黑就……I have no idea.

   B. 老师讲课太无聊或太枯燥。Because the lesson is too boring.

   C. 前一天睡得太晚。Because I slept too late the previous night.

   D. 没有学习动力了。Because I lose my passion for learning.

4. 那你晚上一般几点钟上床睡觉呢？ When do you usually go to bed at night?

   A. 9：30～10：30，早睡早起身体好

   B. 10：30～11：30，也不算太晚啦

   C. 11：30～12：30，绝望的修仙党

   D. 12：30～第二天凌晨，基本已经超神了

5. 你为什么选择在这个点睡觉？ Why do you choose to go to bed at this time?

   A. 和好朋友或室友聊天。Because I chat with my friends or roommates.

> B. 学业压力大，作业写不完。Because the study load is too much for me.
>
> C. 失眠体质，睡眠质量差。Because I suffer from insomnia.
>
> D. 不睡觉的时间用来各种放飞自我。Because I use the spare time to have fun.

步骤二：利用数据，介绍问题

经过调查探究，学生已经获得了关于该问题的初步数据，对问题解决有了更全面的认识和了解。接下来，笔者鼓励学生用一段话详细描述自己小组的问题，并提醒学生在描述中必须强调问题的普遍性，以及解决该问题的紧迫性。对于问题的普遍性，学生可直接使用调查问卷中得到的数据，而对于解决问题的紧迫性，笔者提示学生可使用描述法或假设法。描述法指的是具体描述该问题，使其具象化、视觉化；假设法指的是假设该问题一直无法解决，会造成怎样严重的后果，或者假设读者亲近的人出现了这样的问题，该怎么办，等等。这两种方法都可以调动读者的情感诉求，唤起他们的情绪和想象力，使他们更加重视该问题。

步骤三：解读问题，找出原因

从问题的发现到政策型主张的提出不是一蹴而就的。作为读者，我们可以直接从他人的文章里找到政策型主张，然而当我们指导学生进行政策型议论文写作时，就必须思考如何帮助学生提出合理的政策型主张。要想提出合理的主张，必须在找到问题后进行仔细的分析和解读，从而找出问题产生的原因。

因此，笔者在步骤一就提示学生，设计调查问卷时可以加入原因探究的问题。有了问卷的数据支撑，学生能够较为客观地分析问题产生的原因。根据"上课犯困"小组的调查结果，学生主要得出三个原因：一是前一天睡得太晚，二是有些课太枯燥，三是午后自然犯困。对第一个原因作出进一步分析后，发现选择"学业压力大"和"放飞自我"的学生最多。学生找到问题产生的原因后，就能合理地思考政策型主张，较好地向班主任提出建议。可见，解读问题这一步非常关键，既能使主张的提出更有效，也能使整个写作过程更贴近现实生活,真实可信。

当然,并不是所有政策型议论文都要经历原因分析这一步,有的问题是不可逆的,比如上一节语篇节选中提到的地球问题,作者的假设就是地球有一天要毁灭,探讨的是毁灭之后该怎么办,而不是如何逆转这个问题(即如何拯救地球)。其实,从战略学意义上说,不可逆的问题通常探讨的都是下策(即英文中常说的 Plan B),也就是假设问题的发生不可避免该怎么办,比如与同学发生了肢体冲突该怎么办,超市积压了大量临期产品该怎么办,等等。而可逆的问题通常讨论的都是上策,即最好想办法避免问题再次发生,比如尽量不与同学发生肢体冲突,尽量不产生大量临期产品,等等。因此,如果遇到不可逆问题,作者无须分析原因,直接提出政策型主张即可。还有一类政策型议论文,就是前文提到的带有策划性质的议论文,比如学校的空置教室有什么用,拿到一笔奖金建议怎么用,这类话题也不需要分析原因,直接提出政策型主张即可。

步骤四:分析读者,提出主张

找到问题的原因后,接下来笔者鼓励学生提出政策型主张,同时提示学生要考虑到政策执行者,比如政策执行者有怎样的经历和经验,有多大的权限,有多强的执行能力等。此外,还应考虑政策执行者能调动哪些资源,有哪些难处,还有哪些问题需要解决等,这些都会影响政策型主张的效力。

经过教师的提示,"上课犯困"小组意识到写作对象是班主任。班主任不可能改变其他老师的上课方式,也不可能直接更改课表的安排,但可以向学校相关部门提出建议,比如下午第一节课安排艺术课、体育课、实验课等实践类课程,以提振学生的精神。此外,班主任可以和任课老师协调每天的作业总量,使各科作业分配更均衡,从而保证学生的睡眠。最后,班主任可以召开班会,帮助同学们提升早睡早起的意识等。结合以上思考,"上课犯困"小组打算提出以下政策型主张:

① A class meeting should be held to point out the harm of staying up late.

② All the teachers in the class should work together to develop a reasonable class-wide homework policy.

③ Lessons with hands-on activities should be arranged in the early-afternoon class session.

步骤五：给出理由，支撑主张

提出政策型主张后，笔者鼓励学生依照图尔敏论证模型，列出每条政策的根据和保证。以下是笔者带领学生分析得到的逻辑关系。

① **Warrant**: A class meeting can usually raise the awareness and help students realize the bad impact of staying up late on the class performance of the next day.

Ground 1:
Playing games late into the night causes some students to feel sleepy the next day.

Claim of policy:
A class meeting should be held to point out the harm of staying up late.

② **Warrant**: If teachers can coordinate homework assignments, students won't have to stay up too late and will perform better.

Ground 2:
Feeling sleepy in class is in part a result of late-night study.

Claim of policy:
All the teachers in the class should work together to develop a reasonable class-wide homework policy.

③ **Warrant**: It is well-known that hands-on activities can arouse students' interest more and involve students in active learning, so compared with lectures, they can help students to avoid sleepiness.

Ground 3:
The time when students feel especially sleepy is in the first class in the afternoon.

Claim of policy:
Lessons with hands-on activities should be arranged in the early-afternoon class session.

从图尔敏论证模型可以看到，三条政策都有清晰的根据和保证来支撑。第一条政策从后果法来论证，召开班会能让全班学生意识到熬夜玩游戏对第二天课堂表现的不良影响，可以在一定程度上解决上课犯困的问题。第二条政策也是从后果法来论证的，同一班级的任课教师之间可协调作业总量，这样既能保证学生每天分配到合理的作业，从而早点睡觉，也可以在一定程度上解决上课犯困的问题。第三条政策是从原则法来论证的，实践类课程可以让学生主动参与一些项目，提高学习兴趣，防止犯困，这是符合人的生理规律的，因此该政策也得到了较多的支持。

这时，笔者提示学生：以上理由都是从应然角度写的，是否可以从实然角度思考一下政策的实际操作呢？有学生回答，他知道隔壁班就是由班长统计每天的各科作业，如果预计完成时间过长，班长会在下午 4 点前找到班主任请求予以协调。笔者马上作出回应，称这一操作具有可行性，既然别的班级已有先例，就可以作为第二条政策的实然理由。

当然，在步骤四时，笔者已提示学生提出政策时要思考写作对象的经验、权限和政策执行能力。因此，学生在提出这三条政策前已经考虑过可行性，实然理由实际上也已包含在建议里。

除此之外，由于三条根据中的前两条（"晚上打游戏导致部分学生第二天犯困"以及"晚上学习到很晚是第二天上课犯困的原因之一"）是需要进一步证明的事实型主张，笔者提醒学生写作时务必要用调查中得到的数据证明这两点。

步骤六：考虑相反观点，及时作出回应

在完成论证主体部后，笔者询问是否有学生对这三条政策提出反对意见。有同学对最后一条政策提出疑问，说学校可能没有足够的师资力量在每天下午第一节课都安排实践类课程，这属于操作层面的质疑。笔者认为这个质疑很合理，鼓励"上课犯困"小组成员捍卫自己的观点。小组成员反驳称，即便不能为每个班级每天下午第一节课都安排实践类课程，但只要一周有两三天能够改变排课，也比现在的情况要好，笔者对此表示赞成。至此，学生基本上已明白政策型议论文的整体逻辑论证思路了。

步骤七：考虑情感诉求和人格诉求

逻辑环节的分析结束后，笔者提示学生还需要适当增加情感诉求和人格诉求。前文提到，政策型议论文通常包含三部分：问题的描述、政策的提出、对政策的支撑。在每个部分，作者都可以增加情感诉求和人格诉求。首先，在描述问题时，也就是步骤二，笔者可以鼓励学生使用叙述、描写或适当假想的手段强调问题的严重性，并将这个问题和读者的利益联系起来，以引起读者的重视，提升情感诉求。作者也可以提出自己就是该问题的受害者，讲述自己的经历，提升人格诉求。其次，在提出政策时，作者可以表现出对这一政策的了解（比如自己曾经听说过或参与过类似政策的执行），并适当表示自己能理解政策执行者的难处，使读者或政策执行者更愿意接纳这个政策。最后，在支撑政策时，作者可以详细描述该政策可能带来的好处，从而提升情感诉求。

步骤八：组织语篇布局

在最后的布局阶段，笔者引导学生有条理地将政策型议论文的三部分"引入问题—提出政策—支撑政策"融入习作。政策型议论文的布局方式分为以下两种。

表 4-2 布局 1

步骤	要点
引入问题描述	1. Arouse the readers' attention by introducing the problem to be addressed. 2. Emphasize why the problem is worth the readers' attention and why it is urgent to solve the problem.
分析问题的原因（可选）	Analyze the causes of the problem.（Optional）
提出政策 1 + 支撑理由 + 提出反驳（可选）	1. Introduce the first claim of policy. 2. State the ground（which may also be a claim of fact or value）and warrant. Give supporting details to the claim of fact or value. 3. Summarize the possible objections. Respond to the objections either through rebuttal or concessions.
提出政策 2 + 支撑理由 + 提出反驳（可选）	1. Introduce the second claim of policy. 2. State the ground（which may also be a claim of fact or value）and warrant. Give supporting details to the claim of fact or value. 3. Summarize the possible objections. Respond to the objections either through rebuttal or concessions.
结语	1. Sum up the policies. 2. Call for action and/or express hope.

第一种方式是政策型议论文的常规布局，先引入问题，同时强调问题的重要性和紧迫性，再分析原因（这一步是可选的，并非所有政策型议论文都会涉及），然后提出政策型主张，并予以支撑。如果作者预料到读者中会有怀疑的声音，可以适当地对可能出现的相反意见进行反驳。最后，政策

型议论文在结束时一般都要先总结上文，然后号召读者行动起来，或表达对问题解决的期望。

由于政策型议论文的目的通常是号召人们展开行动，因此常常用于演讲稿的撰写。对于演讲稿类的政策型议论文，我们可以借鉴另一种布局方式，即著名的"门罗激励序列"（Monroe's Motivated Sequence）。

普渡大学的传播学教授艾伦·门罗（Allan Monroe）在 20 世纪 30 年代就提出了一套用于激励性演说的演讲稿结构。[①] 他认为当人们遇到一个需要解决的问题时，会自然产生一股寻求解决方案的动力，使受到扰乱的认知状态达到新的平衡或新的和谐。于是，门罗提出了一种演讲方式，也就是"门罗激励序列"，这种方式遵循人类的认知规律，能够更好地达到演讲者的目的，使听众更容易接受演讲者的观点。

这套激励序列由以下五个步骤组成，按其英文首字母可简称为 ANSVA。

① 注意力（attention）：首先，演讲者应以各种方式抓住观众的注意力，比如讲述一个小故事、提出一个发人深省的问题、引用一段引言或数据、说一段幽默的话等。

② 需求（need）：在抓住观众的注意力后，演讲者必须让观众感受到变革的必要。比如，演讲者可以使用一些数据强调问题的重要性或解决问题的紧迫性。在这个步骤，演讲者必须将变革的需求和观众的福祉紧密联系起来，才能达到应有的效果，比如这个问题可能会影响观众的健康、幸福、安全，甚至命运，因此亟待解决。如果这一步实施到位，观众应该在"需求"环节结束时，展现出对这个问题应有的关切，并且急切想知道解决方案。

③ 满足（satisfaction）：在唤起观众对问题的关切后，演讲者就必须要满足观众对解决方案的好奇。这时，演讲者应马上提出准备好的解决方案，并向观众解释该方案是如何操作的。比如，演讲者可以给出一个具体的操作实例，也可以给出一个操作模型，或者给出一些数据或图表来支撑这个解决方案的合理性。总之，在该环节结束后，观众应对这个解决方案有一个大致的了解。

---

① Monroe A H. Monroe's Principles of Speech［M］. Military ed. Chicago, IL: Scott, Foresman and Company, 1943.

④ 形象化设想（visualization）：观众知晓解决方案后，演讲者还需要强化观众对该解决方案的期待，也就是引导观众想象这个方案可能带来的好处。演讲者可以使用生动的语言或图片等工具来调动观众的想象力，向观众展示他们如何能够从中受益，使方案在观众的脑海中具体化、形象化。演讲者还可以使用对比手法，向观众展示使用该方案和不使用该方案将造成怎样的差异，也就是在观众心中播下美好的种子，让他们再也不愿意回到目前的状态。该环节的关键是要让观众真切感受到该方案将带来的好处，因此，演讲者的描述不能过于脱离实际，而要让观众觉得这个设想是可以实现的。

⑤ 行动（action）：该环节是将观众的热切愿望转化为行动的过程，演讲者必须告诉观众具体该做些什么、怎么做。这个环节不必过长，但要足够清晰，能督促观众开展即时行动。

"门罗激励序列"在广告行业的运用尤其广泛。其实很多广告都涉及议论，因为它们多半带有劝说性质，最终目的就是号召人们行动起来去消费。因此，从本质上来说，广告就是一种政策型议论。以常见的食品广告为例，我们可以很清楚地看到"门罗激励序列"的影子。

① 注意（attention）：一个篮球运动员在一场比赛中准备投篮，场面很精彩，进入关键时刻。这样一来，观众的注意力就被吸引过去了。

② 需求（need）：这时，突然传来一阵肚子叫的声音，这个篮球运动员精力不够，球只投到半空中。这个场景使观众意识到问题的严重性，大家开始关心如何解决饿肚子的问题。

③ 满足（satisfaction）：食品名称和精美的食品细节图出现在屏幕上，旁边可能会附上食品配料表或相关数据等。这是在向观众全面展示该食品的营养价值，也就是让观众看到解决方案及其细节。

④ 形象化设想（visualization）：篮球运动员又恢复了精力，成功地完成了投篮。这个场景使观众将该食品与精力恢复联系在一起，从而相信该食品能让人精力充沛，这就是设想解放方案能带来的真实好处。

⑤ 行动（action）：出示购买该食品的渠道，比如网址或门店信息，让观众赶紧下单，这就完成了最后一个号召观众行动的步骤。

"门罗激励序列"的五个环节和政策型议论文的三个部分是相互匹配的。前文提到，政策型议论文包含三个部分：问题的描述—政策的提出—

对政策的支撑。问题的描述其实就是"门罗激励序列"中"注意"和"需求"环节的结合,需要把观众的注意力拉到问题的重要性和紧迫性上。政策的提出就是"满足"环节,即向观众介绍解决方案。对政策的支撑实际上就是"满足"和"形象化设想"环节的结合,其中"满足"环节给出政策操作的具体方式(相当于可行性分析),是实然理由,"形象化设想"环节设想政策可以给观众带来的好处(也就是后果法),是应然理由。

因此,"门罗激励序列"可作为政策型议论文的第二种布局方式。当学生想要将自己的建议用于演讲时,完全可以采用这种布局方式。

表4-3　布局2

步骤	要点
注意 Attention	Use some techniques to gain the attention of the audience by introducing something related to the problem to be addressed.
需求 Need	Emphasize the seriousness of the problem and make the audience feel that there is a need for change.
满足 Satisfaction	Introduce the policy. State the details and feasibility of the policy, i.e. how the policy can be carried out or has been carried out successfully elsewhere.
形象化设想 Visualization	Use vivid imagery to describe the potential benefits of the policy, helping the audience visualize how conditions will improve after the adoption of the policy.
行动 Action	Make a call for action and tell the audience exactly what to do next and how to do it.

第四节　如何评价政策型议论文

前文提到,价值型议论文只需要作者对主张作出"正确还是错误""好还是坏""残忍还是不残忍"的判断,而政策型议论文需要作者自己提出主张,而且一篇政策型议论文中通常会有多个主张,也就是说作者会提出多个政策来解决一个问题。

因此，评价政策型议论文时，首先要观察作者提出的政策主张是否合理。如前文所说，判断一条政策是否合理的主要依据是该政策能否真正解决问题，那么如何看出一条政策是否能真正解决问题呢？我们可以观察以下三点：一是作者是否分析出问题产生的真正原因，二是作者是否考虑到政策执行者所能调配的资源以及政策执行者自身的需求，三是作者是否考虑到政策执行者本身的经验、权限和问题解决能力等。如果三个前提都考虑到了，这条政策的方向基本正确。接下来要观察政策的支撑理由是否到位，能否解释清楚该政策的合理性。我们可以从以下三个方面判断：一是后果法，二是原则法，三是可行性。如果支撑理由能够涵盖这三个方面，基本上可以肯定这条政策是能够解决问题的。

最后，除了逻辑合理之外，在评价政策型议论文时，我们还要观察习作是否使用了情感诉求和人格诉求来提升议论效果。情感诉求在政策型议论的三个部分都能使用：在描述问题时，作者可以用较为生动的语言来调动读者的想象力，也可以将问题和读者切身利益相结合，以调动读者的情感；在提出政策时，作者可以表达自己考虑到了读者或政策执行者的顾虑和难处；在支撑政策时，作者既可以描述该政策可能为读者带来的具体好处，也可以用自己的经历来支撑政策的合理性。同样，人格诉求也可以在这三个部分使用：在描述问题时，作者可以表达自己比其他人更了解这个问题的严重性；在提出政策和支撑政策时，作者可以通过各种方式展示自己对该政策的了解。教师评价学生习作时，如果发现学生在情感诉求和人格诉求方面做得不够到位，可以将以上这些方法作为提示教给学生，给予学生改进意见。以下评价清单可供参考。

表4-4 政策型议论文评价清单样例

Aspects		Guiding questions	√/×
Organization	Introduction and conclusion	• Does the writing have an opening and closing statement? • Does the ending leave the readers with a powerful thought?	
	Transitions	• Does the writing use transitions to get from one paragraph to the next?	
	Paragraph unity	• Does the writing include only one topic in each paragraph?	

（续表）

Aspects		Guiding questions	√ / ×
Content	The problem	• Does the writing introduce the problem to be addressed? • Does the author emphasize the importance of the problem and show the need for change?	
Content	Logos	• Is the claim of policy reasonable? (Is the cause of the problem addressed? Are the policy practitioners' experience and capabilities taken into consideration?) • Is the claim of policy properly supported? (Is the warrant consequence-based or principle-based? Is the feasibility of the policy taken into account?) • Are the grounds (which may be claims of fact or value) further supported? • Does the writing respond to possible objections?	
	Pathos	• Does the writing use some techniques to tap the readers' imagination and emotions (e.g. using vivid imagery to describe the problem, showing appreciation of the difficulty that the policy practitioners might have)?	
	Ethos	• Does the writing show that the author knows the problem well enough to propose the policy? • Does the writing show that the author is familiar with the implementation of the policy?	
Language	Word choice and sentence variety	• Does the author use precise words and appropriate vocabulary for the subject? • Are sentences varied in length and structure?	
	Cohesion and coherence	• Does the writing use words, phrases, or clauses to create cohesion and clarify the relationships among claims, grounds and warrants?	

（续表）

Aspects		Guiding questions	√／×
Language	Tone	• Is the tone (including style and voice) appropriate for the purpose and the readers?	
	Convention/ CUPS	• Are there errors in capitalization, usage, punctuation, and spelling (CUPS)? If so, do these errors interfere with others' understanding of the writing?	

评价清单的目的不仅仅是给学生一个等第或成绩，而是为他们提供一个更好的修改思路。作为评价者，教师不仅要依据评价清单中的条目判断学生习作是否存在某方面的问题，还要提出一些中肯的修改意见。第二章曾经提到，学生评价固然可贵，但永远不能代替教师评价，教师无论从认知能力、写作经验还是语言能力都远远超过大多数学生。而且，政策型议论文比事实型议论文和价值型议论文复杂得多，学生可能需要经过多次写作实践才能真正理解要领，因此，教师一定要在评价中发挥应有的作用，给予学生恰当的修改建议。在此过程中，教师也要把握好度，对于能力较弱的学生，不要一次性将评价清单上发现的所有问题都列出来，以免学生产生畏难情绪。教师应当依据学生的水平，指出习作中存在的问题时应分轻重缓急，从最重要的问题开始解决。

本章小结

本章介绍了政策型议论的概念，指出了政策型议论文与事实型、价值型议论文的不同之处。政策型议论文一般包含三个部分：问题的描述、政策的提出、对政策的支撑。政策的提出即政策型议论文的主张，该主张需要建立在对问题的合理分析之上。

为了使政策主张更有说服力，政策型议论文的支撑理由需要包含应然和实然两方面，不仅要分析该主张是否在理论上可行，还要分析该主张是否具备可操作性。并且，政策型议论文的支撑理由通常又是一个事实型或价值型主张，需要进一步的论证。

　　在政策型议论文写作教学中，探究法是一种较为有效的教学方法。教师可鼓励学生从身边的问题出发自行开展探究，并通过政策型议论文写作达成真实的交际目的。学生通过调查找出问题的严重性及问题产生的原因，然后通过小组合作找到问题的解决方案，再对解决方案进行证明。

第五章　如何写好驳论文

第二章到第四章分别介绍了高中英语事实型、价值型和政策型议论文的分析、写作和评价方式。这三类议论文都属于立论，而本章将简要介绍英语驳论文的写作方式。严格地说，驳论文也包含事实型、价值型和政策型三类，只不过驳论文还有个"树靶子"的过程，也就是先树立待批驳的观点，再加以驳斥，进而提出自己的观点。

第一节　什么是驳论文

驳论文，顾名思义，涉及对他方观点的反驳。从图尔敏论证模型来看，驳论文实际上就是反驳条件的扩充版。反驳条件又叫作相反意见，当这条相反意见得到足够的根据和保证支撑时，就可以自成体系，成为一个新的论点，也就是驳论文。

以第二章第三节的事实型议论文写作案例为例，事实型主张是"女性在就业市场上受到歧视"（Women are discriminated against in the job market），该议论文的部分逻辑关系如下图所示。

Backing: "to discriminate" is defined as "to treat a person or group differently from another in an unfair way".

Warrant: When people receive different amount of money for the same work or work of equal value, it is called discrimination.

Ground:
Women generally earn less than men do.

Claim:
Women are discriminated against in the job market.

针对上图中的根据"女性总体来说比男性赚得少"（Women generally earn less than men do），有人可能就会质疑，认为现代女性群体的收入并不比男性低，甚至拿出更多证据来证明这一点。有了大量证据后，这个人将他的相反意见写成一篇文章，证明女性在职场上并没有受到歧视，这篇文章就是一篇驳论文。由此可见，驳论文一般由两部分组成：首先指出对方观点错误的实质，继而提出自己的观点并加以论证。

驳论文在日常生活中并不少见，比如你对小区附近要建一个垃圾焚烧点表示不满，打算写一封信给有关部门提出抗议，那么你在这封信中必须指出建造垃圾焚烧点是错误的，并指出其错误实质，再提出自己的观点。又如某公司就一则新的人事方案征求员工意见，员工提出意见的过程实际上也是驳论的过程，首先必须指出方案中的不合理之处，再提出自己的建议。

学生在校园生活中也常常会接触到驳论，比如很多学校都会组织辩论赛，辩论稿的撰写就是驳论文的写作过程。学生需要先找到对方观点中的漏洞，指出其错误实质并反驳，然后提出自己的观点并予以论证。

第二节　如何分析并开展驳论文写作

在高中英语教材中，驳论文仅在《高中英语》（牛津上海版）高三第一学期第2单元的阅读板块中出现过，该语篇的体裁就是一篇辩论稿，辩论的题目是"A woman's place is in the home"（女性的位置应该在家里），作者属于反方，也就是认为"女性的位置不应该在家里"。开篇作者先对正方的三个理由作了简单的总结，为后续提出反对意见打下基础。

Read this transcript of a student's speech in a class debate.

Replying to such a well-argued speech is not easy, but I will try.

As you know, I'm speaking against this motion. I wish to make three main points. First, we cannot accept this traditional role for women in a modern society. Second, I wish to refute the argument that women are weaker than men. Third, I shall discuss whether or not women should stay at home to take care of children.

可以看到，正方的主张是"女性的位置应该在家里"，给出的三条理由分别是"古往今来女性的角色都是在家庭中"（the traditional role for women）、"女性比男性弱"（weaker than men）以及"女性更擅长照顾孩子"（taking care of children better.）。

为了更好地驳斥正方的观点，我们可以用图尔敏论证模型对正方的议论展开分析，从而找出正方论证中的漏洞。

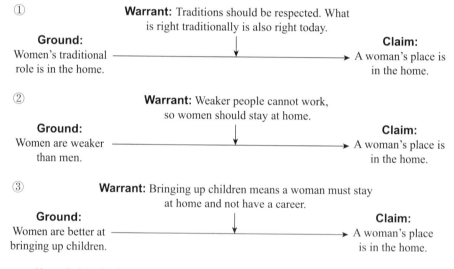

① **Warrant:** Traditions should be respected. What is right traditionally is also right today.

Ground: Women's traditional role is in the home. → **Claim:** A woman's place is in the home.

② **Warrant:** Weaker people cannot work, so women should stay at home.

Ground: Women are weaker than men. → **Claim:** A woman's place is in the home.

③ **Warrant:** Bringing up children means a woman must stay at home and not have a career.

Ground: Women are better at bringing up children. → **Claim:** A woman's place is in the home.

第三章提到，提出相反意见有两种方式：一种是质疑根据，一种是质疑保证。那么，这三条理由分别有什么漏洞呢？我们不妨先尝试一下。第一条理由的根据是较难质疑的，因为从人类历史看，女性的传统角色的确都是在家中。但保证却是有问题的，所有传统都要延续吗？现代社会一定要全盘接受传统吗？事实显然并非如此，对于传统一定是"取其精华，去其糟粕"。第二条理由的根据本身就值得怀疑，"弱"是一个很宽泛的形容词，女性或许在体力上比男性弱一些，但几乎没有证据能证明女性在思维上、情感上、品质上也比男性弱，所以这条根据是站不住脚的。同样，这条理由的保证也站不住脚，就算女性体力比男性弱，并不意味着弱者不能工作，弱者同样可以从事对体力要求不高的工作。第三条理由的根据本身较难反驳，因为婴儿刚出生时基本上都比较依赖母亲，这是常识。但保证是完全可以反驳的，女性带孩子和外出工作矛盾吗？并不矛盾，现代家庭有很多女性能够做到工作生活两不误。

至此，正方议论中的逻辑漏洞基本上都被找出来了。带着这样的预设，我们可以继续阅读语篇，看这篇辩论稿是否成功地找到了这些逻辑漏洞。

In proposing the motion, Jane suggested that we should be proud of our history and respect the traditional role of women. Well, I want to remind her of some other facts about the past. Girls born into many poor families were not wanted. They were sometimes killed or sold as slaves. After they got married, many women were like servants in their husband's family. These wives had such a low status that they were confined to their houses, and had to do as they were told. New wives sometimes committed suicide. Are these traditions which we should support today? I don't think so. We can be proud of our history without clinging to these old traditions.

针对正方的第一条理由，作者针对保证提出反对意见，认为不是所有传统都应该保留。提出观点后，作者用了大量的实例证明，所谓女性居家的传统不过是女性不受尊重的屈辱历史。最后，作者抛出一个反问句：这样的传统我们今天还应该支持吗？从而表明了己方的观点。这段驳论的思路如表 5-1 所示。

表 5-1　第一条理由的反驳思路

Pro side	Opposing view	Supporting details
Warrant: Traditions should be respected. What is right traditionally is also right today.	Not all traditions should be supported today.	• Girls were not wanted and sometimes killed or sold as slaves. • Married women were like servants and had such a low status that they were confined to the houses. • New wives sometimes committed suicide.

针对第二条理由,作者是这样反驳的。

Jane also mentioned the old argument that women are so weak that they are unsuitable for many jobs. I must disagree. Looking around, we can still see some women doing manual labour on farms and building sites. Thus, women can do heavy, physical work, and do it well, in the same way as men do. Furthermore, statistics show that women have a longer average life expectancy than men. So how can we say women are weaker? Though men may be better at weightlifting, few jobs actually require physical strength these days.

和我们前文分析的一样,作者同时反驳了正方的根据和保证:先举例说明女性并不比男性弱,指出根据的不全面;再提出如今很少有工作需要大量体力劳动,驳斥了保证。这样一来,对方的观点完全站不住脚。整个思路如表 5-2 所示。

表 5-2　第二条理由的反驳思路

Pro side	Opposing view	Supporting details
Ground: Women are weaker than men.	Women are not weaker than men.	• Women do manual labour on farms and building sites. • Women can do heavy, physical work. • Women have longer life expectancy.
Warrant: Weaker people cannot work, so women should stay at home.	Women may be weaker at weightlifting, but few jobs require physical strength these days.	/

从上表可以看到,如果能补上更多细节来支撑"很少有工作需要大量体力劳动",该段论证就更加完整了。下面是作者对第三条理由的反驳。

In his speech, James tried to pay us a compliment when he said that since women are superior to men at bringing up children, they should stay at home. I concede that many women are better at taking care of children.

However, a recent study has shown that working women spend only five hours less a week with their children than non-working women. Thus, a child is not damaged if his or her mother works. Every woman should have the right to work out her own priorities. In our city, over 51% of the female population now have jobs. Many of them also manage to run a home, and so they carry a double burden. Very few men could manage this.

　　和我们前文分析的一样，作者并没有驳斥根据，而是承认女性在抚养孩子方面确实更在行。接下来，作者针对保证提出异议，表示女性完全可以边抚养孩子边工作，并引用调查结果和相关数据予以支撑。整个思路如表 5-3 所示。

表 5-3　第三条理由的反驳思路

Pro side	Opposing view	Supporting details
Warrant: Bringing up children means a woman must stay at home and not have a career.	Women can take care of children and work at the same time, with no damage to children.	• A recent study has shown that working women spend only five hours less a week with their children than non-working women. • In our city, over 51% of the female population now have jobs. Many of them also manage to run a home, and so they carry a double burden.

　　至此，语篇对正方三个论点的驳斥基本结束。作者在结尾处首先总结了对方逻辑中的三个漏洞，然后提出一个己方的新主张，也就是"女性不工作是对宝贵资源的浪费"（We are wasting our valuable resources if we don't let women play their full part）。最后，作者提出号召：女性的位置不应该只在家里，而应该出现在各行各业。

Thus, I have shown that some traditions of the past were unfair, and that women are not the weaker sex. I believe we are capable of doing any job a man can do. As Simon pointed out in his speech, there is still so much discrimination against women that their abilities are often wasted. As a community, we are wasting our valuable resources if we don't let women play their full part. A woman's place is not only in the home, but also in the office, in the design studio, in the bank and in the managing director's chair. I urge you to vote against the proposition. Thank you.

通过以上分析可以看出，这是一篇较为成功的驳论文。作者将正方的理由一一"解剖"，指出对方错误的实质，并使用举例、引用等多种支撑方法予以回击。

对于高中学生来说，开展英语驳论文写作的机会可能并不多，但教师平时可以带领学生阅读一些精彩的辩论稿，指导他们厘清正方观点和反方观点，分析作者是如何找出他方论证中的漏洞并加以驳斥的。同时，教师也可以创设一些日常学习和生活中常见的情境，让学生尝试分析。比如前文提到小区附近建垃圾焚烧点，教师可以鼓励学生先找到正方这样做的理由（也就是在小区附近建垃圾焚烧点的理由），再提示学生分析立论中根据和保证的不合理之处，最后提出反驳方案。

本章小结

本章介绍了驳论文的基本概念，驳论文实际上就是相反意见的提出。接下来，本章以高中英语教材上的语篇为驳论文写作范例，借助图尔敏论证模型，进行了详细的分析。从分析结果看，相反意见的提出通常有两种方式：一种是驳斥根据，一种是驳斥保证。在驳斥对方的过程中，作者应给出相应的支撑细节，并在适当的时候提出己方观点。

教师在日常教学中，既可以搜集一些驳论文教学素材，比如精彩的英语辩论稿，指导学生分析辩论稿的作者是如何总结并驳斥对方观点的，也可以创造一些生活中需要驳论的情境，鼓励学生进行思辨。

下篇

实践篇

导言

一、实践篇和理论篇是如何衔接的

实践篇呈现了完整的高中英语议论文写作教学课程实施过程，是理论篇的具体展开。理论篇第一章介绍了高中英语议论文写作教学的相关知识，包括英语议论文写作的概念和特征及议论文写作中重要的逻辑分析工具——图尔敏论证模型，后四章分别以具体案例的形式阐述了如何将以上知识应用于事实型议论文、价值型议论文、政策型议论文和驳论文的分析、写作和评价。

在实践篇中，这四类议论文将进一步体现在具体的英语写作话题中。实践篇共提供了 15 个常见的写作话题，以序列化的方式呈现，方便读者深入理解并应用理论篇中的内容，也有助于新手教师在英语议论文写作教学方面快速上手。

这 15 个教学案例均采用任务型写作话题。任务型写作话题"有特定的情境设计、有具体的写作任务、有确定的写作主体、有明确的读者对象、有实用的写作文体"[①]，是最贴近高中生日常英语写作实践的话题任务，包含学生在教材中所遇到的各种带有明确交际功能的实用英语写作（如推荐信、建议信、申请信等）。这些写作话题，究其本质，也都离不开"议论"二字。

二、15 个教学案例是如何安排的

15 个写作话题如表 0-1 所示。

表 0-1　15 个写作话题

话题 1	在派对上，男主人约翰突然跌下楼梯，昏迷不醒，有一位目击者对警察说约翰是在醉酒后失足滑下了楼梯。根据图片，写一份案件报告，描述事故现场，说明目击者是否说谎，并给出理由。

[①] 周素颖. 任务型写作的特点与训练方法［J］. 教学月刊·中学版，2020（6）：35–39.

话题2	近来，天空日报（*Sky Daily*）正在收集虚假广告受害者的案例，准备做一期专题报道。假设你是 Anne，给报社写一封信，讲述你的经历，证明你遭遇了虚假广告。
话题3	如今，各种各样的数字艺术作品层出不穷，比如手机录制的小视频、平板手写笔创作的画、电脑软件制作的图案、相机拍摄的照片等。校报拟开辟专栏讨论话题"数字艺术作品是否算作真正的艺术"，写一篇稿件，说明你对该话题的态度，并给出理由。
话题4	近年来，盲盒（mystery boxes）的受欢迎程度不断攀升，尤其受到中学生的热捧。校报"热点分析"栏目正在征集该话题稿件，写一篇稿件，描述该现象，并分析原因。
话题5	近年来，越来越多的硕博毕业生选择成为中小学教师，有人说这是教育的进步，也有人说这是一种人才浪费，你赞成高学历人才投身基础教育吗？天空日报（*Sky Daily*）"社会万象"栏目正在征集该话题稿件，向报社投稿，谈谈你的看法，并给出理由。
话题6	在李华18岁生日到来之际，父亲准备送他一份礼物，父亲给他两个选项：新款智能手机或去英国旅行，并让李华自己作出选择。假如你是李华，写一封信给父亲，说明你的选择和理由。
话题7	你校即将进行学生会主席选举，现在校内征集候选人。写一封信给学生处，推荐一名同学作为候选人，并阐明推荐理由。
话题8	如今，青年创业项目层出不穷，你的好友张磊所在的学校开设了一个学生企业家项目（student entrepreneurship project），本期项目与开设书店有关，张磊打算申请，正在犹豫是开一家网上书店还是实体书店，现通过邮件向你征求意见。写一封回信给他建议，并给出理由。
话题9	你所在的读书社想要选出5本"伟大的著作"作为本学年社员必读书目。写一封信给社长，推荐你心目中"伟大的著作"，简述该著作，并说明推荐理由。
话题10	在读完《雾都孤儿》小说节选 *Oliver Wants More* 之后，你认为"奥利弗想要更多"的行为是有勇气的行为吗？请给出理由。
话题11	请围绕"我们发现的班级问题"写一封信给班主任，描述班级目前存在的一个问题，分析原因，并给出解决方案，说明理由。
话题12	最近，你们小区的池塘受到污染，飘出阵阵臭味。写一封信给居委会，反映这一情况，分析原因，并给出合理建议，说明理由。

（续表）

话题 13	王婷最好的朋友摔碎了她的手表，而这个手表是王婷奶奶送给她的生日礼物。王婷不知道该怎么办，写信向校报"烦恼热线"栏目求助。假设你是校报编辑，写一封回信给王婷，提出你的建议和理由。
话题 14	你们学校和社区孤儿院是结对单位，最近学校打算发起"孤儿募捐日"（a fundraising day for orphans）活动。作为学生会的一员，写一份活动策划书供校方参考，提出募捐日当天活动的详细安排，并给出理由。

| 话题 15 | 学生会打算成立一个英语报社，定期发行英语校报（目前的计划如下所示），并向全校同学征求意见。写一封信给学生会，提出你的意见和建议，并给出理由。 |

	主要版面	时事头条（Current Events）、娱乐新闻（Entertainment News）、好书导读（Book Guide）、校园生活（Campus Life）、备考专练（Test Prep）
话题 15	发行时间	每周五
	发行量	每班 5 张

这 15 个教学案例共分为四组：

第一组为事实型议论文写作教学案例，即话题 1—话题 4。

第二组为价值型议论文写作教学案例，即话题 5—话题 10（其中话题 10 为价值标准写作教学案例）。

第三组为政策型议论文写作教学案例，即话题 11—话题 14。

第四组为驳论文写作教学案例，即话题 15。

每组话题内部也按严谨的逻辑层次编排，并在开头部分作出说明。

三、15 个教学案例遵循怎样的体例

在每个教学案例的开始，笔者都给出了该教学时段的"学习目标汇总"（Learning Objectives）。不同于以往的学习目标，"学习目标汇总"分为整体目标和分项目标两部分。在整体目标（Can-do statements）中，笔者先列出三条目标，即学生上完本节课后能做什么。接着将整体目标中涉及的具体知识和能力指标进行细化，形成分项目标，使读者对本节课涉及的概念知识一目了然。分项目标主要从思维焦点（Thinking focus）、表达焦点

（Expression focus）、功能焦点（Function focus）和风格焦点（Style focus）四个维度切入。整体目标和分项目标的设置有助于师生在课前和课后更好地对照其中的条目审视自身的教学和学习情况。

随后，每个案例遵循过程性写作教学（process writing）的流程，按照以下十个步骤展开：

① 准备开始写作（Preparing to Write）

② 了解写作话题（Understanding the Prompt）

③ 搭建思维模型（Constructing the Model）

④ 撰写提纲（Producing an Outline）

⑤ 提升效果（Adding the Impact）

⑥ 聚焦语言（Focusing on Language）

⑦ 组织布局（Designing the Layout）

⑧ 互动评价（Evaluating the Drafts）

⑨ 分享范文（Sharing the Samples）

⑩ 尝试相似话题（Suggested Writing Prompts）

每个步骤的概述如表 0-2 所示：

表 0-2　教学步骤与概述

教学步骤	概述
准备开始写作 Preparing to Write	教师借助高中英语教材中的议论语篇、学生日常生活情境，以及探究性任务等多种方式，帮助学生铺垫写作背景或初步理解某一论证方法。
了解写作话题 Understanding the Prompt	教师带领学生分析写作目的、作者身份和目标读者，引导学生思考应使用何种语气和语调来开展写作，提升学生的读者意识。
搭建思维模型 Constructing the Model	教师带领学生展开思考，启发学生找出写作话题的论证核心，构建逻辑思路，并根据图尔敏论证模型搭建思维框架，给出板书示范。
撰写提纲 Producing an Outline	教师鼓励学生根据板书示范独立撰写提纲，同时邀请部分学生在黑板上当场完成提纲，并对提纲的内容和语言给予指导和评价。案例中给出的参考提纲并不是唯一的提纲列举方法，而是众多提纲中的一种。

101

（续表）

教学步骤	概述
提升效果 Adding the Impact	教师提醒学生从多个角度增加议论的情感诉求和人格诉求，提升议论效果。同时鼓励学生思考相反意见，并学会驳斥相反意见。
聚焦语言 Focusing on Language	教师根据经验，预设学生在写作中可能遇到的语言难点，并为学生准备好相应的语言支架。
组织布局 Designing the Layout	教师引导学生思考如何对写作内容进行合理布局，形成一篇思路清晰的读者友好型习作。
互动评价 Evaluating the Drafts	教师引导学生根据前七个步骤中提及的重点对习作开展自评或互评。
分享范文 Sharing the Samples	教师分享学生优秀习作，并鼓励学生依照评价清单中的条目列举优秀习作中值得学习的地方。同时，笔者给出了教师评价，该评价实际上是对评价清单的应用示范。
尝试相似话题 Suggested Writing Prompts	该板块从写作话题 3 开始出现（因前两个话题是给材料作文，非独立写作），教师在课堂结束后给出与本话题相似的话题，鼓励学生开展独立写作。

　　15 个教学案例中包含详细的教学流程和教学语言示范，可帮助教师真正理解如何在高中课堂上有效开展英语议论文写作教学，比如如何引导学生从写作话题中剥离出需要论证的核心，并有效利用思维模型搭建写作框架等。

四、与普通教案相比，这 15 个教学案例有什么特点

　　常见的教案通常以文字或表格形式呈现，分步骤展现教学活动和活动目标，但教师们普遍认为仅仅通过教案上的简短描述很难还原优秀教师的课堂。为了方便新手教师更快地开展教学实践，本书的 15 个教学案例将教案、学案和相关活动资源整合在一起，按照课堂的时间顺序呈现，并辅以课堂师生对话摘录和板书示范，以期为教师提供更具体的教学参照。

以下是这 15 个教学案例的相关说明：

仿宋字体部分是笔者对活动的说明或评论，一般置于活动前后。

■ 该项目符号之后的内容代表教师活动（Teacher's activities）。

◇ 该项目符号之后的内容代表学生活动指令（Students' activities）以及该活动涉及的具体活动资源（如图片、教材语篇、配对题等）。

☆ 该项目符号之后的内容代表该教学活动的参考答案。

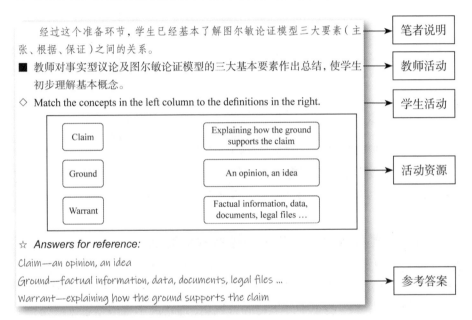

考虑到多数高中大班教学的特点，笔者还特地设立了"课堂再现"和"板书演示"两个板块，提供课堂上师生互动的示范及板书结构参考，方便教师借鉴。

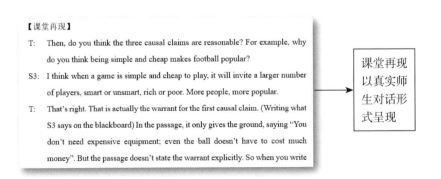

【板书演示】

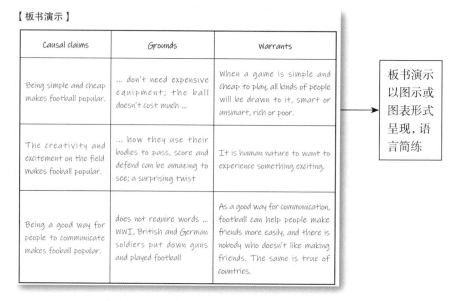

Causal claims	Grounds	Warrants
Being simple and cheap makes football popular.	... don't need expensive equipment; the ball doesn't cost much ...	When a game is simple and cheap to play, all kinds of people will be drawn to it, smart or unsmart, rich or poor.
The creativity and excitement on the field makes fooball popular.	... how they use their bodies to pass, score and defend can be amazing to see; a surprising twist	It is human nature to want to experience something exciting.
Being a good way for people to communicate makes fooball popular.	does not require words ... WWI, British and German soldiers put down guns and played football	As a good way for communication, football can help people make friends more easily, and there is nobody who doesn't like making friends. The same is true of countries.

板书演示以图示或图表形式呈现，语言简练

这 15 个教学案例不仅能成为教师教学的帮手，也可以作为学生自学的材料，学生可以根据每一步的指令和要求尝试开展写作。

五、在具体教学中如何使用这些教学案例

每个案例建议在 2 个课时（即两个 40 分钟）内完成，教师可以按照案例中每个步骤的活动指令，利用活动资源，依次开展教学。其间，教师要尽量循循善诱，让学生的思维外显化和可视化，即帮助学生搭建思维模型，并在语言表达和语言风格上辅以适当的"脚手架"。

需要注意的是，"课堂再现"部分只是展现了多种课堂师生对话方式中的一种，其意图是辅助教师打开思路，开展启发式、探究式、参与式的教学。在实际课堂上，教师还需要考虑学生的语言水平、思维层次、背景知识储备等因素，适时调整对话的风格和难度，必要时也可以适当使用母语进行解释，鼓励学生转换语码。但不论怎样调整，课堂对话都有一定的原则，即由浅入深、由表及里、由易到难地讲解高中英语议论文写作相关知识，引导学生主动思考。同样，"板书演示"部分也只是展示了众多可能的板书方式中的一种，并非所有课堂都必须按照这样的方式进行，教师可以依据学生的需求灵活调整板书的设计。

除此之外，限于案例写作的体例，"互动评价"出现在第八个步骤，

但在实际的教学过程中，教师应当确保评价贯穿整个课堂。比如，教师在写作课开始时就要在黑板上预留出一块专门的位置，用于记录在课堂上和学生共同讨论得出的评价清单，即在前七个步骤的教学中即时生成评价要点。

最后一个步骤，即"尝试相似话题"是选做步骤，教师可以在每个案例的教学结束后，鼓励学生尽量完成该步骤的写作话题，帮助他们实现从教师辅助下的写作到独立写作的转变。

第六章 事实型议论文教学案例

写作话题 1 案件报告

学习目标汇总 Learning Objectives

Can-do statements

By the end of this session, students will be able to say:

- I can understand and apply the three basic elements of the Toulmin Model (the claim, the ground and the warrant).
- I can describe the crime scene with some degree of accuracy.
- I can write a case report with clear reasoning.

Thinking focus	Expression focus	Style focus
Logos: The relationship between claims, grounds and warrants *Ethos*: Using personal experiences	**Describing the crime scene:** **Verbs:** *inspect the scene, is dressed neatly, slip down the stairs* **Adjectives:** *not broken, neat, not messy, disturbed*	**Formal register:** generally impersonal and unemotional, avoiding contractions and abbreviations

准备开始写作 Preparing to Write

　　本节课是学生第一次接触事实型议论文写作，此前他们从未接触过图尔敏论证模型的概念。因此，教师可以设计一个有趣的课前小任务，利用侦探漫画，使学生在探案过程中理解什么是事实型议论，并向学生介绍图尔敏论证模型的三大基本要素。

■ 教师向学生展示一张漫画，告诉他们这是玛丽的房间，玛丽回到家发现有人闯进过她的房间。教师让学生把自己假设成案件现场的警察，讨论并回答闯入者是否为了钱财而来。

◇ This is a picture of Mary's room. Upon returning home, Mary found that her room had been broken into and she immediately reported to the police. Suppose you were the policeman, examine the picture and find out whether the intruder broke into the room for money. Have a discussion with the partner.

【课堂再现】

T: Sherry, do you think the intruder broke into Mary's room for money?

S1: No, my partner and I don't think so.

T: So you mean the intruder didn't come for money, right? This is a "claim" you and your partner has made.（Drawing a table and writing "Claim" and "didn't come for money" on the first column）Then, do you have evidence to support the claim?（Writing "Ground" on the second column）

S1: We see the jewelry is still in the jewelry box.

T: So what? Maybe the intruder took the money and ignored the jewelry.

S1: But generally speaking, if an intruder aims for money, he will be greedy for anything that is valuable, including the jewelry which is put in such an eye-catching place on the dressing table.

T: Great! Sherry, you have just finished the reasoning process. We can call the process the "warrant"（Writing "Warrant" on the blackboard）which is a link between the claim and the ground. The warrant ensures that the ground is useful and relevant. Sherry, you have just successfully finished an argument of fact.（Writing "An Argument of Fact" on top of the table）

【板书演示】

An Argument of Fact

Claim	Ground	Warrant
… didn't come for money.	The jewelry is still in the box.	Generally speaking, if an intruder aims for money, he will be greedy for anything valuable, including the jewelry which is put in such an eye-catching place on the dressing table.

经过这个准备环节，学生已经基本了解图尔敏论证模型三大要素（主张、根据、保证）之间的关系。

■ 教师对事实型议论及图尔敏论证模型的三大基本要素作出总结，使学生初步理解基本概念。

◇ Match the concepts in the left column to the definitions in the right.

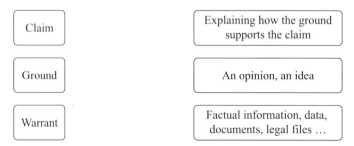

Claim		Explaining how the ground supports the claim
Ground		An opinion, an idea
Warrant		Factual information, data, documents, legal files …

☆ *Answers for reference:*

Claim—an opinion, an idea

Ground—factual information, data, documents, legal files ...

Warrant—explaining how the ground supports the claim

了解写作话题 Understanding the Prompt

写作 话题	在派对上，男主人约翰突然跌下楼梯，昏迷不醒，有一位目击者对警察说约翰是在醉酒后失足滑下了楼梯。根据图片，写一份案件报告，描述事故现场，说明目击者是否说谎，并给出理由。①

■ 教师告诉学生，本节课的写作任务是一个比玛丽的房间更复杂的案件。教师让学生先读题，然后围绕话题具体内容提问，确保每个学生都理解写作话题所陈述的背景和要求。

◇ Think and answer the following questions.

1）Who is the victim? What happened to the victim?

2）What does the witness say?

---

① 话题改编自 "Slip or Trip"（Hillocks G. Teaching Argument Writing, Grades 6–12 [M]. Portsmouth, NH: Heinemann, 2011.）

3）What is your identity as the writer? Who is the target reader?

4）What tone and voice should be used in the writing?

5）Could you use one sentence to sum up what you are going to write?

I am going to write a _____ to describe the scene,

_____.

☆ *Answers for reference:*

1) The victim is John. He fell to the bottom of the stairs at a party and is now unconscious.

2) The witness says that John was drunk and slipped down the stairs.

3) I (the writer) am a policeman. The target reader is probably the chief inspector of the police station.

4) The tone should be formal and the voice should be serious, impartial, and authoritative since this is a case report.

5) I am going to write a case report to describe the scene, decide whether the witness IS or IS NOT lying and give reasons.

搭建思维模型 Constructing the Model

■ 教师鼓励学生使用图尔敏论证模型，先观察图片并与小组成员讨论图片中的可疑之处，再确定主张。

◇ Examine the picture carefully, discuss with the group members and find out whether the witness is lying.

【课堂再现】

（After the discussion）

T: Do you think the witness is lying?

S1: Yes, we think so.

T: Why do you think so?

S1: Because the witness says John slipped down the stairs, but it is strange that John held the wine glass in his right hand.

T: Why is it strange?

S1: If a person slipped down the stairs, he would normally try to save himself and throw away the glass.

T: Interesting discovery. I think your reason has convinced me. What about the next group? Do you have different opinions?

S2: We also think the witness is lying. John's feet shouldn't be on the stairs.

T: Could you explain a little bit more?

S2: Because if you slipped, your feet would be towards the floor, not up on the stairs.

…

T: So, the majority of you think that the witness is lying, right?

【板书演示】

Claim	Ground	Warrant
… is lying.	John held the glass tightly in his right hand.	If a person slipped down …, he would normally get rid of … and try to hold the handrail.

撰写提纲 Producing an Outline

■ 教师鼓励学生将讨论的内容按照图尔敏论证模型的三大要素列成提纲。

◇ Produce an outline using the Toulmin model of argumentation.

Claim	Grounds	Warrants

在该环节，学生常常会存在以下问题：

（1）出现多个主张。比如有学生可能会写 The witness is lying and the witness pushed John，这就涉及两个主张，而题目只要求说明目击者是否说谎,并没有要求找出案件真相。此外,即使题目有要求,两个主张也应该分开提出并证明。

(2)根据中出现主观性形容词。比如 The position of John is strange,这个表述是不准确的,"奇怪"本身需要定义,不适合出现在案件报告中。

(3)根据和保证不匹配。有些学生的几条根据和保证相互混淆,造成上一条根据对应下一条保证,教师在点评时务必要注意。

(4)保证中出现新的主张。有时学生会在保证中加上一些主观想法,而且不加以说明,这类问题也是教师应该指出的。

■ 教师将部分学生的提纲进行投屏,指导学生当场分析提纲中不合理的地方,共同生成针对提纲修改的评价清单,并鼓励学生根据评价清单进行修改。

◇ Work out a checklist and revise the outline based on the checklist.

☆ *Possible checklist:*

Guiding questions	√ / ×
1. Does my writing have one clear claim or multiple claims?	
2. Does my ground contain subjective words? If so, what are they?	
3. Does my warrant support the ground?	
4. Does my warrant contain new claims?	

☆ *Possible outline:*

Claim	Grounds	Warrants
The witness is lying.	The wine glass is still in John's hand.	When people sense they are slipping down, they will drop what they are holding to save themselves.
	John's feet are pointing towards the stairs.	If a man slips on the stairs, he will land on the buttocks and his feet will be towards the floor.
	Nothing on the wall is disturbed.	When someone falls unexpectedly, he will find something to hold to keep balance and the objects on the wall will be disturbed.

提升效果 Adding the Impact

　　对于案件报告的写作，学生只是假设自己的身份是警察，并没有实际的探案经验，因此并不一定能使用人格诉求这一修辞要素。但是，教师可以询问学生是否从长辈的工作中了解过类似的案情分析，或者是否看过类似的书籍等。

■ 教师询问学生是否了解过警察或侦探是如何判断案情的，如有类似经历，可适当在报告中提及，增加话语的可信度。

◇ Think and answer the following questions:

Have you ever known or heard about how the police or detectives solve cases?

If you have related experience, you can mention your experience in your report to establish credibility with the readers.

聚焦语言 Focusing on Language

■ 从词到句：教师鼓励学生用英文表达与现场描述相关的短语和句子。

◇ From words to sentences: Try translating the following phrases and sentences.

某人被发现不省人事	＿＿＿＿＿＿＿＿＿＿＿＿
详细检查现场	＿＿＿＿＿＿＿＿＿＿＿＿
衣物整齐	＿＿＿＿＿＿＿＿＿＿＿＿
他手紧握着酒杯。	＿＿＿＿＿＿＿＿＿＿＿＿
他脚朝向楼梯。	＿＿＿＿＿＿＿＿＿＿＿＿
目击者说他滑下楼梯。	＿＿＿＿＿＿＿＿＿＿＿＿

☆ *Answers for reference:*

某人被发现不省人事	somebody is found unconscious ...
详细检查现场	inspect the scene carefully / careful inspection of the scene
衣物整齐	... is dressed neatly / ... is wearing ... that is neat
他手紧握着酒杯。	He was holding a wine glass tightly.

他脚朝向楼梯。 His feet are pointing towards the stairs.

目击者说他滑下楼梯。 The witness said that he slipped down the stairs.

■ 从句到段：教师让学生尝试将根据和保证连接起来，写成一段话。

◇ From sentences to paragraphs: Try connecting the ground and the warrant in a short paragraph.

Ground	Warrant
The wine glass is still in John's hand.	When people sense they are slipping down, they will drop what they are holding to save themselves.

_____

_____

_____

_____

☆ *Answers for reference:*

The wine glass is still in John's hand. <u>As a rule</u>, when people sense they are slipping down, they will usually drop what they are holding in order to save themselves.

Other connectors besides "as a rule":

- As we all know / As is known to all, ...

- It is common sense that .../ It is generally acknowledged that ...

- Generally speaking, ...

- Normally, ...

组织布局 Designing the Layout

本节课是学生第一次尝试事实型议论文写作，此前他们并未接触过案件报告类写作。因此，教师可以给出一个基本的框架，并辅以语言支撑，帮助学生快速进入写作状态。

■ 教师给出参考布局格式，提示学生写初稿时应注意该写作话题的要求：描述事故现场，说明目击者是否说谎，并给出理由。

◇ Write the report with the reference layout shown below. Note that your report should include the description of the scene, the statement of whether the witness is lying and the reasons.

Dear chief inspector,

    At 11 pm last night, John was found unconscious at the bottom of the staircase in his home. He was _____

_____

_____

    A witness says that _____

_____ After careful inspection of the scene, I believe the witness _____

    First, _____

_____

_____

    Second, _____

_____

_____

    Third, _____

_____

_____

    Therefore, _____

More investigation is needed to get the details about the case.

互动评价 Evaluating the Drafts

    理论篇中已给出了事实型议论文的评价清单。这个环节中，教师可以依据具体的写作话题调整清单，并列出需要检查的最重要部分。

■ 教师鼓励学生依据评价量表进行自我评价或同伴评价。

◇ Evaluate the drafts in pairs or in groups with the following checklist.

（请参见本书理论篇第二章第四节事实型议论文评价清单样例，选取合适的维度，鼓励学生围绕习作初稿开展自评与互评。）

分享范文 Sharing the Samples

■ 教师分享优秀范文，供学生交流、评价、学习。

◇ Read the sample writings of your classmates and learn from them.

Dear chief inspector,

At 11 pm last night, John was found unconscious at the bottom of the staircase in his home. He was lying on his back, facing up, with his feet on the second and third step. He was holding a wine glass in his right hand and the glass was not broken. In addition, he was wearing a robe that was neat, not messy. Nothing on the wall was disturbed.

A witness says that John was drunk and slipped down the stairs. After careful inspection of the scene, I believe the witness was lying.

First, the glass was still in John's right hand. Generally speaking, when one slips on the stairs, he won't be able to still hold something in his hand unless it is very important. The glass is obviously not something of great importance. If John slipped down the stairs, he should try to get hold of something in order to keep balance and meantime throw away the glass.

Second, John's feet are pointing towards the stairs. From my years of observation, if a man slips down the stairs, he will normally land on the buttocks, and his feet will be pointing

---

towards the floor, not up on the stairs. So it cannot be true that John was slipping down the stairs.

Third, nothing on the wall was disturbed. As a rule, when someone encounters an unexpected fall, he would try to grab anything to save himself. Besides, John looks big and the stairs are narrow. So it is quite possible that John would knock something on the wall if he actually slipped down the stairs.

Therefore, the witness is lying. More investigation is needed to crack the truth about the case.

◇　Write down what you have learned from this sample writing.

> > > 　教师点评

　　这篇习作结构完整，较好地完成了写作话题的要求，即描述事故现场，说明目击者是否说谎，并给出理由。每个理由段落都围绕一个要点，并且段落之间使用了转折词 first、second、third，过渡自然。

　　从逻辑上看，三条理由都能围绕"目击者在说谎"的主张来写。而且，理由的陈述方式清晰，都是先给出根据，再进行详细的论证，即保证。根据和保证能够相互匹配，彼此之间过渡自然，清楚地解释了为何现场和目击者的证词相悖。

　　从语言上看，习作在描述事故现场时用到了 lie、face up、hold、wear 等动词，以及 not broken、neat、not messy、disturbed 等描述性形容词，语言较为精确、客观。在论述过程中，代词和连接词（如 generally speaking、as a rule 等）的使用能够确保习作衔接流畅，使读者读起来不费劲。此外，习作使用了较为正式的表达，用词严谨，语言逻辑性强，句型结构正确，在书写中未使用缩略形式，是一份较正式的案件报告。

写作话题 2　虚假广告

学习目标汇总 Learning Objectives

Can-do statements

By the end of this session, students will be able to say:

- I can understand "unstated warrants" and "conditions of rebuttal"/ "counter-argument" in the Toulmin Model.
- I can describe the characters' changing actions and emotions to enhance the effect of the reasoning process.
- I can write an argument of fact to warn other customers against the purchase of a product.

Thinking focus	Expression focus	Function focus
Logos: The unstated warrant and conditions of rebuttal *Pathos*: Describing the changing mood of the characters	**Describing the characters' changing actions and emotions:** **Actions:** *switch to Channel 12, promote a limited offer, subscribe ...* **Emotions:** *excited, amazed, disappointed, surprised ...*	**Ways of introducing warrants** **Paragraph transitions:** *firstly, to begin with, secondly, furthermore, in addition, to sum up, on the whole*

准备开始写作 Preparing to Write

　　经过前一节课的学习，学生已经基本知晓了图尔敏论证模型，并成功地将主张、根据、保证三大要素应用于案件报告的写作。在本节课中，教师将带领学生结合教材中阅读文本的内容情境，进一步体验事实型议论文的写作。

■ 教师要求学生阅读《高中英语》（新世纪版）高一第二学期第 8 单元语篇 *An Added Bonus* 并回答问题。

◇ Read the following passage *An Added Bonus* and answer the following questions.

1）How many characters are there in the passage? Who are they?

2）What was advertised on Channel 12? Did the advertisement attract them?

3）What is the added bonus? Are they satisfied with the bonus?

以下为语篇节选：

> Anne and Joe King sat back in their easy chairs, watching television in their cozy living-room. Anne used the remote control to find a programme of interest.
>
> "Why don't we watch *The Family Friction*?" said Anne.
>
> "I hate watching soap dramas," said Joe. "Especially this one where couples argue over money."
>
> "Okay," said Anne, as she switched to Channel 12.
>
> "And now," said a good-looking announcer on the TV screen, "*Round-the-World*, the magazine of the world, is proud to announce its limited offer. For the bargain price of $10, half the newsstand price, you can subscribe to one year ..."

【课堂再现】

T: So who can tell me how many characters there are in the passage?

S1: There are two characters.

T: Who are they?

S1: Anne and Joe King.

T: And they were watching TV, right? So what was advertised on TV?

S1: *Round-the-world*, the magazine.

T: Yes, the subscription of the magazine *Round-the-World*. Are they interested in the magazine? Tom, what do you think?

S2: Yes, I think they are interested in the magazine. Anne said "that sounds amusing".

T: What sounds amusing?

S2: The World Atlas.

T: Good. It was the free gift "the World Atlas" that attracted them to subscribing to the magazine. That is the "added bonus", right? (Pointing to the words "added bonus" on the blackboard) But are they satisfied with the gift?

S2: No, they are not.

T: How can you tell?

S2: Because it is different from the TV.

T: You mean it is different from what was advertised on TV, right?

■ 教师提出关键问题 "这则广告是否为虚假广告"，让学生开展对子活动并讨论，引出写作话题。

◇ Have a discussion with the partner and take your stand on the question "whether this TV advertisement is false advertising or not".

了解写作话题 Understanding the Prompt

写作话题	近来，天空日报 (*Sky Daily*) 正在收集虚假广告受害者的案例，准备做一期专题报道。假设你是 Anne，给报社写一封信，讲述你的经历，证明你遭遇了虚假广告。

■ 教师要求学生仔细读题，然后围绕写作话题具体内容提问，确保每个学生都理解写作话题的要求。

◇ Think and answer the following questions.

1) What is the purpose of this writing?

2) What is your identity as the writer? Who are the target readers?

3) What tone and voice should be used?

4）Could you use one sentence to sum up what you are going to write?

> I am going to write a _____
>
> _____.

☆ *Answers for reference:*

1) The writing purpose is to share the experience and possibly warn the readers of the newspaper not to believe in the *Round-the-World advertisement*.

2) I (the writer) am Anne who is an angry customer. The target readers are the editor of *Sky Daily* and if the writing piece gets published, the readers of the newspaper will also be the target readers.

3) The tone should be relatively formal since the relationship between the writer and the reader is not so close. The voice should be personal and emotional; the author can present himself as an angry customer.

4) I am going to write a letter to *Sky Daily* to share my experience of being cheated and prove that the TV advertisement is false advertising.

搭建思维模型 Constructing the Model

■ 教师鼓励学生将上节课学到的图尔敏论证模型的三大要素应用于逻辑构思，并与小组成员一起讨论写作话题中的根据和保证。

◇ Have a discussion with the group members and try to state the grounds and the warrants.

【课堂再现】

（After the discussion）

T: As we have discussed before, most of you think this TV advertisement is false advertising. So what grounds does your group find?

S1: The atlas looks like a postage stamp, but it looks tremendous on TV.

T:（Writing what the student says on the blackboard）Yes, we can find this information in the passage. Then why is it false advertising?

S1: Isn't it obvious?

T: It may seem obvious. But when we are writing to prove that this advertisement belongs to the category of false advertising, we need to further explain it, making everything clear to our readers. That is, we need to explicitly state the warrant. Like in this one, we can go on to explain that "the TV advertisement gave the audience a wrong impression on purpose". (Writing the warrant on the blackboard)Any other ideas from other groups?

S2: The TV advertisement said that you can have the world at your fingertips, and the atlas they received is really so small that it can be put on fingertips.

T: Great. Your group has found another ground. So what does this ground say about the false advertising?

S2: It is just ... "at your fingertips" is a 成语, which doesn't mean something actually at your fingertips.

T: I can get what you mean. You want to say that the advertiser actually played with the words, and replaced the figurative meaning of the idiom "at your fingertips" with its literal meaning, right? That can be a good warrant. You have done a very good job explaining. Have you found that the warrant is actually the definition of false advertising?

　　从以上对话可以看出,学生在思考根据和保证时,保证往往是难点。从笔者的教学经历来看,高中生常常漏掉保证,或者觉得保证很明显,不需要说出来。教师要向学生强调,在写作中,有的保证属于某种常识,确实很明显,可以作为隐性保证;但多数时候,作者要尽量将隐性保证挖掘出来,并进行清楚的陈述,这样才能形成完整的思维链,让读者较为容易地跟上作者的论证思路。在这个环节,教师的总结非常关键,当学生找不到合适的思路来写保证时,教师必须提出参考思路,帮助学生形成逻辑闭环。

■ 教师向学生强调,有的保证看似很明显,但为了让读者在短时间内更快地跟上作者的论证思路,必须将隐性保证陈述出来。随后,教师总结道,对于该写作话题,隐性保证实际上就是虚假广告的定义。

◇ Write down the function of warrant in this writing topic.

☆ *Answers for reference:*

In this writing topic, the warrant is actually the definition of "false advertising".

撰写提纲 Producing an Outline

■ 教师鼓励学生将讨论的内容按照图尔敏论证模型的三大要素列成提纲，并邀请两位学生在黑板上书写提纲。

◇ Produce an outline using the Toulmin model of argumentation.

Claim	Grounds	Warrants

　　教师邀请学生在黑板上书写提纲可以带来一些便利和好处：首先，在提纲初稿完成后，教师可以直接带学生在黑板上一起探讨如何修改提纲内容；其次，教师可以当场指出提纲中的语言错误，并提醒班级其他学生避免类似错误。

■ 教师和学生一起探讨黑板上提纲初稿的修改，指出根据和保证中不匹配的地方，并帮助学生提升语言表达。同时，教师要指出学生提纲中明显的语言错误。

◇ Revise the outline and try to avoid the mistakes the teacher has mentioned.

☆ *Possible outline:*

Claim	Grounds	Warrants
The TV advertisement is false advertising.	The atlas we received was as big as a postage stamp. However, it looked tremendous in the advertisement.	The TV advertisement gave the audience a wrong impression on purpose, which may tempt the audience into subscribing.

（续表）

Claim	Grounds	Warrants
The TV advertisement is false advertising.	The TV advertisement said that "you can have the world at your fingertips", while the atlas we received was actually so small that it could be put on fingertips.	It played with the words and replaced the figurative meaning with the literal meaning.
	The TV advertisement said that every chief tourist attraction in the world could be found in the atlas, but actually nothing could be found without a microscope.	The advertisement exaggerated the function of the product and cheated the customers.

　　提纲撰写的重点是内容，但教师也要在适当的时机指出其中涉及的语言使用。比如，在该提纲的根据部分，学生肯定会使用对比的写作手法，即把广告上看到的地图和包裹中收到的地图进行对比。教师在黑板上修改提纲时，最好和学生一起分析其中的语言特点，提示学生可使用 but（in fact）、however、while 等副词和连词来强调两者的对比。

提升效果 Adding the Impact

　　描述主人公的情感变化可以提升习作的情感诉求，从而增强表达效果，教师可以提示学生仔细阅读语篇，体会人物情感，在习作中表现出"生气的顾客"的语气。

■ 教师让学生再次阅读语篇 An Added Bonus，体会人物情感，并建议学生在习作中适当使用情感描述的语言。

◇ Read the passage An Added Bonus again, feel the emotions of the hero and include some emotive language in the writing.

■ 教师询问学生对"该广告为虚假广告"的主张是否有异议，并让学生思考如何回应。

◇ Think about the possible objections against the claim that this TV advertisement is false advertising and come up with ideas to respond to the objections.

Objections:

_____

_____

Responses:

_____

_____

☆ *Answers for reference:*

Objections:

The atlas is only a free gift. The main part of the TV advertisement is the subscription of the *Round-the-World* magazine. So you cannot say the TV advertisement is false advertising.

Responses:

It is true that the atlas is a free gift, but it is a vital part of the TV advertisement. Almost half of the ad time is devoted to the introduction of the "amazing" atlas. Without this free offer, we wouldn't have subscribed to the magazine in the first place.

　　理论篇中曾提到，相反意见是图尔敏论证模型的重要组成部分，合理应对相反意见是提升表达效果的一个重要方式。因此，教师可以在这个环节提出图尔敏论证模型的又一要素——相反意见，也叫反驳条件。教师应让学生学会思考相反意见的提出，并告诉学生，如果能在议论中承认相反意见的存在，并适当予以反驳，可以增加议论的强度，使读者更信任作者的观点。

聚焦语言 Focusing on Language

■ 教师鼓励学生使用第一人称概述教材语篇中呈现的人物经历，并强调需要提及人物的动作和情感变化。

◇ Summarize the characters' experience in the passage in the first person, with the help of the following table.

Action	Emotion
switch to Channel 12 a good-looking announcer is promoting a limited offer ... subscribe before midnight, an added bonus, the World Atlas locate places I plan to visit	excited/amazed/thrilled ↓ disappointed/surprised/astonished

☆ *Answers for reference:*

The other day, my brother and I were watching Channel 12 and saw a good-looking announcer promoting a limited offer, *Round-the-World* magazine for a bargain price with an added bonus, a free World Atlas. I thought it handy to have an atlas at home, so I subscribed immediately. Two weeks later, a small package arrived. After opening it, we were hugely disappointed.

■ 从句到段：教师让学生尝试将根据和保证连接起来，写成一段话。

◇ From sentences to paragraphs: Try connecting the ground and the warrant in a short paragraph.

Ground	Warrant
The atlas we received was as big as a postage stamp. However, it looked tremendous in the TV advertisement.	The TV advertisement gave the audience a wrong impression on purpose, which may tempt the audience into subscribing.

_____

_____

_____

_____

☆ *Answers for reference:*

The atlas looked tremendous on TV. However, when we got the package, we were astonished to find that the atlas was as big as a postage stamp. <u>It is clear that</u> the advertisement purposely enlarged the atlas in front of the camera to give the audience a wrong impression.

Other connectors besides "it is clear that ...":

- ..., which I believe is a classic way of false advertising ...

- I suppose that ... / I consider it ...

- That is to say ...

- It is common knowledge that ...

组织布局 Designing the Layout

■ 教师给出参考布局格式，提示学生写初稿时应注意该写作话题的要求：讲述你的经历，证明你遭遇了虚假广告。

◇ Write the letter with the reference layout shown below. Note that your letter should include the narration of your experience of encountering false advertising and the reasons to prove that it is false advertising.

Dear editor,
    The other day, my brother Joe and I _____

_____

_____

_____ I

want to warn other customers that the *Round-the-World* TV advertisement is false advertising.

Firstly / To begin with, _____

_____

_____

_____

Secondly/Besides/Furthermore/Moreover, _____

_____

_____

_____

Thirdly / In addition, _____

_____

_____

_____

To sum up / In summary / To conclude / On the whole / In short, _____

_____

_____

以上参考布局重点突出了段落转折语，教师可以重点强调段落转折语的重要性，并根据学生情况提供更多的参考转折语。在之后的案例中，将不再特意补充段落转折语。

互动评价 Evaluating the Drafts

■ 教师鼓励学生依据评价量表进行自我评价或同伴评价。

◇ Evaluate the drafts in pairs or in groups with the following checklist.

（请参见本书理论篇第二章第四节事实型议论文评价清单样例，选取合适的维度，鼓励学生围绕习作初稿开展自评与互评。）

分享范文 Sharing the Samples

■ 教师分享优秀范文，供学生交流、评价、学习。

◇ Read the sample writings of your classmates and learn from them.

The other day, my brother Joe and I were watching Channel 12 and saw a good-looking announcer promoting a limited offer, *Round-the World* magazine for a bargain price with an added bonus, a free World Atlas. I thought it handy to have an atlas at home, so I subscribed immediately. Two weeks later, a small package arrived. After opening it, I was hugely disappointed. I want to warn other customers against this product because the *Round-the-World* TV advertisement is false advertising.

Firstly, the atlas looked tremendous on TV. However, when we got the package, we were astonished to find that the atlas was as big as a postage stamp. It is clear that the advertisement purposely enlarged the atlas in front of the camera to give the audience a wrong impression, thus misguiding the customers.

Secondly, the ad mentioned that the atlas included maps of every chief tourist attraction in the world and the metropolises and capitals of the countries, while the real one is so small that only with a microscope can we see the content of the maps clearly. That is to say that the company has exaggerated the functions of the atlas, which obviously aimed to fool the customers.

Thirdly, the advertiser was clearly manipulating the phrases and terms. The idiom "having sth at your fingertips" means having something ready and available to use easily, not something so small that can actually be put on your fingertips. The advertiser clearly replaced the figurative meaning of the idiom with its literal meaning.

To sum up, the atlas is not an added bonus, but useless trash. I believe the TV advertisement *Round-the-World* is false advertising. Although I have canceled the subscription and got my money back, I still want to warn others not to waste their valuable time on such products.

◇ Write down what you have learned from this sample writing.

 教师点评

　　这篇习作结构完整，较好地完成了写作话题的要求，即讲述经历，证明自己遭遇了虚假广告。每个段落都围绕一个主题来写，特别是理由段落，三条理由各自独立，互不重复。并且段落之间过渡清楚、自然，使读者能够较容易地跟上作者的论证思路。

　　从逻辑上看，三条理由都能围绕"该广告是虚假广告"的主张来写。而且，理由的表述方式清晰：第一条和第二条理由都是先给出根据，再写保证；第三条理由则先给出保证，即虚假广告的定义之一"歪曲广告词"，再给出证据，说明该广告如何歪曲广告词以达到欺骗消费者的目的。两种写法都清楚地解释了该广告为何为虚假广告。

　　从语言上看，该习作的语气把握得较好，在讲述被骗经历时，对 *An Added Bonus* 的语篇内容进行了较好的概括，并且将人物情感（thought it handy、hugely disappointed 等）融入其中，提升了习作的情感诉求；在理由阐述中也使用了情感类表达，如 were astonished to find，并通过 however、while、not ... but ... 等词语来展示收到的地图和广告中的地图之间的差别。此外，在论述的过程中，作者使用了一些从句和连接短语（it is clear that ...、that is to say 等），确保根据和保证之间衔接流畅。

写作话题 3　数字艺术

学习目标汇总 Learning Objectives

Can-do statements

By the end of this session, students will be able to say:

- I can prove the grounds with evidence and state the function of warrant in an argument of fact.
- I can describe the history of art and technology in detail.
- I can write an argument of fact discussing whether digital art is art.

Thinking focus	**Expression focus**	**Function focus**
Logos: The relationship between grounds and evidence, warrants and definition *Pathos*: Using concrete language	**About traditional art and digital art:** *technological tools at our fingertips, digital paintings and videos, unique way of expression, a combination of art and technology ...*	**Introducing definition:** *is defined as, by definition, refers to* **Ways of stating the claim:** *embrace the view, strongly believe, express my preference for* **Ways of introducing counter-arguments:** *Some may argue that ..., It is true that ..., Admittedly*

准备开始写作 Preparing to Write

　　经过前两节课的学习，学生对事实型议论文有了基本的认识，也初步尝试了图尔敏论证模型的应用。如果教师亲自实践过，会发现这两节课的写作话题学生比较容易上手。为什么呢？因为这两个话题相当于"给材料作文"，学生可以直接观察到议论中所需的论据（写作话题 1 中，学生通过看漫画找出论据；写作话题 2 中，学生通过阅读得出论据），不需要凭自己的经历或日常的思考得出论据。然而现实生活中，大量的写作话题都是独立写作。独立写作不仅考查学生的思维能力，更考验学生的知识面、阅读积累、语言表达，以及平时是否养成了对身边事开展思考的习惯。教师在独立写作话题的教学中要给予学生更多的输入和引导；同时，教师本人也要成为一个善于思考、勤于积累的阅读者和写作者，这样才能在课堂的师生对话中给予学生更多养分。本节课的写作任务开始前，教师首先通过教材中的阅读语篇引导学生思考艺术和技术之间的关系。

■ 教师要求学生阅读《高中英语》（外研社版）选择性必修第一册第 4 单元语篇 *Art and Technology* 并回答问题。

◇ Read the following passage *Art and Technology* and answer the following questions.

1）Why is the passage titled "Art and Technology"？

2）What is the question that has been repeatedly raised in the passage？

3）Do you think this question is worth discussing？

以下为语篇节选：

> Think "art". What comes to your mind? Is it Greek or Roman sculptures in the Louvre, or Chinese paintings in the Palace Museum? Or maybe, just maybe, it's a dancing pattern of lights?
>
> The artworks by American artist Janet Echelman look like colourful floating clouds when they are lit up at night. Visitors to one of her artworks in Vancouver could not only enjoy looking at it, they could also interact with it–literally. They did this by using their phones to change its colours and patterns. Exhibits such as these are certainly new and exciting, but are they really art? ...

【课堂再现】

T: OK, can anybody tell me why the passage is titled "Art and Technology"？

S1: Because it talks about the relationship between art and technology.

T: So what is their relationship?

S1: Emmm ... Many artworks are now created using technological tools.

T: That's right. It is closely related to the central question of the passage. So what is the question that has been repeatedly raised by the author?

S1: I think it is the question "are they really art"?

T:（Writing the sentence on the blackboard）Yes, that's the first time the author has raised the question. Can you tell me what "they" refers to?

S1: "Exhibits such as these".

T: So what does "these" refer to? Can you use your own words?

S1: I think "these" refers to artworks using technology.

T: Good. Now can you make the author's question "are they really art" complete?

S1: Are artworks using technology really art?

T: That's right.（Writing S1's answer on the blackboard）So what is the second time the author has raised the question?

S2: Can a video of someone slicing a tomato played in slow motion really be called "art"?

T: Right, here the author raises the question again. This time the artwork is the video. Do you think the question is worth discussing?

S3: I do. I do think the question is worth discussing. Actually, I never really thought about the question before. But these examples mentioned here really make me think a lot. It is true that in our daily life there are many so-called artworks like the exhibits and videos. But can they really be called art?

T: I agree with you. We are going to have a discussion on this topic today.

了解写作话题 Understanding the Prompt

写作 话题	如今，各种各样的数字艺术作品层出不穷，比如手机录制的小视频、平板手写笔创作的画、电脑软件制作的图案、相机拍摄的照片等。校报拟开辟专栏讨论话题"数字艺术作品是否算作真正的艺术"，写一篇稿件，说明你对该话题的态度，并给出理由。

■ 教师要求学生仔细读题, 然后围绕写作话题具体内容提问, 确保每个学生都理解写作话题的要求。

◇ Think and answer the following questions.

1) What is the purpose of this writing?

2) What is your identity as the writer? Who are the target readers?

3) What tone and voice should be used?

4) Could you use one sentence to sum up what you are going to write?

I am going to _____

_____.

☆ *Answers for reference:*

1) The writing purpose is to express one's opinion on whether digital artworks can be called art and possibly influence others' thoughts on this topic.

2) I (the writer) am a student in the school. The target readers are the readers of the school newspaper.

3) The tone should be relatively formal since the writing is going to be published in the school newspaper. The voice can be objective and logical.

4) I am going to submit a piece of writing to the school newspaper to express my opinion on the topic "whether digital artworks can really be called art" and give my reasons.

搭建思维模型 Constructing the Model

■ 教师引导学生思考艺术的定义, 即该话题的保证, 鼓励学生开展小组讨论, 确定小组关于该话题的观点。

◇ Think about the warrant of this writing topic, have a discussion with the group members and take your stand on this topic.

【课堂再现】

(Before the discussion)

T: Before you begin your discussion, I want to ask you a question. What do you think is the key to answering the question "Are they really art"? (Pointing at the blackboard)

S1: I think we need to know what "art" refers to here.

T: That's right. Remember the false advertising we have discussed in the previous class? We gave the definition of false advertising. Similarly, for this writing topic, in order to prove that something does or does not belong to the category of art, we need to first identify what "art" is. That is the warrant for this topic.

S1: Can we use dictionaries to find out the definition of "art"?

T: Yes, of course you can. But meanwhile you can also organize your thoughts by thinking about the contrast between an oil painting and a digital painting. Why is there no objection against oil paintings being categorized as art? What are the differences between oil paintings and digital painting?

在上一节课中，学生已知晓要证明某广告是虚假广告，必须指出该广告虚假在哪里，也就是虚假广告的定义。其实，在事实型议论文的提纲中，该定义就是保证。本节课中，教师应进一步帮助学生巩固这一论证思路。需要注意的是，本节课的写作思路与上节课略有不同：在上一个写作话题中，学生可以先从阅读语篇中找出论据，从而总结出虚假广告的定义；而本节课是独立写作话题，没有阅读语篇可供查阅。因此，教师可以鼓励学生先思考艺术的定义，然后根据定义寻找相应的根据。

【课堂再现】

(After the discussion)

T: So have you reached a conclusion about the definition of art?

S1: We referred to the e-dictionary and chose the definition in the Merriam-Webster Dictionary. It defines art as "the conscious use of skill and creative imagination especially in the production of aesthetic objects". (Writing key words on the blackboard)

T: So why do you choose this definition?

S1: Because it mentioned the imagination and skill. We think they are the most important when it comes to defining art.

T: So you mean as long as a piece of artwork involves the use of imagination and skills, it can be called art, right? So do you think the digital artworks can be called art?

S1: Yes, I think in this sense, digital artworks can be called art because no matter what tools you are using, the creators of digital artworks all use their imagination and skills to complete the work.（Writing what S1 says on the blackboard）

T: Good. Any other group has different ideas?

S2: We discussed why oil paintings and other traditional artworks are considered art. We think that's because the artists have learned how to paint for many years and put in great efforts, but for digital paintings, photographs or videos, anybody can make videos. They don't need to learn the skill for many years.

T: That is an interesting thought. You think whether something should be called art is related to the efforts you put in when learning the skill, right? Any different ideas?

S3: I disagree. Photographers also put in great effort when they learn photography. My uncle is a photographer, and he says it takes a lot of practice to produce a good photograph.

T: I see. Jane uses her uncle's example to raise objections. The example increases the credibility of her words. I want to remind everybody to use some examples to prove your ground, better if you are familiar with digital art yourself.

　　由于学生在语言水平上存在差异，这个环节的师生对话在不同班级或不同学校可能会表现出不同的难易程度，教师应根据学生的语言水平在课堂上给予学生不同的辅助。当然，教师本人也要先对这个话题进行充分的思考和研究，这样才能在内容和语言方面当场给予学生合适的建议。总之，该环节的关键是要帮助学生理清思路，为后续撰写提纲打下基础。

【板书演示】

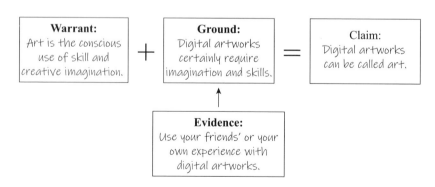

教师要借助该话题提示学生图尔敏论证模型中的根据是可以进一步展开的，从而引出证据的概念。教师还可以提示学生，使用个人经历作为根据的证明能提升话语的可信度，增加议论中的人格诉求。教师在板书中可以通过图示引导学生关注这一点。

撰写提纲 Producing an Outline

■ 教师鼓励学生将讨论的内容按照图尔敏论证模型的三大要素列成提纲，并邀请两位学生在黑板上书写提纲。

◇ Produce an outline using the Toulmin model of argumentation.

Warrants	Grounds + Evidence	Claim

■ 教师和学生一起探讨黑板上提纲初稿的修改，指出根据和保证中不匹配的地方，并帮助学生提升语言表达。同时，教师要指出学生提纲中明显的语言错误。

◇ Revise the outline and try to avoid the mistakes the teacher has mentioned.

☆ *Possible outline:*

Warrants	Grounds + Evidence	Claim
The Merriam-Webster Dictionary defines art as "the conscious use of skill and creative imagination especially in the production of aesthetic objects".	Digital artworks require the use of skills and creative imagination. My own experience of drawing with the app Procreate can prove this. I need all the drawing knowledge and skills. The only difference was whether I draw on a piece of real paper or on a tablet. Digital artworks can be called art.	Digital artworks can be called art.

（续表）

Warrants	Grounds + Evidence	Claim
Art is a means of self-expression.	Digital artworks can help people express themselves as well as, if not better than, traditional art. With the app Procreate, I can express my emotions and feelings anytime anywhere.	Digital artworks can be called art.

提升效果 Adding the Impact

■ 教师引导学生尽可能使用具体的语言描述来加强议论的情感诉求，唤起读者的感性思维。

◇ Use concrete language to enhance *pathos*, helping trigger the audience's feelings. The following is an example of using concrete language.

e.g. If you want to take a high-quality photo, you don't simply set the camera on the auto mode. Instead, you must have the knowledge related to the optics, composition, photo treatment, etc. and have to be familiar with the hardware, including the lenses, tripods and lighting equipment.

■ 教师提示学生思考反方可能存在的质疑，并让学生思考如何回应。

◇ Think about the possible objections against the claim and come up with ideas to respond to the objections.

Objections:

_____

_____

Responses:

_____

_____

☆ *Answers for reference:*

Objections:

Art is a unique expression of heart. Any traditional artwork is a one-of-a-kind piece and the original work is sometimes priceless. However, digital artworks can be easily replicated, printed, or copied, not to mention photographs which only capture the reality instead of creating things.

Responses:

It is true that digital artworks can be copied easily and drawings on tablets can be printed out millions of times. But that doesn't contradict the uniqueness of artworks. What changes is simply the distribution method. Isn't it a good thing that one's artworks can be more widely distributed?

聚焦语言 Focusing on Language

　　如果学生是第一次接触该话题，且语言基础较弱，教师可以适当补充一些有关艺术和技术主题的翻译，帮助学生尽快进入写作状态。同时，教师可以提示学生再次回到教材语篇 *Art and Technology* 进行语言聚焦，鼓励他们收集与主题相关的表达。

■ 教师让学生尝试翻译以下句子，引入数字艺术作品是否为艺术的话题。

◇ Translate the following sentence about the relationship between art and technology into English.

1）艺术和技术有着复杂的、相互影响的历史。

2）技术的发展使得艺术和技术之间的界限越来越模糊。

3）在数字时代，越来越多的艺术家开始依靠技术来输出创造力。

☆ *Answers for reference:*

1) Art and technology have a complex history of influencing each other.

2) Technological developments have blurred the line between art and technology.

3) In the digital age, more and more artists are relying on technology for their creative output.

■ 从词到句：教师指导学生将有关艺术定义的句子翻译成英文。

◇ From words to sentences: Try making the following sentences on the definition of art complete by translating the Chinese into English.

---

1) Art _____（通常被定义为）the creation or expression of something beautiful.

2) _____（照字典上的定义）, art is the expression or application of human creative skill and imagination.

3) Art, _____（本质上来说）, is an expression of emotions.

4) Art _____（指的是）a diverse range of human activities in creating visual, auditory or performing artifacts.

☆ *Answers for reference:*

1) is commonly defined as   2) By definition in the dictionary
3) at (its) root / basically   4) refers to

组织布局 Designing the Layout

■ 教师给出一些有关开篇表达自己观点的句型，让学生尝试翻译。

◇ Please translate the following Chinese into English.

开篇表达自己观点	1) _____（基于我本人接触数字艺术的经历）, I _____（强烈地认为）that digital art is real art. 2) While this issue has sparked a debate in our school, I _____（持有这样的观点）that digital art is real art. 3) I am writing to _____（表达我对……观点的偏好）that digital art is real art.

☆ *Answers for reference:*

1) Based on my experience with digital art; (am among one of those who) strongly believe

2) hold/embrace the view / am in favour of the opinion

3) express my preference for the view

■ 教师给出一些有关引出相反意见的表达，让学生尝试翻译。

◇ Please translate the following Chinese into English.

引出相反意见	1）_____（有人可能会争论说）that true artworks are priceless.
	2）_____（我承认），digital artworks can be easily copied.
	3）_____（确实如此）that art is a unique expression.

☆ *Answers for reference:*

1) Some people may argue　2) Admittedly　3) It is true

■ 教师给出参考布局格式，提示学生写初稿时应注意该写作话题的要求：对"数字艺术作品是否算作真正的艺术"的态度，并给出理由。

◇ Write the essay with the reference layout shown below. Note that your essay should include the stand you take as a writer and the reasons you give.

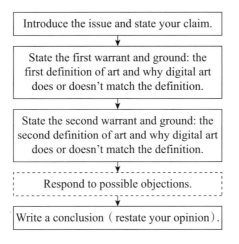

虚线框为可选段落，作者也可以选择不对相反意见作出回应。

互动评价 Evaluating the Drafts

■ 教师鼓励学生依据评价量表进行自我评价或同伴互评。

◇ Evaluate the drafts in pairs or in groups with the following checklist.

（请参见本书理论篇第二章第四节事实型议论文评价清单样例，选取合适的维度，鼓励学生围绕习作初稿开展自评与互评。）

分享范文 Sharing the Samples

■ 教师分享优秀范文，供学生交流、评价、学习。

◇ Read the sample writings of your classmates and learn from them.

Today, technological advances have led to a combination of art and technology. More and more artworks are produced through the use of cameras, videos, tablet apps and other digital techniques. However, can those digital artworks really be called art? As an art lover who has experiences in producing both traditional and digital paintings, I believe the answer is yes.

The Merriam-Webster Dictionary defines art as "the conscious use of skill and creative imagination especially in the production of aesthetic objects". Digital paintings fit right in the definition. I used to have snobby resistance against drawing with an iPad, but one day a friend of mine suggested I have a try on her iPad. As it happened, I took to it instantly and didn't feel anything different except that I wasn't holding a brush. The same creativity and painting skills go into my work.

What's more, art, at its root, serves as a platform for people to express their emotions or thoughts, whatever medium they use. Digital artworks serve the same function and are no less expressive. Whether I draw on a canvas or on iPads, I can

---

always feel the urge of expressing my emotions and feelings and it can always arouse my passion of communicating with the world.

Some people may argue that digital artworks don't require any effort to be made. Part of it is true since anybody can take a picture with their phones. However, creating a photo of high quality requires the same amount of skills, talent and efforts as any traditional art piece does. Being a highly-skilled professional photographer takes years of practice and hard work.

Therefore, I think it is fair to say that digital artworks can be called art.

◇ Write down what you have learned from this sample writing.

▶▶▶ **教师点评**

这是一篇校报投稿。作者在首段先简述了近年来艺术和技术之间相互影响的关系，然后开门见山地抛出校报的讨论主题"数字艺术作品是否算作真正的艺术"，并马上给出自己的主张。在第二段和第三段，作者分别给出两个理由；第四段，作者对可能出现的相反意见进行了回击。最后，作者对该话题进行总结，并重申了一遍主张。可以看出，整篇习作结构清晰。在段落之间的转折中，作者用到了 what's more、some people may argue、therefore 等信号词，使读者能较为容易地跟上作者的思路。

从内容上看，在第二段和第三段的理由段落中，作者按照图尔敏论证模型，先给出保证（即艺术的定义），再给出相应的根据，并辅以自身的具体事例加以说明，逻辑线索清晰。此外，教师使用了一些较为具体的语言（have snobby resistance、took to it instantly、draw on a canvas 等）来描述自身的经历，唤起读者的想象力，提升了情感诉求。

从语言上看，作者语言运用纯熟，在描述具体事例时，使用了 I used to ... 和 as it happened 表达前后态度转变，用词恰当。在连接根据和保证时，作者

使用了 ... fit right in the definition 和 serve the same function 等短语来表达数字艺术符合艺术的定义，衔接流畅。

尝试相似话题 Suggested Writing Prompts

写作话题	电子竞技（electronic sports）近年来发展速度极快，在年轻人中热度很高，因此也产生了许多话题，其中最具争议的是电子竞技是否能算作体育运动。校报拟开辟专栏讨论该话题，写一篇稿件，说明你对该话题的态度，并给出理由。

写作话题 4　盲盒流行

学习目标汇总 Learning Objectives

Can-do statements

By the end of this session, students will be able to say:

- I can apply the elements in the Toulmin Model to a causal argument.
- I can use detailed description of mystery boxes to enhance the credibility of my argument.
- I can write an argument of fact analyzing the causes of the popularity of mystery boxes from different angles.

Thinking focus	Expression focus	Function focus
Logos: Applying the four elements of the Toulmin Model learned and analyzing causes from different angles in a causal argument	**About popularity:** *become increasingly popular, witness the popularity, a hot trend, find one's way to ...*	**Introducing causes and results:** *the reason why ... is that ..., ... results*

***Pathos*: Using specific examples ***Ethos*: showing a strong base of knowledge		*in ..., ... account for ...*

准备开始写作 Preparing to Write

前两节课的写作话题主要涉及事实型议论文中的概念议论（什么是虚假广告？什么算作艺术？）。概念议论是事实型议论文中最重要的类型之一，概念议论中的保证实际上就是概念的定义。而事实型议论文中另一个重要类型是因果议论，因果议论讨论的是某件事是因何发生的。本节课，教师将从教材中的因果议论语段出发，帮助学生思考因果议论的特点。

■ 教师要求学生阅读《高中英语》（外研社版）必修第二册第 3 单元语篇 *A Game for the World* 并回答问题。

◇ Read the following passage *A Game for the World* and answer the following questions.

1）According to the passage, what are the three causes behind football's popularity?

2）When introducing the reasons, what sentence patterns does the author use?

以下为语篇节选：

These days, football is one of the most popular sports in the world. Given that Neil Armstrong wanted to take a football to the Moon, we could even say that it is also the most popular sport out of this world!

That football is such a simple game to play is perhaps the basis of its popularity. It is also a game that is very cheap to play. You don't need expensive equipment; even the ball doesn't have to cost much money. All over the world you can see kids playing to their hearts' content with a ball made of plastic bags; just like Pelé did when he was a boy ...

【课堂再现】

T: So, according to the passage, what are the three causes behind football's popularity?

S1: The first one is that football is such a simple game to play.

T: Just simple, anything else?

S1: It says it is also a game that is very cheap to play.

T: Right, football is a simple and cheap game to play. (Writing the first reason on the blackboard) Go on, the second and the third reason?

S1: The second reason is the creativity and excitement on the field and the third reason is that football has become one of the best ways for people to communicate.

T: (Writing what S1 says on the blackboard) Good. It is not difficult to find the three reasons. They are all clearly stated at the beginning of each paragraph. Can you highlight the sentence patterns for us?

S2: Sure. The first is "sth is the basis of its popularity", the second one is "Another factor behind football's global popularity is ...", and the third one is "What's more, football has become one of the best ways ..."

T: Good. So here we have three causal claims. (Writing "3 causal claims" on the blackboard)

【板书演示】

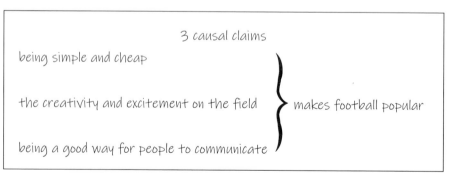

■ 教师引导学生思考这三个因果主张是否合理。

◇ Think about whether the three causal claims are reasonable or not.

【课堂再现】

T: Then, do you think the three causal claims are reasonable? For example, why do you think being simple and cheap makes football popular?

S3: I think when a game is simple and cheap to play, it will invite a larger number of players, smart or unsmart, rich or poor. More people, more popular.

T: That's right. That is actually the warrant for the first causal claim. (Writing what S3 says on the blackboard) In the passage, it only gives the ground, saying "You don't need expensive equipment; even the ball doesn't have to cost much money". But the passage doesn't state the warrant explicitly. So when you write a causal argument yourself, you'd better add the warrant to make your reasoning process clearer to the readers. Then how about the second and the third claim? What is the warrant? You can have a quick discussion ...

【板书演示】

Causal claims	Grounds	Warrants
Being simple and cheap makes football popular.	... don't need expensive equipment; the ball doesn't cost much ...	When a game is simple and cheap to play, all kinds of people will be drawn to it, smart or unsmart, rich or poor.
The creativity and excitement on the field makes football popular.	... how they use their bodies to pass, score and defend can be amazing to see; a surprising twist	It is human nature to want to experience something exciting.
Being a good way for people to communicate makes football popular.	does not require words ... WWI, British and German soldiers put down guns and played football	As a good way for communication, football can help people make friends more easily, and there is nobody who doesn't like making friends. The same is true of countries.

通过分析教材语篇中因果议论的逻辑关系，教师可以帮助学生进一步理解因果议论的特点，为新的因果议论写作话题做好准备。该环节可以在写作课上完成，也可以在前一天的阅读课上完成。

了解写作话题 Understanding the Prompt

写作话题	近年来，盲盒（mystery boxes）的受欢迎程度不断攀升，尤其受到中学生的热捧。校报"热点分析"栏目正在征集该话题稿件，写一篇稿件，描述该现象，并分析原因。

■ 教师要求学生仔细读题，然后围绕写作话题具体内容提问，确保每个学生都理解写作话题的要求。

◇ Think and answer the following questions.

1) What is the purpose of this writing?

2) What is your identity as the writer? Who are the target readers?

3) What tone and voice should be used?

4) Could you use one sentence to sum up what you are going to write?

I am going to _____

_____.

☆ *Answers for reference:*

1) The writing purpose is to convince others that certain causes lead to the popularity of mystery boxes.

2) I (the writer) am a student in the school. The target readers are the readers of the school newspaper.

3) The tone should be relatively formal since the writing is going to be published in the school newspaper. The voice can be objective and logical.

4) I am going to submit a piece of writing to the school newspaper to describe the increasing popularity of mystery boxes and analyze the possible reasons behind it.

搭建思维模型 Constructing the Model

■ 教师鼓励学生开展小组讨论，引导学生从多角度思考盲盒流行的原因。

◇ Have a discussion with the group members and come up with as many causes as possible.

【课堂再现】

（Before the discussion）

T: Before you begin the discussion, I want you to come back to the reading passage about football's popularity again. From what aspects do you think the three causal claims are made? Let's start with the first claim: football is a simple and cheap game to play.

S1: Emmm ... I think it talks about the features of football itself.

T: That's right, the feature of the sport itself. What about the second claim? The creativity and excitement on the field makes it popular. Is it still about the football itself?

S2: No, it is about ... Let me think. It is about the feelings that football brings.

T: Yes, the feelings that football brings to the audience, right? You see, we have two aspects already. What about the third claim?

S3: The third claim is about ... about what football can bring to the world?

T: It especially mentions the relationship between countries, right? It actually talks about the society as a whole. You see, the three claims analyze football's popularity from different angles or parties related to football: the football itself, the audience, and the society as a whole. Therefore, when you are trying to figure out the causes of something, you can apply the same strategy.

　　讨论前的教师引导环节可依据班级学生的程度进行调整。如果学生思维活跃，教师可以略过这个环节。如果学生在讨论时常常无话可说，那么教师可以按照以上方式引导学生。这里，教师指导学生从足球的阅读语篇出发，思考语篇中因果主张提出的角度，即从写作话题涉及的不同相关方出发（足球运动本身的特点、观众的情绪特点以及社会的交际需求）思考原因，学生在讨论时可以参考这一思维路径。

【课堂再现】

(After the discussion)

T: So what causes has your group figured out?

S1: Well, we think the feature of the mystery box itself leads to its popularity.

T: Would you care to elaborate?

S1: Well, since they are called "mystery boxes", you never know what is inside. The curiosity is so great and sometimes you are lucky enough to get the rare stuff.

T: I see. Chances are that you will be the lucky one to get the big prize, right? (Writing what S1 says on the blackboard)

S1: Exactly.

T: Have you had such an experience?

S1: Actually, I have. I once wanted a special model airplane and the shopkeepers told me only one in ten boxes contained the model I wanted. I decided to buy one and try my luck. Guess what? I really got the model I wanted!

T: Lucky for you. So we have the causal claim, the ground, and the evidence. (Writing what S1 says on the blackboard) Now we need the warrant. Why does the big prize make the box popular among teenagers?

S1: Because many students have emmm ... how to say 猎奇心理 ?

T: You mean many people are adventurous, especially teenagers like you, and they all want to try their luck, right? Thank you. You've just given us a reasonable warrant. (Writing on the blackboard) ...

【板书演示】

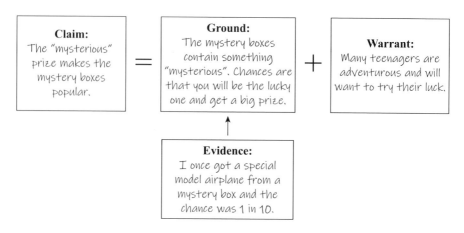

150

撰写提纲 Producing an Outline

■ 教师鼓励学生将讨论的内容按照图尔敏论证模型的三大要素列成提纲，并邀请两位学生在黑板上书写提纲。

◇ Produce an outline using the Toulmin Model of argumentation.

Causal Claims	Grounds + Evidence	Warrants

■ 教师和学生一起探讨黑板上提纲初稿的修改，确保主张、根据和保证相互匹配，并帮助学生提升语言表达。同时，教师要指出学生提纲中明显的语言错误。

◇ Revise the outline and try to avoid the mistakes the teacher has mentioned.

☆ *Possible outline:*

Causal Claims	Grounds + Evidence	Warrants
The possibility of getting a big prize makes mystery boxes popular.	Mystery boxes contain something "mysterious". Chances are that you will be the lucky one and get a big prize. I once got a model airplane and the chance was 1 in 10.	Anybody will want to try their luck, especially middle school students who are particularly adventurous.
The excitement and fun when the owners unpack the boxes makes mystery boxes popular.	Only the one who opens the box can experience the feeling of surprise and a sense of fulfillment.	Teenagers have strong curiosity and the excitement of unpacking is simply irresistible. It is a wonderful diversion from the dull study life.

（续表）

Causal Claims	Grounds + Evidence	Warrants
The communicative function makes mystery boxes popular.	Owners can exchange what's in their boxes with classmates or with friends on the Internet.	Mystery boxes help them make friends with people who share similar interests and find a sense of belonging.

提升效果 Adding the Impact

■ 教师引导学生尽可能使用具体的例子来加强议论的情感诉求，唤起读者（特别是不理解盲盒现象的读者）的想象力。

◇ Use specific examples to enhance *pathos*, sharing your experience with mystery boxes, which will help arouse the audience's imagination.

■ 教师引导学生尽量细致地描述盲盒的外形和内容等，树立作者熟悉该话题的形象，加强议论的人格诉求。

◇ Describe mystery boxes using as many details as possible, including its appearances and content to enhance *ethos* of the argument, to show that you are knowledgeable about the subject of writing. An example is done for you.

e.g. Mystery boxes come in various colours and wrappings.

聚焦语言 Focusing on Language

■ 教师让学生尝试用括号中的单词补全句子，来表达某物的流行。

◇ Complete the sentences using the words in the brackets to describe the popularity of a certain object.

表达某物流行	1）Recent years, mystery boxes _____ _____ .（popularity） 2）Over the last decade, mystery boxes _____ _____（popular）.

（续表）

表达某物流行	3）Mystery boxes _____ _____ in recent years.（trend） 4）Recent years _____ of mystery boxes among teenagers.（witness） 5）Over the last few years, mystery boxes _____ _____ the desks of millions of middle school students.（way） 6）Over the last few years, the mystery box phenomenon _____ _____ a multi-billion-dollar business.（balloon） 7）To gain customers' attention, _____ _____（各种品牌都将它们的产品包 进）mystery boxes.（pack） 8）Increasingly in recent years, _____ _____（越来越多的品牌卖产品）as mystery boxes.（sell）

☆ *Answers for reference:*

1）have been gaining popularity

2）have become increasingly popular

3）have become a hot trend

4）have witnessed the increasing popularity

5）have found their way to

6）has ballooned into

7）various brands are increasingly packing their products into

8）a growing number of brands have begun selling their products

■ 教师给出以下引出原因的句型结构，供学生在写作时参考。

◇ Learn the sentence patterns about how to introduce causes, and use them in your own writing.

The reason why ... is that ...

The popularity is the result of ...

It is ... that results in its popularity.

... account for the phenomenon.

... is the basis of its popularity.

One/Another factor behind its popularity is ...

Part of its appeal/popularity lies in ...

组织布局 Designing the Layout

■ 教师给出参考布局格式，提示学生写初稿时应注意该写作话题的要求：
描述盲盒流行这一现象，并分析原因。

■ Write the draft with the reference layout shown below. Note that your
draft should include the description of the popularity of mystery boxes and
analyzing the reasons behind it.

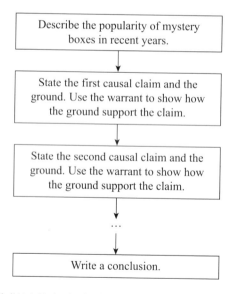

省略号部分是指因果主张的数量不定，一般来说，两条或三条理由比
较常见，作者只要将现象背后的理由分析清楚即可。

互动评价 Evaluating the Drafts

■ 教师鼓励学生依据评价量表进行自我评价或同伴评价。

◇ Evaluate the drafts in pairs or in groups with the following checklist.

（请参见本书理论篇第二章第四节事实型议论文评价清单样例，选取合适的维度，鼓励学生围绕习作初稿开展自评与互评。）

分享范文 Sharing the Samples

■ 教师分享优秀范文，供学生交流、评价、学习。

◇ Read the sample writings of your classmates and learn from them.

Over the last few years, mystery boxes have found their way to the desks of millions of teenagers. To gain their attention, all kinds of brands are increasingly packing their products into mystery boxes. The boxes come in different colours and wrappings, which look especially appealing.

From my point of view, several reasons account for this hot trend. Firstly, the mystery box, as its name suggests, contains something "mysterious". Chances are that somebody will be the lucky one and get a big prize out of the many boxes. Once, I bought a mystery box and I really got the model I had been dreaming of. It is human nature that people will want to try their luck, especially middle school students who are particularly adventurous.

Secondly, part of its appeal is the excitement and fun when the owners unpack the boxes. Only the one who opens the box can experience the feeling of surprise and a sense of fulfillment. Middle school students are in a period in life which is characterized by strong curiosity, so the excitement of unpacking is simply irresistible. And such a feeling is a pleasant

---

diversion from the dull school work.

Furthermore, mystery boxes are one of the easiest ways for teenagers to increase social contact. Owners can exchange what's in their boxes with classmates or with friends on the Internet. In the information age, people have become more distant from one another, and mystery boxes help students make friends with those who share similar interests and find a sense of belonging.

Therefore, it is only natural that mystery boxes have become a hot trend. However, as a student, it is essential for us not to get addicted to them.

◇ Write down what you have learned from this sample writing.

 教师点评

这篇习作结构完整，较好地完成了写作话题的要求，即描述盲盒流行这一现象，并分析原因。第一段是现象描述，最后一段是总结，中间三个原因分析段落中，每个段落都围绕一个因果主张来写，三个原因各自独立，互不重复。在段落之间的转折中，作者用到了 firstly、secondly、furthermore等信号词，使读者能较为容易地跟上思路。

从内容上看，三个因果主张分别从盲盒本身的吸引力、人的情感特点以及学生的社交需求提出，每个主张的证明都按照根据＋保证的方式展开，逻辑清晰。此外，作者通过自身的故事以及对盲盒外形和功能的具体描述，有意识地提升了议论中的情感诉求和人格诉求。

从语言上看，作者使用表达因果关系的短语（account for ..., part of its appeal is ..., ... are one of the easiest ways）引出盲盒流行的原因。在陈述根据和保证的时候，作者还使用了 as its name suggests、chances are that ...、is characterized by ...、a sense of belonging 等短语和句型，体现了较好的语言驾驭能力，令人眼前一亮。

尝试相似话题 Suggested Writing Prompts

写作 话题	微信（WeChat）走进了人们的生活，为大家带来了诸多便利，但有些人也随之成了微信控（WeChataholic）。校报"热点分析"栏目正在征集该话题稿件，写一篇稿件，描述该现象，并分析原因。

第七章 价值型议论文教学案例

写作话题 5 择业述评

学习目标汇总 Learning Objectives

Can-do statements

By the end of this session, students will be able to say:

- I can understand the element "qualifier" in the Toulmin Model and learn to apply the Toulmin Model to the argument of value.

- I can understand "arguing from consequences" and "arguing from principles" and use them to develop warrants.

- I can describe the education-related social phenomenon with some degree of accuracy.

- I can write an argument of value commenting on whether a phenomenon is desirable or not.

Thinking focus	Expression focus	Function focus
Logos: Understanding the element "qualifier" and the relationship between warrants and value criteria; anticipating the "counter-argument" *Pathos:* Using specific examples or quotes	**About education and talent cultivation:** *high-degree holders, basic-level education / K-12 education, job seekers with a doctorate, design the curriculum, highly disciplined, encourage the initiative ...*	**Introducing phenomenon:** *... has been brought to attention, a growing trend, witness a phenomenon ...* **Introducing opposing views:** *spark different reactions, opinion is divided over ...*

准备开始写作 Preparing to Write

前四节课的写作话题属于事实型议论文，接下来的六个写作案例将围绕价值型议论文的写作教学展开。价值型论题主要讨论"什么是好的""什么是正确的""什么是道德的"等价值问题。因此，教师首先要引导学生思考价值型论题的价值标准是如何得出的。

■ 教师要求学生阅读《高中英语》（沪外教版）必修第二册第 2 单元语篇 *Zoos: Cruel or Caring?* 并回答问题。

◇ Read the following passage *Zoos: Cruel or Caring?* and answer the following questions.

1）What is the author's attitude towards zoos?

2）What reasons does the author give?

以下为语篇节选：

> Last weekend I visited a zoo with a friend. When we were there, we debated whether or not zoos were a good thing. When I was little,

I loved going to zoos. Now, at the age of 20, I still enjoy visiting them. However, I am aware that there are lots of people who don't support these establishments.

Animal welfare is a growing concern in today's society. There are many people who believe that zoos are cruel ...

【课堂再现】

T: According to the passage, what is the author's attitude towards zoos?

S1: The author thinks that "overall, zoos are a good thing".

T: Right, that's the claim of this argument. The argument explores whether something is good or not. We call such an argument "an argument of value". (Writing on the blackboard) An argument of value explores the worth or value of a certain thing. Then, let me ask you another question: why does the author put "overall" here?

S1: Because the passage says "there are many people who believe that zoos are cruel".

T: Yes, zoos also have their bad sides. By using the word "overall", the author wants to tell us that the claim may not be true in all circumstances. In the Toulmin Model, we call such words "qualifier". (Writing on the blackboard) It is used to limit the certainty of a claim. Do you understand?

S1: So is it a new element in the Toulmin Model?

T: Brilliant. That's right. The claim, ground and warrant are the three fundamental elements in the Toulmin Model. Today, we will learn a new element "qualifier", which is used to modify the claim. Actually, the qualifier serves to strengthen the credibility of the author, helping the author build an image of a careful, unbiased thinker. (Writing on the blackboard) I am sure you know a lot of common qualifiers, like "some", "most", "usually", "in general", "sometimes", "typically" and so on. (Writing on the blackboard) Can you come up with more qualifiers?

S1: Maybe "Generally speaking"?

T: Right. Let me add to them. (Writing on the blackboard) Now that we know the claim and the qualifier, can you find the grounds for the claim "overall, zoos are a good thing"? Alice, have a try.

S2: The first one is that a trip to the zoo can be an educational experience. The second is that zoos are involved in many conservation projects. The third one is that many zoos attempt to replicate an animal's natural habitat.

T: Good. The topic sentences are quite obvious. So how do the three grounds support the claim that "overall, zoos are a good thing"? In other words, why "an educational experience" can prove that "zoos are good"?

S2: Because it tells us that zoos can bring benefits to students, and for the second ground, it tells us that zoos can benefit the endangered animals. And the third ground, well, I think the third one tells us that zoos are not so cruel. They also respect animals' way of living.

T: (Writing on the blackboard) Brilliant. You just gave us three pieces of warrants to match the grounds. Now think about this question: what function does the warrant serve in an argument of value?

S3: I think the warrant here actually deals with the definition of "good".

T: You touched upon something very important. In an argument of value, we call the definition "the criteria". The three pieces of warrants here are actually the criteria to judge whether zoos are "good" or not. Generally speaking, if something brings benefits, it is good in some ways, right?

S4: Right.

T: So we call it "arguing from consequences". (Writing on the blackboard) We can judge whether a thing is good or bad when it leads to good or bad consequences. Since the zoo can bring benefits to students and endangered species, it is good. Then, what about the third warrant? Does it argue from consequences too?

S4: No, I don't think so. I think it tries to respond to the opposing view that "it is cruel to remove animals from their natural habitats".

T: You are right. It is a response to the opposing view by saying "many zoos attempt to replicate an animal's natural habitat". But it also uses another method—"arguing from principles". (Writing on the blackboard) It means that a thing is good or bad because it follows or violates certain principles. Being removed from natural habitats is against animals' natural disposition. So when zoos replicate animals' natural habitats, it follows the principle of respecting others' way of living. So to conclude, these are the two ways of developing criteria in an argument of value—arguing from consequences and arguing from principles. I want you all to bear in mind.

【板书演示】

An argument of value

Qualifier: some, most, usually, in general, sometimes, typically ...

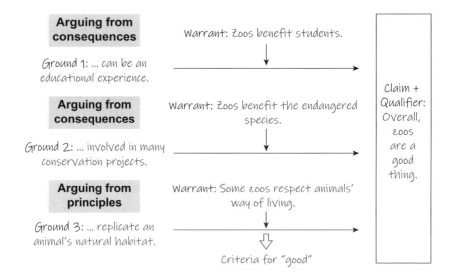

本节课是学生第一次接触价值型议论文，因此教师以阅读课作为引入，带领学生分析该价值型议论文背后的写作思路。不论课堂对话怎样展开，教师都需要帮助学生明白以下三点：

（1）什么是价值型议论文；

（2）图尔敏论证模型中的一个新要素——限定（qualifier）；

（3）价值型议论文的保证就是价值标准，而有关好坏的价值标准可以从两种途径来思考：后果法和原则法。

了解写作话题 Understanding the Prompt

写作 话题	近年来,越来越多的硕博毕业生选择成为中小学教师,有人说这是教育的进步,也有人说这是一种人才浪费,你赞成高学历人才投身基础教育吗? 天空日报(*Sky Daily*)"社会万象"栏目正在征集该话题稿件,向报社投稿,谈谈你的看法,并给出理由。

■ 教师要求学生仔细读题,然后围绕写作话题具体内容提问,确保每个学生都理解写作话题的要求。

◇ Think and answer the following questions.

1）What is the purpose of this writing?

2）Who are the target readers?

3）What tone and voice should be used?

4）What is the type of claim?

5）Could you use one sentence to sum up what you are going to write?

I am going to _____

_____.

☆ *Answers for reference:*

1) The writing purpose is to express the attitude towards the phenomenon of high-degree holders teaching in primary or secondary schools.

2) The target readers are the readers of Sky Daily and possibly the general public.

3) The tone should be relatively formal since the writing is going to be published in a newspaper. The voice can be objective and logical.

4) It is actually a claim of value: the topic asks you to judge whether the phenomenon is GOOD or BAD.

5) I am going to submit a piece of writing to Sky Daily to express my opinion on whether it is good or bad for high-degree holders to pursue a career in primary and secondary schools.

该环节的关键是帮助学生意识到常见的"赞成与反对"（pros and cons）类型的议论文从本质上来说就是价值型议论文。事实上，赞成或反对某件事体现了一个人对某件事价值的判断。一般来说，如果利大于弊就应该赞成；反之，则应该反对。教师可以引导学生将该写作话题转化为价值型议论文，然后从后果法和原则法引导学生思考该话题的利弊。

搭建思维模型 Constructing the Model

■ 教师引导学生从后果法和原则法思考对该话题的态度及其理由，并鼓励学生开展小组讨论。

◇ Find out your attitudes towards the phenomenon by using either a consequence-based argument or a principle-based argument or a combination of both. Have a discussion with the group members.

【课堂再现】

（After the discussion）

T: So does your pair support high-degree holders becoming teachers in primary and secondary schools?

S1: Well, Jenny and I think this is a good phenomenon because it leads to good consequences.

T: What good consequences?

S1: Primary and secondary school students can receive the benefits. High-degree holders are usually good students themselves, so they have some good qualities to pass on to students.

T: Yes. And when you describe those good qualities, you can be more specific, like what kind of good qualities do they have?

S1: Like strong self-discipline and they know the subject better than other people.

T: Right, they are highly disciplined and dedicated to what they learn.（Writing on the blackboard）Then, how can students benefit? Can you be more specific?

S1: Well, students need such teachers to teach them and encourage them. When they meet with some problems in study, they will want to find a teacher who can understand them and give them suggestions.

T: Good. That is the warrant. (Writing what S1 says on the blackboard) When you write, you should be specific in expressing your thoughts. Instead of simply saying they can benefit students, you should show the readers HOW they can benefit students. Clear? Now has any group tried to argue from principles?

S2: We think that every job is equal and everyone has the right to make their own career choice. That's the principle.

T: Yes, that's right. Then, why do you think those graduates make such a career choice?

S2: I think it must be that they find the career meaningful. I have a cousin who is a PhD. Last year, she got two job offers, one at a research lab and one as a high school teacher. And in the end she chose to be a high school teacher.

T: Has she told you the reasons?

S2: She said she loved having lively conversation with teenagers.

T: Good! That's the example serving as evidence.

【板书演示】

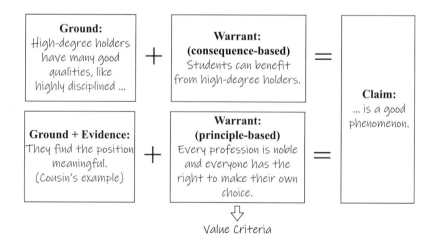

撰写提纲 Producing an Outline

■ 教师鼓励学生将讨论的内容按照图尔敏论证模型的四大要素列成提纲，并邀请两位学生在黑板上书写提纲。

◇ Produce an outline using the Toulmin model of argumentation.

Warrants (Value Criteria)	Grounds + Evidence	Claim + Qualifier

■ 教师和学生一起探讨黑板上提纲初稿的修改，确保提纲中有明确的价值标准（保证），并且保证和根据相互匹配。同时，教师要帮助学生提升语言表达，并指出学生提纲中明显的语言错误。

◇ Revise the outline with the help of the teacher and try to avoid the mistakes the teacher has mentioned.

☆ *Possible outline:*

Warrants (Value Criteria)	Grounds + Evidence	Claim + Qualifier
It can bring benefits to students. Students need the best teachers to broaden their horizon and teach them the value of self-discipline and perseverance, etc.	High-degree holders are usually highly disciplined and dedicated learners. They understand the teaching subject better.	Generally speaking, high-degree holders being involved in K-12 education is a good phenomenon.
Each profession is noble and respectable. Each job seeker's wish should be respected.	Many graduates give up well-paid jobs in research labs for teaching positions, which means teaching in primary and secondary schools is a meaningful job for them.	

提升效果 Adding the Impact

■ 教师引导学生使用身边的具体例子或引言来加强议论的情感诉求，使读者和作者共情。

◇ Use specific examples or quotes in your life to enhance *pathos* of the argument, allowing the audience to identify with the writer. The following is an example of using quotes.

e.g. "I will give what I learned during my PhD — learning methods, cutting-edge research in IT — to my students, who might go into the computer chip sector in the future," my cousin said. "It's worth it."

■ 教师提示学生思考反方可能存在的质疑，并让学生思考如何回应。

◇ Think about the possible objections against the claim and come up with ideas to respond to the objections.

Objections:

_____

_____

Responses:

_____

_____

☆ *Answers for reference:*

Objections:

1) Someone with a doctorate should spend their career in research or something higher, at least not just teaching children. It's a waste of talents.

2) PhDs are overqualified to teach in secondary schools.

Responses:

1) There is no such thing as talents going to waste. K-12 education

---

> shapes the next generation, who are the future of China. They deserve the best talents to teach them.
>
> 2) Some top secondary schools have designed curricula that require a high level of logic and advanced scientific knowledge, skills typically learned in colleges and universities.

聚焦语言 Focusing on Language

■ 教师让学生尝试用括号中的单词补全句子，来表达某现象的出现。

◇ Complete the sentences using the words in the brackets to describe the emergence of a certain phenomenon.

表达 某现象 出现	1) Recently, an issue _____ that a growing number of graduates ...(attention) 2) In recent years, _____ that many high-degree holders ...(trend) 3) Nowadays, _____ to see that many ...(uncommon) 4) _____ a phenomenon that ...(witness) 5) Recently, a new phenomenon _____ that ...(emerge)
引出 不同 观点	1) This phenomenon _____ .(spark) 2) _____ over whether it is a good choice for .... (divided) 3) Some people maintain/believe/think that ... / hold the view that ..., while others _____ (opposite), regarding it as a waste of talent.

☆ *Answers for reference:*

表达 某现象 出现	1) has been brought to attention 2) there is a growing trend 3) it is not uncommon 4) Recent years have witnessed a phenomenon 5) has emerged

（续表）

引出不同观点	1）has sparked different reactions 2）Opinion is sharply divided 3）take the opposite side

组织布局 Designing the Layout

■ 教师给出参考布局格式，提示学生写初稿时应注意该写作话题的要求：表达是否赞成，并给出理由。

◇ Write the draft with the reference layout shown below. Note that your draft should include expressing whether you think this is a good phenomenon and giving your reasons.

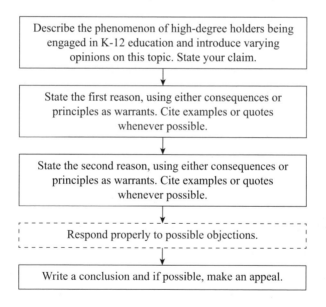

虚线框为可选段落，作者可以选择不对相反意见作出回应，也可以将虚线框与结论段合并，在结论段中简单地对相反意见作出回应。

互动评价 Evaluating the Drafts

■ 教师鼓励学生依据评价量表进行自我评价或同伴互评。

◇ Evaluate the drafts in pairs or in groups with the following checklist.

（请参见本书理论篇第三章第四节价值型议论文评价清单样例，选取合适的维度，鼓励学生围绕习作初稿开展自评和互评。）

分享范文 Sharing the Samples

■ 教师分享优秀范文，供学生交流、评价、学习。

◇ Read the sample writings of your classmates and learn from them.

> Recently, an issue has been brought to attention that increasingly more high-degree holders choose to become teachers in primary and secondary schools. Some people say this is a waste of talents while others hold the opinion that this phenomenon signals a big advancement in education. Generally speaking, I regard this phenomenon as a good trend.
>
> To begin with, advanced-degree holders are usually highly disciplined and dedicated learners. The significant amount of time they spent on their studies usually translates to a deep understanding of their teaching subjects, which makes them outstanding secondary school teachers. They can not only teach knowledge, but also encourage initiative, teamwork and help us students to build self-esteem. In this way, students can benefit enormously from such teachers and the quality of education in our country can be greatly enhanced.
>
> In addition, every profession is noble and everybody has their own right to make career choices. Since the phenomenon has now become a trend, it means more and more graduates find

the position meaningful and worth devoting their life to. A cousin of mine is a PhD student majoring in physics. She said compared with a career in a physics lab, she enjoyed the creative spark she had with teenagers more.

Therefore, it is time for us to throw away the stereotype that high-degree holders must do something higher than simply teaching children. Teaching is a career that shapes the next generation, who deserves the best talents of the country.

◇ Write down what you have learned from this sample writing.

教师点评

这篇习作结构完整，共分为四段。第一段描述越来越多的高学历毕业生投身基础教育的现象，并引入人们对该话题的不同观点，再表明作者自己的观点。第二段和第三段是作者赞成的原因。第四段作出总结（同时简单地对相反意见进行了回击）。在段落转折中，作者用到了 to begin with、in addition、therefore 等信号词，使读者能较为容易地跟上思路。

从内容上看，作者为了证明该现象是好的，给出了两个关于好的标准，分别从后果法和原则法出发：一是该现象能够给学生带来益处，二是该现象符合"工作不分高低贵贱"的原则。作者给出的根据分别和这两条标准相符，并且通过亲戚的择业故事提升了议论的情感诉求和可信度。此外，作者考虑到了相反意见，在结尾段简单予以回应，称应该抛弃这种刻板印象（stereotype）。由于相反意见的存在，作者对主张进行了限制，添加了限定 generally speaking，可见议论的严谨性。

从语言上看，作者使用了较为具体的语言：首先，在描述高学历毕业生的特点时，作者用到了具体的形容词和词组，如 highly disciplined and dedicated、a deep understanding of ...；其次，在描述学生的需求时，作者用到了 encourage initiative, teamwork 和 build self-esteem 等动宾短语；最后，在表达求职者态度时，作者用到了 find sth meaningful and worth doing 这一宾语加宾补的句型，可见作者语言运用的纯熟度。

尝试相似话题 Suggested Writing Prompts

写作话题	近年来，越来越多的父母开始在社交平台上"晒娃"，对此，人们观点不一。天空日报"社会万象"栏目正在征集该话题稿件，向报社投稿，谈谈你的看法，并给出理由。

写作话题 6   礼物选择

学习目标汇总 Learning Objectives

Can-do statements

By the end of this session, students will be able to say:

- I can understand how choice-making topics relate to the argument of value.
- I can write a personal letter to express my preference for a birthday gift.
- I can adjust the tone of my writing to make it sound more personal and intimate.

Thinking focus	Expression focus	Style focus
Logos: Understanding the value criteria related to choice-making, anticipating the "counter-argument" *Pathos:* Using concrete language *Ethos:* Showing familiarity with the gift choices given	**About the importance of a 18th birthday:** *an important milestone, a test of my independence and capability, mark one's entry into adulthood*	**Personal and intimate tone:** Using the second pronoun, emotive adjectives, the active voice, etc.

准备开始写作 Preparing to Write

前一个写作话题要求作者对是否赞成一个社会现象发表看法，其本质是对这一现象的好坏进行价值判断，属于价值型议论文。事实上，生活中很多情境在本质上都属于价值型议论，比如报考学校时，我们可能需要在 A 学校和 B 学校之间作出选择，这种取舍其实就是在探讨哪所学校更适合自己。这类选择情境就是价值型论题，教师应在课堂导入时点明这一点。此处，教师在写作课导入时，还可以利用日常事物的取舍，引导学生理解这类论题的价值标准，即"为谁选"或"为什么场合而选"。

■ 教师以生活中的例子引发学生思考人们是如何作出选择的。

◇ Think about how people make choices in daily life and answer the teacher's questions.

【课堂再现】

T: I hear that the canteen has prepared two main courses for today's lunch: fried chicken drumsticks and the steamed fish. I am going to ask you which one you will choose. Charlie, which will you choose?

S1: Well, I think I will choose the steamed fish.

T: Could you tell us why?

S1: I want to lose weight, so fried stuff doesn't suit me.

T: Jane, what about you?

S2: I prefer fried chicken drumsticks.

T: Why?

S2: I don't like eating fish because of the ... 鱼刺 .

T: You mean you hate fish bones, right?

S2: That's right. And I like the smell of fried food.

T: So, did you see? When we make choices between the two dishes, we are actually judging which one is more suitable for us. So choice making, at its root, is value judgment. (Writing on the blackboard) You are actually asking yourself which one is suitable for you. So what do you think are the criteria for "suitable"? Charlie, you first.

S1: I think for me, healthy food is suitable.

T: (Writing what S1 says on the blackboard) Jane, what about you?

S2: Convenient and delicious food is suitable for me.

T: (Writing what S2 says on the blackboard) So, we can see, to make the right choice, we need to know for whom we are choosing. Different people have different value criteria. Sometimes, the criteria will also vary with the occasion.

【板书演示】

Choice making → value·judgment (Which one is more suitable?)

Criteria: healthy food is suitable
convenient food is suitable → For whom are you choosing?

了解写作话题 Understanding the Prompt

写作话题	在李华 18 岁生日到来之际，父亲准备送他一份礼物，父亲给他两个选项：新款智能手机或去英国旅行，并让李华自己作出选择。假如你是李华，写一封信给父亲，说明你的选择和理由。

■ 教师要求学生仔细读题，然后围绕写作话题具体内容提问，确保每个学生都理解写作话题的要求。

◇ Think and answer the following questions.

1) What is the purpose of this writing?

2）What is your identity as the writer?

3）Who is the target reader?

4）What tone and voice should be used?

5）Could you use one sentence to sum up what you are going to write?

I am going to _____

_____.

☆ *Answers for reference:*

1) The writing purpose is to justify the choice of the 18th birthday gift.

2) I am a son who is turning 18.

3) The target reader is "my" father.

4) The tone can be intimate since this is a letter between a father and a son and the voice should sound like a teenager who is writing to his father.

5) I am going to write a letter to "my" father to tell him "my" birthday gift choice and give my reasons.

搭建思维模型 Constructing the Model

■ 教师引导学生讨论并思考该写作话题的价值标准，即"为谁选"或"为什么场合而选"，然后根据标准作出选择。

◇ Think and discuss with the partners the value criteria for this writing topic（for whom or for what occasion you are choosing）, and make the gift choice according to the criteria.

【课堂再现】

（After the discussion）

T: So if you were Li Hua, which gift would you choose?

S1: I would choose a new phone.

T:（Writing on the blackboard）What are your criteria for choosing?

S1: First, this is a gift for me. I am a fan of the latest technology.

T: Good. Your interest and preference are part of the criteria. (Writing on the blackboard) And what else?

S1: Second, this is a gift for the 18th birthday. After the birthday, I will go to college. So I think the gift should be something useful for the college life.

T: Good. That's the second criteria for gift choosing. (Writing on the blackboard) So, why do you think a smartphone is useful for the college life?

S1: Well, after I go to college, I might be a long distance away from home. With a new smartphone, I can video chat with my parents. Also, many things in college have to be done with a smartphone.

T: What kind of things? You can't just write "many things" in your writing. You have to be specific, remember?

S1: Like I may need to record some of the lectures, hand in my paper by email and apply for the summer internship with the smartphone.

T: That sounds much better. Everybody, keep in mind: when you are writing the grounds, you should be as specific as possible. Is there any group that chooses a trip to Britain as the birthday gift?

S2: We do.

T: So what are your criteria for choosing?

S2: We think the 18th birthday means independence and responsibility. So the gift should represent independence.

T: So you think a trip to Britain can help you achieve independence?

S2: Actually, it is a test of my independence, to show my parents that I can prepare a trip independently.

T: Sounds reasonable. Any other criteria?

S2: Visiting Britain is always my dream. 18th birthday is a big birthday. It deserves a dream-come-true gift.

T: If I were your father, I would agree. Yes, the 18th birthday gift should be a dream-come-true gift. Now the two groups have set us an example of developing value criteria in a clear way. Now it is your turn to produce your outline for writing.

【板书演示】

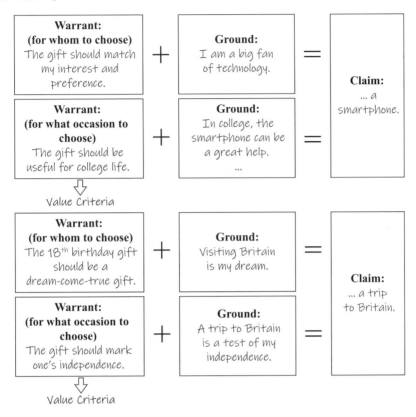

撰写提纲 Producing an Outline

■ 教师鼓励学生将讨论的内容按照图尔敏论证模型的三大要素列成提纲，并邀请两位学生在黑板上书写提纲。

◇ Produce an outline using the Toulmin model of argumentation.

Warrants (Value criteria)	Grounds + Evidence	Claim

■ 教师和学生一起探讨黑板上提纲初稿的修改，确保提纲中有明确的价值标准（保证），并且保证和根据相互匹配。同时，教师要帮助学生提升语言表达，并指出学生提纲中明显的语言错误。

◇ Revise the outline with the help of the teacher and try to avoid the mistakes the teacher has mentioned.

☆ *Possible outline:*

Warrants (Value Criteria)	Grounds + Evidence	Claim
The 18th birthday marks one's entry into adulthood, when one is free to chase one's dream.	My dream is to become an electronic engineer and the smartphone can bring my dream closer to me.	I choose a smartphone as my 18th birthday gift.
The 18th birthday gift should be something practical for my future study.	The smartphone can bring convenience to my college life, like checking emails from professors, following the latest updates on a certain subject.	

提升效果 Adding the Impact

■ 教师引导学生使用具象化的描述（如智能手机的特征描写或出国旅游的准备事务等），让读者想象某礼物可能带来的好处，加强议论的情感诉求；同时，具象化的描述也可以突出作者对礼物的深刻理解，提升人格诉求，增加议论的可信度。

◇ Use vivid imagery (e.g. the features of the smartphone or the detailed preparations for traveling abroad) to help the reader visualize the benefits the gift might bring, tapping the reader's imagination and enhancing *pathos*. Meanwhile, show your deep understanding of the gift to increase the credibility of your writing, enhancing *ethos*. The following is an example done for you.

e.g. Making a travel plan involves applying for visa, booking accommodation, packing and unpacking, designing the schedule and routes for travel, etc., which is a reliable test of my independence and capability as a soon-to-be adult.

■ 教师提示学生思考反方可能存在的质疑，并让学生思考如何回应。

◇ Think about the possible objections against the claim and come up with ideas to respond to the objections.

> Objections:
> _____
> _____
>
> Responses:
> _____
> _____

☆ *Answers for reference:*

> Objections:
> The trip abroad might bring unexpected trouble or even dangers.
> Responses:
> I am going to live an independent life in college. The trip can just serve as a test of my flexibility to deal with emergencies.

聚焦语言 Focusing on Language

■ 教师让学生尝试修改以下句子，使语言更亲切，更符合父子之间的通信。

◇ Revise the following sentences to make them sound more intimate and conversational between a son and a father.

1) To celebrate my birthday, I hear that you have provided two gifts for me to choose from.

→ _____

_____ .

2) The 18th birthday is so significant that the gift should match my dream.

→ _____ (agree) the 18th birthday is an important milestone in my life and it would mean a great deal to me _____ (if).

3) My dream is to become an editor in a travel magazine.

→ _____ (know) my dream has always been to become an editor in a travel magazine.

4) I have been preparing for this trip for years.

→ _____ (truth), I have been preparing for this trip for years.

5) Regarding your concern that I might overuse the phone and neglect my study, you can put your mind at ease.

→ _____ (if) I might overuse the phone and neglect my study, _____ (want) and put your mind at ease.

☆ *Answers for reference:*

1) → <u>You are so generous to let me choose a gift for my 18th birthday. / I want you to know how much I appreciate your kindness and thoughtfulness to let me choose a gift for my 18th birthday.</u>

2) → <u>I think we both agree</u> (agree) the 18th birthday is an important milestone in my life and it would mean a great deal to me <u>if the birthday gift can help realize my dream</u> (if).

3）→ You know（know）my dream has always been to become an editor in a travel magazine.

4）→ To tell you the truth（truth）, I have been preparing for this trip for years.

5）→ If you have concerns that（if）I might overuse the phone and neglect my study, I want to ask you to trust me（want）and put your mind at ease.

在前几个写作案例中，学生习惯了使用较为正式、客观的语气，可能在使用亲切的语气方面会遇到困难。这时，教师应提示学生，在亲人或朋友之间的信件写作中，可以通过使用偏口语化的短句、带有情感的形容词、主动语态、第二人称等来创建对话式的语言。

组织布局 Designing the Layout

■ 教师给出参考布局格式，提示学生写初稿时应注意该写作话题的要求：选择礼物，并给出理由。

◇ Write the draft with the reference layout shown below. Note that your draft should include choosing a gift and giving the reasons.

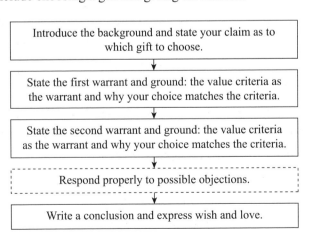

虚线框为可选段落，作者可以选择不对相反意见作出回应，也可以将虚线框与结论段合并，在结论段中简单地对相反意见作出回应。

互动评价 Evaluating the Drafts

■ 教师鼓励学生依据评价量表进行自我评价或同伴互评。

◇ Evaluate the drafts in pairs or in groups with the following checklist.

（请参见本书理论篇第三章第四节价值型议论文评价清单样例，选取合适的维度，鼓励学生围绕习作初稿开展自评和互评。）

分享范文 Sharing the Samples

■ 教师分享优秀范文，供学生交流、评价、学习。

◇ Read the sample writings of your classmates and learn from them.

Dear father,

You are so generous to let me choose a present for my 18th birthday. Meaningful and rewarding as a trip to Britain may seem, I still want to choose a new smartphone.

First off, I think we both agree that the 18th birthday marks a person's entry into adulthood, when I will become an independent individual to chase my dream. You know my dream has always been to become an electronic engineer one day, and I am a big fan of the cutting-edge technology. To tell you the truth, I have been eyeing a smartphone for months, which is equipped with a 5.8-inch display, a camera with an extra-wide angle and the latest artificial intelligence technology. Therefore, a smartphone will be a memorable 18-year-old birthday gift to me.

Moreover, after celebrating this birthday, I will start college life. A smartphone will be such a practical present. The

---

phone I am using now is out-of-date and gets stuck often. With a new smartphone, I can video chat with you and my friends more conveniently, and stay connected better. Besides, much communication and school work in college require smartphones to complete, like checking emails, applying for academic projects and doing online interviews.

I sincerely hope that you can grant me this wish. If you have concerns over my overexposure to the phone, I am going to ask you to trust me. I am old enough to take responsibility for my own behaviour. I love you, father.

◇ Write down what you have learned from this sample writing.

 教师点评

这篇习作结构完整，共分为四段。第一段引入话题并表达作者的选择，第二段和第三段给出理由，最后一段表达希望和对父亲的爱意，同时打消父亲可能存在的顾虑。在段落转折中，作者用到了 first off、moreover 等转折词，使结构更清晰。

从内容上看，作者选择背后的价值标准清晰：第一条标准是该生日礼物应该结合个人的兴趣和志向，第二条标准是该生日礼物应该对 18 岁以后的大学生活有用。作者给出的根据与这两条价值标准相匹配：首先，解释了智能手机如何符合"我"的兴趣和志向，并且对智能手机的新功能作了具体的描述，还提到"我"已经关注了几个月，进一步说明"我"对该礼物的了解以及想得到该礼物的热切愿望；其次，具体阐述了大学生活的哪些方面将会需要智能手机，并对需求进行了列举，使读者更加信服，提升了人格诉求。最后，作者还考虑到了父亲可能持有的相反意见，给出了相应回应，并表达了对父亲的爱，进一步提升了情感诉求。

从语言上看，作者的语气把控较为到位，字里行间流露出对父亲的深厚感情。首先，作者使用了 I think we both agree that、you know my dream has always been ...、to tell you the truth、going to ask you 等短语，用第一人称和第二人称体现出父子之间的熟悉程度。从一则亲人之间的通信来看，作者的用词和句型都较有日常对话感，比如 I have been eyeing a smartphone、I will start college life、such a practical present、get stuck often、stay connected better 等。除此之外，作者在描述智能手机的功能及列举大学生活需求时都使用了较为具体的语言，提升了议论的可信度。

尝试相似话题 Suggested Writing Prompts

写作 话题	你的好友李华在一所住宿制学校读书，学校允许高三学生自行选择住宿或走读，李华正在为此犹豫。写一封邮件给李华，给出你对高三年级住宿还是走读的建议，并给出理由。

写作话题 7　人选推荐

学习目标汇总 Learning Objectives

Can-do statements

By the end of this session, students will be able to say:

- I can understand how a recommendation letter relates to the argument of value.
- I can describe the qualities of the recommended candidate.
- I can write a recommendation letter with clear value criteria.

Thinking focus	Expression focus	Function focus
Logos: Understanding the element "backing" and its relationship with "warrant" in an argument of value *Ethos:* Showing familiarity with the recommended candidate	**About qualities of a leader:** **Linking verb+predicative:** *is an effective communicator / an inspiring person, is far-sighted/committed* **Verb+noun:** *possess strong communicative ability, have great vision, represent the image of the school, set a good example for others to follow*	**Opening a recommendation letter:** *Having heard ..., I am writing to ..., XXX is the best fit* **Closing a recommendation letter:** I have no doubt that ..., take my recommendation into consideration

准备开始写作 Preparing to Write

　　前两个写作话题属于价值型议论文，但略有不同：写作话题 5 是对现象的赞成或反对，核心价值问题是"该现象是好是坏"；写作话题 6 是关于礼物的选择，核心价值问题是"哪个礼物更适合自己"，也就是"哪个更好"。在日常生活中，我们不仅为自己作选择，还常常为别人作选择，或给出选择意见，这就是本案例涉及的推荐信写作，其本质也是价值型议论文，教师可以引导学生思考这类话题的核心价值问题是什么。

■ 在本节写作指导课开始的前一天，教师布置一份简单的作业，让学生思考如下问题：如果要推选班里的一名同学担任学生会主席，你会推荐谁？简单陈述一条理由（不超过 20 个字）。

◇ Write down the candidate that you want to recommend as chairman of the Student Union and briefly state the reasons（no more than 20 words）.

I want to recommend ...	because ...

了解写作话题 Understanding the Prompt

写作 话题	你校即将进行学生会主席选举，现在校内征集候选人。写一封信给学生处，推荐一名同学作为候选人，并阐明推荐理由。

■ 教师要求学生仔细读题，然后围绕写作话题具体内容提问，确保每个学生都理解写作话题的要求。

◇ Think and answer the following questions.

1）What is the purpose of this writing?

2）Who is the target reader?

3）What tone and voice should be used?

4）Could you use one sentence to sum up what you are going to write?

I am going to _____

_____.

☆ *Answers for reference:*

1) The writing purpose is to recommend a person for the position of chairman of the Student Union.

2) The target reader is the teacher in the Student Office.

3) The tone should be formal and objective since this is a letter between the Student Office and a student, and the voice should sound supportive.

4) I am going to write a recommendation letter to the Student Office to recommend a candidate for the position of chairman of the Student Union and explain why he/she is worth recommending.

搭建思维模型 Constructing the Model

■ 教师根据前一天作业布置的结果，引导学生思考该写作话题的价值标准。

◇ Answer the teacher's question and think about the value criteria for this writing topic.

【课堂再现】

T: I have read what you have written in your homework yesterday. Some of you recommend Alice and the reason is that Alice is the top student in our school. (Writing on the blackboard) Others recommend Tom and the reason is that Tom is handsome and good at sports. (Writing on the blackboard) If I were the teacher in the Student Office, who would I choose? Elaine, who would you choose?

S1: I would choose Alice.

T: Why Alice?

S1: Because being handsome doesn't seem to be right. Does a chairman need to be handsome?

T: Right, you hit the most important point, the value criteria. In the previous writing topic, the choice of birthday gifts, we discussed the importance of "for whom or for what occasion we are choosing". The same is true of this writing topic. So for what position are we choosing?

S1: We are choosing a candidate for chairman of the Student Union.

T: So what should be the value criteria?

S1: I think the criteria should be what kind of chairman we need.

T: Right. In other words, we should ask ourselves what qualities a chairman of the Student Union needs.

【板书演示】

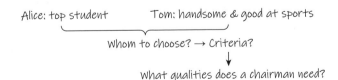

　　该环节的关键在于引导学生思考推荐信写作中的核心价值问题，即"推荐人是否适合该岗位"或"该岗位需要怎样的人"。

■ 教师引导学生讨论学生会主席需要怎样的品质（即价值标准），并根据标准重新思考推荐人选。

◇ Think and discuss with the partners the qualities that a chairman of the Student Union needs（i.e. the value criteria）, and recommend someone according to the criteria.

【课堂再现】

（After the discussion）

T: So what qualities do you think a chairman of the Student Union should have?

S1: We think a chairman should be able to balance study and student work.

T:（Writing what S1 says on the blackboard）Why do you think this is an important quality?

S1: Because a chairman is very busy. He needs to handle complaints from students, collect students' needs, plan student activities, and attend conferences and so on. If he struggles with his homework, he would not be able to spare time for a chairman's tasks.

T:（Writing what S1 says on the blackboard）Brilliant. You just gave us a very detailed explanation of why this quality is needed. In the Toulmin Model, this is called "backing".（Writing on the blackboard）The backing is used to support the warrant. Understand?

S1: Does that mean when the warrant is not so clear, we need to use backing to further explain it?

T: That's right. Now according to this criterion, who do you want to recommend?

S1: We want to recommend Jane.

T: Why Jane?

S1: Jane is efficient in learning. We are her roommates, so we know she finishes homework quickly and goes to bed before 22:30 almost every evening. We believe she has enough time to deal with a chairman's responsibilities.

T: That's good. I see you not only give the ground but also give the concrete evidence. That can increase the credibility of your words.

【板书演示】

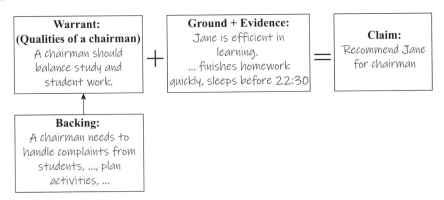

该环节的关键是教学生理解图尔敏论证模型中的一个新要素,即支撑。教师要让学生明白,支撑是用来确保保证的有效性的,当保证站不住脚或需要进一步解释时,就需要支撑。此外,对于思维能力较弱的学生,教师可以在这个环节给出以下有关学生领袖品质的表述,给予学生一些提示和启发。或者,教师可以直接让学生从这些品质中挑选出自己认为最重要的三条,再鼓励学生补充支撑,具体说明。

☆ *Phrases to describe the qualities of student leaders:*

√ *be sensitive to others' needs and offer support to students*

√ *set a good example for others to follow*

√ *be energetic and be able to balance study and student work*

√ *represent the image of the school*

√ *possess strong communicative ability*

√ *have great vision so that proper plans can be made for the future*

√ *be good at team building / inspire and engage group members / get other students to be willing to follow his lead*

√ *have a strong sense of responsibility and make sure other members in the group also perform their duties*

√ *respect others and make every member in the Student Union feel valued*

撰写提纲 Producing an Outline

■ 教师鼓励学生将讨论的内容按照图尔敏论证模型的四大要素列成提纲，并邀请两位学生在黑板上书写提纲。

◇ Produce an outline using the Toulmin model of argumentation.

Claim	Warrants + Backing	Grounds + Evidence

■ 教师和学生一起探讨黑板上提纲初稿的修改，确保提纲中有明确的价值标准（保证＋支撑），并且保证和根据相互匹配。同时，教师要帮助学生提升语言表达，并指出学生提纲中明显的语言错误。

◇ Revise the outline with the help of the teacher and try to avoid the mistakes the teacher has mentioned.

☆ *Possible outline:*

Claim	Warrants + Backing	Grounds + Evidence
I recommend Tom.	... should possess strong communicative ability + a chairman needs to negotiate students' needs with the school	Tom is a good communicator + being monitor for two years, good at dealing conflicts
	... should be able to inspire and engage group members + getting others to be willing to follow his/her lead	Tom is an inspiring person + making good public speeches
	... should look smart + a chairman is the public face of the school and represents the image of the student body	Tom is one of the most good-looking boys in our class.

提升效果 Adding the Impact

■ 教师引导学生通过直接陈述、描述或举例展示自己对被推荐人的了解，以增加推荐的可信度。

◇ Use direct statement, description or examples to show that you know the candidate enough to recommend him/her, increasing the *ethos* of the argument. The following are examples.

e.g.

Direct statement	As his roommate, I know his daily schedule very well.
Description	He has thick eyebrows and determined look, which radiates natural self-confidence.
Example	As our monitor, he once came up with a creative way to solve a "class crisis".

聚焦语言 Focusing on Language

如果学生语言能力较弱，描述被推荐人的品质有困难，教师可以提供以下语言练习。

■ 教师让学生尝试翻译下列短语，来描述被推荐人的品质。

◇ Translate the following phrases to describe the qualities of the recommended candidate.

使用系表结构	名词作表语： • is _____（有效的沟通者） • is _____（支持型领导） • is a top student • is _____（一心多用者） • is an inspiring person • is a responsible student • is _____（模范学生） • is a great public speaker ……	形容词作表语： • is _____（有远见的） • is _____（擅长团结同学） • is sincere • is passionate about what he does • is _____（致力于他所做的事） • is _____（精通活动策划） ……

（续表）

使用 动宾 结构	• _____（有同理心） • shows great respect for others • _____（坚持自己认为是正确的事） ......

☆ *Answers for reference:*

	名词作表语： • an effective communicator • a supportive leader • is a top student • a multi-tasker • is an inspiring person • is a responsible student • a model student • is a great public speaker	形容词作表语： • far-sighted • good at uniting classmates • is sincere • is passionate about what he does • committed to what he is doing • expert at activity planning ......
使用 系表 结构		
使用 动宾 结构	• have empathy • shows great respect for others • stick to what he thinks is right	

■ 从词到句：教师让学生通过翻译补全下列句子，来丰富有关价值标准的表达。

◇ From words to sentences: Try making the following sentences complete by translating the Chinese into English to add to the sentence variety.

1）A _____ chairman _____（一个合格的主席应该 / 必须）be energetic and be able to balance study and student work.

2）The _____ of a chairman _____（主席这个职位需要）great vision so that proper plans can be made for the future.

3）The _____ that _____（主席应该具备的品质）is a strong sense of responsibility and he should make sure other members in the group also perform their duties.

☆ *Answers for reference:*

1) qualified; should / needs to　　2) position; calls for　　3) quality; a chairman should possess/be equipped with

■ 从句到段：教师让学生用一句话补全段落，使保证与根据之间的语言更连贯通顺。

◇ From sentences to paragraphs: Try adding a sentence between the warrant and the ground to make the paragraph coherent.

A qualified chairman needs to be energetic and able to balance his/her study and student work. _____ He is a multi-tasker. Not only is he a top student in our grade, but also he is president of the debate club.

☆ *Answers for reference:*

- It goes without saying that Xiao Ming is one of the most energetic students.

- Xiao Ming happens to be such a student leader.

- As Xiao Ming's classmate, I am always impressed by his energy.

- Xiao Ming is one of the few students who can manage several things at the same time.

这个活动是为了让学生意识到，不能将提纲中的内容直接组合成段落，保证和根据之间需要一些过渡句，才能使段落更连贯。

组织布局 Designing the Layout

■ 教师给出参考布局格式，提示学生写初稿时应注意该写作话题的要求：推荐人选，并给出推荐理由。

◇ Write the draft with the reference layout shown below. Note that your draft should include recommending the candidate and giving reasons.

```
┌─────────────────────────────────────────────────────┐
│  Introduce the background and recommend the candidate for │
│           chairman of the Student Union.              │
└─────────────────────────────────────────────────────┘
                          ↓
┌─────────────────────────────────────────────────────┐
│  State the first warrant (+backing) and ground (+evidence): │
│  the quality that a chairman needs and how the candidate matches │
│              the required quality.                    │
└─────────────────────────────────────────────────────┘
                          ↓
┌─────────────────────────────────────────────────────┐
│  State the second warrant (+backing) and ground (+evidence): │
│  the quality that a chairman needs and how the candidate matches │
│              the required quality.                    │
└─────────────────────────────────────────────────────┘
                          ↓
┌─────────────────────────────────────────────────────┐
│       Write a conclusion and express hope.            │
└─────────────────────────────────────────────────────┘
```

　　推荐信中理由段落的数量没有限制，一般以两到三段为宜。

■ 教师让学生完成以下两个练习，并为推荐信写一个合适的开头段。

◇ Write an appropriate opening paragraph with the help of the exercises below.

1. Decide which of the following is an appropriate beginning for the letter.

> * Hi, I know you are looking for candidates for chairman of the Student Union. I want to recommend one.
> * The choice of a chairman is such an important matter in the school that an appropriate person should be recommended.
> * On hearing that the election for chairman of the Student Union is coming soon, I am writing to give/offer my recommendation.

☆ *Answers for reference:*

The third one is the best because it states the background and the purpose of the letter. The first one is too informal and the second one is irrelevant.

2. Please translate the following Chinese into English.

| 推荐人选 | 1) In my opinion, Alice is ＿＿＿＿＿＿＿＿＿＿＿＿＿＿（是这个职位的最佳人选）. |
| | 2) Alice, ＿＿＿＿＿＿＿＿＿＿＿＿＿＿（三班的班长）, is ＿＿＿＿＿＿＿＿＿＿＿＿＿＿（就是我想推荐的人选）. It is ＿＿＿＿＿＿＿＿＿＿＿＿＿＿（丰富的经验和独特的品质）that ＿＿＿＿＿＿＿＿＿＿＿＿＿＿（使她脱颖而出 / 给我留下深刻的印象）. |

☆ *Answers for reference:*

1) the best fit for this position

2) monitor of Class 3; the candidate I want to recommend; her rich experience and unique qualities; make her stand out / leave a deep impression on me

   教师可以鼓励学生在开头段使用同位语（monitor of Class 3）和强调句（it is her ... that ...）来突出被推荐人的品质。

■ 教师让学生补全句子，并为推荐信写一个合适的结尾段。

◇ Add an ending by making the following sentences complete, using the words in the brackets.

总结 上文	1）The above qualities _____ for the position.（exceptional） 2）Therefore, I _____ that the Student Union will take on a new look with Alice as the leader.（convinced） 3）With _____, I have no doubts that she will become an excellent student leader.（qualities）
期盼 采纳	1）Hope you can _____.（take） 2）I sincerely hope you will _____.（consider） 3）I would _____ if you can consider my recommendation.（appreciate）

☆ *Answers for reference:*

总结 上文	1) make her an exceptional candidate 2) am convinced 3) so many valuable qualities mentioned above
期盼 采纳	1) take my recommendation into consideration/account 2) consider my recommendation 3) appreciate it very much

互动评价 Evaluating the Drafts

■ 教师鼓励学生依据评价量表进行自我评价或同伴互评。

◇ Evaluate the drafts in pairs or in groups with the following checklist.

（请参见本书理论篇第三章第四节价值型议论文评价清单样例，选取合适的维度，鼓励学生围绕习作初稿开展自评和互评。）

分享范文 Sharing the Samples

■ 教师分享优秀范文，供学生交流、评价、学习。

◇ Read the sample writings of your classmates and learn from them.

Dear Student Office,

On hearing that the election for chairman of the Student Union is drawing near, I am writing to offer my recommendation. In my opinion, Alice is the best fit for this position. It is her rich experience and unique qualities that make her stand out.

A qualified chairman needs to be energetic and able to balance his/her study and student work. It goes without saying that Alice is one of the most energetic students in our school. She is a multi-tasker. Not only is she a top student in our grade, but also she is president of the debate club.

The major task of the Student Union is to design activities to enrich students' life, so this position calls for someone who is sensitive to students' needs and respect others' opinions. As Alice's deskmate, I know she is a sympathetic listener. Many classmates turn to her for help when they meet with trouble.

A chairman should also possess the ability to inspire and engage the group members. Alice happens to be such an inspiring leader. The speeches she has delivered in our class are so powerful that many students feel energized and are willing to follow her lead.

With so many valuable qualities mentioned above, I have no doubts that she will become an excellent student leader. I sincerely hope you will consider my recommendation.

◇　Write down what you have learned from this sample writing.

 **教师点评**

这篇习作结构完整，共分为五段。第一段交代了背景和来信目的，并给出推荐人选，第二段到第四段给出理由，最后一段作出总结并表达希望。在段落转折中，作者虽然没有使用诸如 first、in addition 等转折词，但从第二段到第四段都以学生会主席应具备的品质开头，读者很容易就能跟上思路，并且最后一段用 with 结构总结上文，转折自然。

从内容上看，作者在三个理由段落中皆采用了先陈述保证再配以相应根据的写法。三条保证和支撑（即价值标准）非常清晰，且不重复，分别是学生会主席应该有能力平衡好学习和学生工作、学生会主席需要对学生的需求保持敏感以及学生会主席要有激励他人的能力。作者给出的根据也能与保证一一对应。在人格诉求方面，作者通过 As Alice's deskmate, I know ...，以及 The speeches she has delivered in our class ... 这样的句子来体现自己对被推荐人选的熟悉程度，增加了议论的可信度。

从语言上看，作者的语言运用较为熟练。在描述学生会主席应具备的品质时，作者用到了不同的表达方式（sb needs to ...，... calls for ...，should possess）。在描述 Alice 的品质时，作者用到了 an energetic student、a sympathetic listener、an inspiring leader 等偏正短语，用词准确。此外，三个理由段落读起来通顺连贯，这与作者大量使用连接句是分不开的，如 it goes without saying that ...、As Alice's deskmate、Alice happens to be ...。整体上看，这篇习作的用词体现了作者对 Alice 的欣赏和支持，语气颇为恰当。

尝试相似话题 Suggested Writing Prompts

写作话题	可爱的熊猫形象"冰墩墩"作为北京冬奥会的吉祥物家喻户晓。你的班主任受此启发，想组织学生为本班挑选一个动物形象作为班级吉祥物（mascot）。写一封信给班主任，建议你心中设想的动物形象，并给出理由。

写作话题 8　创业建议

学习目标汇总 Learning Objectives

Can-do statements

By the end of this session, students will be able to say:

- I can derive the value criteria from different angles, including arguing from consequences, arguing from principles and considering the readers' needs.
- I can describe how a small business works in general.
- I can write a letter of suggestion to a friend with clear value criteria.

Thinking focus	**Expression focus**	**Style focus**
Logos: Different methods of developing value criteria *Pathos:* Using listing and detailed description *Ethos:* Showing understanding of the reader(s)	**About business operation:** *cater to the fast-paced life, manage the daily operations of the store, drafting a business plan*	**Friendly tone:** Using conversational language.

准备开始写作 Preparing to Write

　　前三个写作话题分别是现象判断、礼物选择、人选推荐，它们从本质上来说都是价值型议论。要对一个事物或一个现象作出是好是坏的判断，必须要知道"好"或"坏"的标准是什么，而后果法和原则法能够提供较为具象的标准。以礼物选择和人选推荐这两个话题为例，学生了解到，当选择对象较为具体时，选择对象本身就成了价值标准形成的依据，比如礼物是为"我"的 18 岁生日而选，人选是为学生会主席的岗位而选。因此

"我"的兴趣爱好、18 岁生日的特点，以及学生会主席的岗位要求，都是价值标准形成的关键。如果价值标准较为复杂，还需要使用支撑来进一步解释。在新的写作话题开始之前，教师可以帮助学生回顾一下前几节课所学的内容。

■ 教师带领学生回顾前三个价值型议论文写作话题练习中所学的内容。

◇ Review what has been learned in the writing lessons of the three arguments of value.

【课堂再现】

T: In the previous three writing sessions, we have touched upon some important points in the argument of value. Do you remember, Bonnie?

S1: Well, let me think ...

T: Maybe my question is too general. Let me narrow it down a bit. Do you remember how we analyze the phenomenon of college graduates choosing to become teachers in primary and secondary schools?

S1: Yes.

T: Why do we say that is a good phenomenon?

S1: Because it can bring benefits to students and it respects the job seeker's wish.

T: That's right. So what methods did we use?

S1: Let me think...

T: Lucas, can you help her?

S2: OK. Bringing benefits to students is arguing from consequences and respecting the job seeker's wish is arguing from principles.

T: That's right. When we are not sure how to set the criteria for good or bad, we can try the two methods. If something brings good consequences or follows certain principles, it is good. Then what about the topic of birthday gift choosing? What did you learn from that?

S2: I think it teaches us that when we make a choice, we need to consider for whom or for what occasion we are choosing, because it determines the value criteria.

T: Great. The same is true of a recommendation letter. When we recommend someone, we need to consider what position we recommend him or her for. Then if the value criteria are not so clear, what can we do?

S3: We can use "backing" to support the criteria.

T: Right, backing is a new element we have learned in the Toulmin Model last time. Today, we are going to apply what we have learned and write on a new topic.

了解写作话题 Understanding the Prompt

写作话题	如今，青年创业项目层出不穷，你的好友张磊所在的学校开设了一个学生企业家项目（student entrepreneurship project），本期项目与开设书店有关，张磊打算申请，正在犹豫是开一家网上书店还是实体书店，现通过邮件向你征求意见。写一封回信给他建议，并给出理由。

■ 教师要求学生仔细读题，然后围绕写作话题具体内容提问，确保每个学生都理解写作话题的要求。

◇ Think and answer the following questions.

1）What is the purpose of this writing?

2）What is your identity as the writer?

3）Who is the target reader?

4）What tone and voice should be used?

5）Could you use one sentence to sum up what you are going to write?

I am going to _____
_____.

☆ *Answers for reference:*

1) The writing purpose is to give suggestions to a friend who is hesitating over which kind of bookstore he is going to open.

2) I am a friend of Zhang Lei.

3) The target reader is "my" friend, Zhang Lei.

4) The tone can be personal and friendly since this is a letter between two friends and the voice should sound supportive.

5) I am going to write a letter to "my" friend to help him make a choice between opening an online bookstore and a physical one, and give reasons to convince him.

搭建思维模型 Constructing the Model

根据前三节课的教学内容，再结合课前的师生对话，教师可以鼓励学生独立开展有关价值标准的讨论。当然，如果教师通过观察，仍然觉得学生独立开展讨论有困难，可以在学生讨论前加强引导。

■ 教师引导学生讨论并思考该写作话题的价值标准，并根据标准在网上书店和实体书店中作出选择。

◇ Think and discuss with the partners the value criteria for this writing topic, and make a choice between an online bookstore and a physical one according to the criteria.

【课堂再现】

（After the discussion）

T: So what is your suggestion for Zhang Lei?

S1: We think an online bookstore is a better choice.

T:（Writing on the blackboard）What are your criteria for choosing?

S1: First, Zhang Lei is the one who applies for the project, so this business should be suitable for him.

T: That's a reasonable criterion. So why do you think an online bookstore suits him better?

S1: Because he is a student who doesn't have much business experience. Opening an online bookstore is much easier than opening a physical one, like you don't have to consider where to rent a shop or how to manage the staff.

T: I get your point. You mean opening a physical bookstore involves a lot of business knowledge and experience like renting a shop and managing staff. (Writing on the blackboard) Good. Alice's group gives us one piece of warrant and backing. William, what about your group?

S2: We also choose an online bookstore for Zhang Lei.

T: So your criteria?

S2: We think that online bookstore is the future trend for the book business.

T: I see. You mean the business should follow the trend in current society. (Writing on the blackboard) Identifying the market trend is an important principle for doing business, so that's arguing from principles. Can you give us more details about this trend?

S2: Nowadays, people are reluctant to go from door to door to find something they want. Instead, they simply tap their phone screens. So online bookstores provide people with greater convenience.

T: Good. And also, you can think about the purpose of this business project, which will also help you develop the value criteria.

【板书演示】

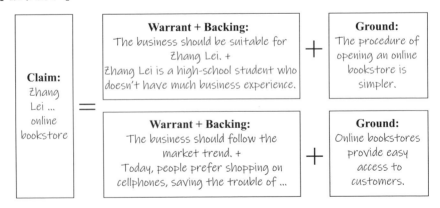

在该写作话题中，教师需要着重引导学生思考：价值标准既包含对一件事物本身好或坏的判定（后果法和原则法），也包含一件事物适合谁（选择对象），当价值标准不够清晰时，还需要进一步补充支撑。教师在该环节结束时，可以帮助学生再次复习以上几点，加深学生的印象。

撰写提纲 Producing an Outline

■ 教师鼓励学生将讨论的内容按照图尔敏论证模型的四大要素列成提纲，
并邀请两位学生在黑板上书写提纲。

◇ Produce an outline using the Toulmin model of argumentation.

Claim	Warrants + Backing	Grounds + Evidence

■ 教师和学生一起探讨黑板上提纲初稿的修改，确保提纲中有明确的价值
标准（保证＋支撑），并且保证和根据相互匹配。同时，教师要帮助学生
提升语言表达，并指出学生提纲中明显的语言错误。

◇ Revise the outline with the help of the teacher and try to avoid the mistakes
the teacher has mentioned.

☆ *Possible outline:*

Claim	Warrants + Backing	Grounds + Evidence
I suggest Zhang Lei choosing a physical bookstore.	The business should help Zhang Lei realize his dream.	Zhang Lei has a dream of owning a bookstore with a café inside.
	The project is supposed to help future entrepreneurs accumulate real-life business experience.	Zhang Lei has already opened an online business before and he has already gained enough experience to do a real off-line business.

提升效果 Adding the Impact

■ 教师引导学生使用列举、描写等方式来展示自己对开设书店的理解，提
升话语的可信度，加强议论的人格诉求。

◇ Use writing techniques like listing and description to show your understanding of opening a bookstore, increase the credibility of your words, enhancing the *ethos* of the argument. The following is an example done for you.

e.g. For an online bookstore, the procedure is much simpler. You only need to create a seller account with a big platform, choose a name for your store, add the product images, and maintain a good seller profile, all of which can be done by yourself.

■ 教师引导学生在习作中展示自己对好友张磊性格或经历的了解，以调动读者（也就是张磊）的情感和想象力，加强议论的情感诉求。

◇ Show your understanding of Zhang Lei's personality or experiences to arouse your friend's imagination and emotion, increasing the *pathos* of the argument.

e.g. As your friend, I know that you are business savvy, so you should use this project as a stepping stone to a future you desire.

■ 教师提示学生思考反方可能存在的质疑，并让学生思考如何回应。

◇ Think about the possible objections against the claim and come up with ideas to respond to the objections.

Objections:

_____

_____

Responses:

_____

_____

☆ *Answers for reference:*

Objections:
Online bookstores fail to let people have a specific idea of what they are buying, which is a deadly weakness.

Responses:

Admittedly, online bookstores may not give customers full idea of a book. But you can scan the table of contents and one chapter of a book and upload the images to allow customers to have a preview before they place an order.

聚焦语言 Focusing on Language

■ 教师鼓励学生用英文表达与开设书店和现代购物相关的短语和句子。

◇ Try translating the following phrases and sentences related to bookstore business and shopping.

1）迎合现代人快节奏的生活方式	
2）下单和快递只要动动手指就能完成。	
3）为消费者提供方便的购书渠道	
4）上传图书照片、维护卖家页面	
5）管理每日商店的运营	
6）顾客对商店的好评可以提升商店的名气。	
7）不同的顾客有不同的阅读品味和喜好	
8）在店里营造一种学术氛围	
9）帮助你缓解焦虑，逃避都市的喧嚣，寻找精神世界的避难所	
10）创业不仅仅是注册一家公司而已。	
11）起草商业计划、申请营业执照、确定目标客户、选择租店地点、招聘书店员工、开设资金账户	
12）创造独特的感官体验和口口相传的宣传效果	

☆ *Answers for reference:*

1) cater to the fast-paced life of modern people

2) It only takes several clicks to place an order and select a delivery service.

3) provide customers with easy access to purchasing books

4) upload the images of the books and maintain the seller profile

5) manage the daily operations of the store

6) The positive reviews of customers can help build up the reputation of the store.

7) different customers have different tastes and interest in books

8) create an academic atmosphere in the bookstore

9) help you relieve anxiety, escape from the hustle and bustle in the metropolis and seek spiritual refuge

10) Starting a business is more than just registering it.

11) drafting a business plan, applying for the business license, identifying the target customers, selecting a proper location to rent a shop, hiring staff and setting up a business account

12) create distinctive sensory experience and word-of-mouth marketing effects

组织布局 Designing the Layout

■ 教师给出参考布局格式，提示学生写初稿时应注意该写作话题的要求：给出开网店还是实体店的建议，并给出建议理由。

◇ Write the draft with the reference layout shown below. Note that your draft should include giving suggestions on which type of bookstores to open and giving reasons.

```
┌─────────────────────────────────────────────────┐
│  Introduce the background and give your suggestion on  │
│  whether to open an online bookstore or a physical one. │
└─────────────────────────────────────────────────┘
                        ↓
┌─────────────────────────────────────────────────┐
│  State the first warrant (+backing) and ground (+evidence): │
│  the criteria for choosing the type of bookstore and how the │
│              choice matches the criteria.              │
└─────────────────────────────────────────────────┘
                        ↓
┌─────────────────────────────────────────────────┐
│   State the second warrant (+backing) and ground   │
│  (+evidence): the criteria for choosing the type of bookstore │
│          and how the choice matches the criteria.          │
└─────────────────────────────────────────────────┘
                        ↓
┌─────────────────────────────────────────────────┐
│         Respond properly to possible objections.         │
└─────────────────────────────────────────────────┘
                        ↓
┌─────────────────────────────────────────────────┐
│          Write a conclusion and express hope.          │
└─────────────────────────────────────────────────┘
```

■ 教师让学生完成以下两个练习，并为建议信写一个合适的开头段。

◇ Write an appropriate opening paragraph with the help of the exercises below.

1. Decide which of the following is an appropriate beginning for the letter.

- Word came that you are hesitating over whether to open an online bookstore or a physical one. I am writing to offer you some suggestions.

- Hearing that you are having trouble determining which project to choose, I'd like to express my opinions.

- I am so happy that you are going to start your own entrepreneurship project. Seeing you are having doubts about the type of bookstore to open, I can hardly wait to share with you my ideas.

☆ *Answers for reference:*

The third one is the best because it is less formal and its voice sounds more like the correspondence between two close friends.

2. Please translate the following Chinese into English.

表达 选择	1）As your friend, I _____ （建议你选择实体书店）. 2）_____ （如果我是你）, I would choose the physical bookstore. 3）In my opinion, an online bookstore _____ （将会给你更好的起点）. 4）_____ （将是个好主意）if you start from an online bookstore.

☆ *Answers for reference:*

1) suggest you choose the physical bookstore

2) If I were you

3) will give you a better starting point

4) It would be an excellent idea

■ 教师让学生判断以下哪个更适合作该建议信的结尾段。

◇ Decide which of the following is an appropriate ending for the letter.

- In conclusion, an online bookstore is a better choice for you. If you have any questions, please don't hesitate to contact me.
- I hope my suggestion can be of help to you. I sincerely wish your business project a big success.
- I would appreciate it very much if you could take my suggestions into account. I look forward to hearing from you.

☆ *Answers for reference:*

The second one is the best because it expresses sincere wish to a friend and the voice sounds supportive. The first ending sounds like writing to a business partner and the third one is used to write to some organizations.

互动评价 Evaluating the Drafts

■ 教师鼓励学生依据评价量表进行自我评价或同伴互评。

◇ Evaluate the drafts in pairs or in groups with the following checklist.

（请参见本书理论篇第三章第四节价值型议论文评价清单样例，选取合适的维度，鼓励学生围绕习作初稿开展自评和互评。）

分享范文 Sharing the Samples

■ 教师分享优秀范文，供学生交流、评价、学习。

◇ Read the sample writings of your classmates and learn from them.

Dear Zhang Lei,

Hope everything goes well with you. Congratulate you on the opportunity to start your own entrepreneurship project. I am glad that you trust me and turn to me for suggestions on whether to open an online bookstore or a physical one. If I were you, I would choose an online bookstore.

First, we have to admit we are students who don't have much business experience, so you'd better start from something simpler. If you choose a physical bookstore, you will have to worry about renting shops, decorating the interior, hiring staff, etc., all of which require abundant experience. In contrast, an online bookstore can save you all the trouble. You can make use of the existing trading platforms and manage the operations of the store on your own.

Second, online shopping is a trend that no businessmen can afford to overlook. There is a reason that they say it is the spring of electronic commerce and the autumn of physical stores. The strongest power in this century surely lies in the Internet Technology, which can be easily told from the popularity of online shopping. With an online bookstore, you can catch the trend, catering to the fast-paced life of modern

---

customers.

　　Hope my suggestions can be helpful to you. Wish your entrepreneurship project a great success.

◇　Write down what you have learned from this sample writing.

　教师点评

　　这篇习作结构完整，共分为四段。第一段问候并祝贺好友获得学生创业项目的机会，并明确提出建议，第二段和第三段给出理由，最后一段表达期待和希望。在段落转折中，作者用到了 first、second 等转折词，使结构更加清晰。

　　从内容上看，作者的逻辑思路清晰，两个理由分别从不同的价值标准出发：第一条价值标准针对选择对象（也就是张磊本人）的特点，张磊和作者一样都是学生，因此作者建议从操作较为简单的网上书店开始；第二条价值标准从做生意的原则出发，即做生意应该遵从市场趋势，而网上购物就是现在的趋势。两条价值标准非常清晰，作者给出的根据也能与价值标准相对应。并且，作者关注到了写作中的情感诉求和人格诉求，不仅详细陈述了开设实体书店可能带来的麻烦（租赁店铺、招募员工等），激发了读者的想象力，还通过"我们不得不承认"（we have to admit ...）来表达对好友张磊的了解，提升了人格诉求。

　　从语言上看，作者的语气把握较为到位，能看出这篇文章是好友之间的信件往来。作者先用英文中朋友之间的常见信件问候语开头（Hope everything goes well with you），并表达了对朋友获得机会的祝贺。更难能可贵的是，作者还对朋友的信任表达了感激。接着作者用较有对话感的短语和句子拉近了和朋友之间的关系，比如 if I were you、you'd better start from ... 以及 there is a reason that they say ...。此外，作者还用较为具体的语言描述开实体店的流程及现代社会的网购潮流，语言使用的熟练度可见一斑。

尝试相似话题 Suggested Writing Prompts

写作话题	你的英国笔友吉姆（Jim）打算学习中文口语，正在犹豫是报名"旅游汉语基础"（大班教学、时间灵活）还是"商务汉语入门"（小班教学、时间固定），现通过邮件向你征求建议。写一封回信给他建议，并给出理由。

写作话题 9 好书推荐

学习目标汇总 Learning Objectives

Can-do statements

By the end of this session, students will be able to say:

- I can find out the value criteria in others' writing and come up with my own value criteria of a great book.
- I can introduce the content of a book and the benefits of reading good books.
- I can recommend a great book with clear criteria and reasoning process.

Thinking focus	Expression focus	Function focus
Logos: Understanding the value criteria for a philosophical issue *Ethos:* Showing a strong knowledge base	**About books and reading:** *is set in, follow the character development, challenge readers' established prejudices, provoke the reader to inquire, offer unique insight into human nature*	**Opening a recommendation letter:** *Hearing ..., I'd like to recommend ...* **Making a conclusion:** *Therefore, I am sure ...*

准备开始写作 Preparing to Write

在前几节课的价值型议论文写作话题中，我们通过后果法和原则法，以及依据选择对象来判定价值标准，这些价值标准通常用于短期的或一次性的价值判断，可能会因为选择对象不同而发生改变。然而，人类社会还有一些价值话题是经久不衰的，比如"什么是伟大的著作""怎样的行为算得上勇敢""怎样的人生是成功的人生"等，其价值标准往往不是短期内就能看出来的。这些价值标准既有普遍的一面，也有个性的一面，比如关于伟大的著作的价值标准，可以是大部分人都认可的经典名著，也可以是少数群体认可的优秀书籍。教师可以带领学生通过归纳法，也就是具体的事例或案例归纳总结出这类经典话题的价值标准。

■ 教师要求学生阅读《高中英语》（新世纪版）高三第一学期第 5 单元语篇 *What Is a Great Book?* 并回答问题。

◇ Read the following passage *What is a Great Book?* and answer the following questions.

1）How many criteria of great books are mentioned? What are they?

2）Do you agree with the criteria?

以下为语篇节选：

> No matter how long your life is, you will, at best, be able to read only a few of all the books that have been written, and the few you do read should include the best.
>
> What makes a book great?
>
> Great books are probably the most widely read. They are not bestsellers for a year or two. They are enduring bestsellers. Therefore, *Gone with the Wind* has had relatively fewer readers compared with the plays of Shakespeare.
>
> A great book need not be a bestseller in its own day. It may take time for its audience to grow. Kepler, whose work on planet motions is now a classic, reportedly said of his book, "It may wait a century for a reader, as God has waited 6,000 years for an observer."
>
> ...

【课堂再现】

T: So who can tell me how many criteria of great books are mentioned in the text? I think the answer is quite obvious.

S1: There are five criteria.

T: Any different opinions?

S2: I don't agree. I think there are altogether four criteria. Paragraph 3 and 4 actually talk about the same thing.

T: I agree. There are altogether four criteria. What are they?

S2: They are "great books are probably the most widely read, great books are popular, great books are the most readable and great books are the most instructive".

T: Good. (Writing on the blackboard) These are the value criteria of great books mentioned by the author. And the author also gives further explanation of the four criteria, which is the "backing". Can you give me some key words about the backing? Bob, have a try.

S3: For the first criterion, "the most widely read" means "enduring bestsellers" like the plays of Shakespeare and Kepler's works. For the second one, ...

T: (Writing on the blackboard while S3 is talking about the backing) Good. Now we have analyzed the four criteria and get to know the author's understanding of a great book. So can you tell me whether you agree with the four criteria?

S3: Well, I think I agree with most of them, but I don't agree with one point.

T: Which one?

S3: The one with *Gone with the Wind*. In my opinion, *Gone with the Wind* is a great book, even greater than Shakespeare's works.

T: Why do you think so?

S3: Because I have read the Chinese version of *Gone with the Wind*. The hero's story gives me great strength. But I don't feel the same when I read Shakespeare's plays. I think a great book should be inspiring.

T: I see. You have actually added to the criteria. That's good. Today you are going to recommend a great book based on your own criteria.

【板书演示】

	Warrants	Backing
Value criteria	Great books are probably the most widely read.	are enduring bestsellers like the plays of Shakespear and Kepler's works on planet motions
	Great books are popular.	deal with human, not academic subjects, be written for common people
	Great books are the most readable.	can be read over and over again at different levels of understanding, can be interpreted from different aspects, like *Gulliver's Travels* and *Robinson Crusoe*
	Great books are the most instructive.	contain something that cannot be found in other books, make basic contributions to human thought

了解写作话题 Understanding the Prompt

> 写作话题　　你所在的读书社想要选出 5 本"伟大的著作"作为本学年社员必读书目。写一封信给社长，推荐你心目中"伟大的著作"，简述该著作，并说明推荐理由。

■ 教师要求学生仔细读题，然后围绕写作话题具体内容提问，确保每个学生都理解写作话题的要求。

◇ Think and answer the following questions.

1) What is the purpose of this writing?

2) Who is the target reader?

3) What tone and voice should be used?

4) Could you use one sentence to sum up what you are going to write?

I am going to _____

_____.

☆ *Answers for reference:*

1) The writing purpose is to recommend a great book as one of the five must-reads for the reading club members.

2) The target reader is the president of the reading club.

3) The tone should be standard, and the voice should be assertive and reasonable.

4) I am going to write a letter to the president of the reading club to recommend a great book that I have in mind, briefly introduce it and explain why it is worth recommending.

搭建思维模型 Constructing the Model

■ 教师引导学生结合以往的阅读经历，讨论并得出自己对"伟大的著作" 的价值标准（包含保证和支撑）。

◇ Recall your past reading experiences and come up with your own value criteria of a great book (including the warrant and backing). You can discuss with your group members.

【课堂再现】

(After the discussion)

T: What are the criteria your group has developed?

S1: The four of us all have different books to recommend. But we find that the four books have one thing in common. They are all classics that have stood the test of time.

T: (Writing on the blackboard) "Stand the test of time", that is a good phrase. Can you elaborate on that?

S1: If a book sells for generations, it means it has rich levels of meaning and inspires people of all ages.

T: (Writing on the blackboard) Right, like the reading passage says, great books are enduring bestsellers. OK, any other groups?

S2: We think great books should convey positive energy.

T: OK, positive energy is 正能量 . (Writing on the blackboard) That's a catchphrase. Can you be more specific?

S2: Like *The Old Man and the Sea*, after I read it, I felt empowered. The perseverance and the bravery of the old man touched me.

T: You mean it gives you strength, right? (Writing on the blackboard) Any other ideas?

S3: Our group thinks great books should teach general readers the knowledge of a certain field and help the advance of humans. Like *The Brief History of Time*, it introduces physics in a simple way.

T: Good. You mean great books should popularize specialized knowledge and help the advance of human civilization, right? (Writing on the blackboard) Any other group has new ideas?

S4: We think readers should be able to gain something deep from great books.

T: You mean great books should help readers gain insight or wisdom, right? (Writing on the blackboard) Can you give me an example?

S4: The book *Sophie's World* makes us think about questions of philosophy, like what is the purpose of life.

T: Good. You mean the book opens reader's mind to the world of philosophy and engages readers with the most fundamental questions of human life. (Writing on the blackboard) We don't have enough time for all groups to express your ideas, but I believe you have all formed your own understanding of what is a great book. I hope the criteria will help you better recommend the book.

【板书演示】

	Warrants	Backing
Value criteria	Great books stand the test of time.	If a book sells for generations, it means it has rich levels of meaning and inspires people of all ages.
	Great books convey positive energy.	give you strength, you feel empowered, *The Old Man and the Sea*
	Great books popularize specialized knowledge and help the advance of human civilization.	teach general readers physics in a simple way

（续表）

	Warrants	Backing
Value criteria	Great books help readers gain insight or wisdom.	opens reader's mind to the world of philosophy and engages readers with fundamental questions

撰写提纲 Producing an Outline

■ 教师鼓励学生将讨论的内容按照图尔敏论证模型的四大要素列成提纲，并邀请两位学生在黑板上书写提纲。

◇ Produce an outline using the Toulmin model of argumentation.

Claim	Warrants + Backing	Grounds + Evidence

■ 教师和学生一起探讨黑板上提纲初稿的修改，确保提纲中有明确的价值标准（保证＋支撑），并且保证和根据相互匹配。同时，教师要帮助学生提升语言表达，并指出学生提纲中明显的语言错误。

◇ Revise the outline with the help of the teacher and try to avoid the mistakes the teacher has mentioned.

☆ *Possible outline:*

Claim	Warrants + Backing	Grounds + Evidence
I recommend Walden.	A great book owns a large and growing audience. They are widely read by people all over the world.	Walden was not a bestseller in its own day but became popular many years later. It was translated into 8 languages and read across continents.

（续表）

Claim	Warrants + Backing	Grounds + Evidence
I recommend Walden.	A great book addresses the common issues and values facing all human beings, benefiting readers for a lifetime.	Walden deals with issues of labour and leisure, self-reliance and individualism, which is thought-provoking.

提升效果 Adding the Impact

■ 教师引导学生通过陈述阅读经历展示自己对被推荐著作的了解，以增加推荐的可信度。

◇ Use your own reading experiences to show your knowledge of the recommended book, increasing the *ethos* of the argument. The following is an example.

e.g. The book is a Pulitzer Prize winner and has been adapted into movies several times. At first, you may be frightened by its thickness like I was, but once you start to read it, you will be attracted by its plot, which is full of twists and turns.

聚焦语言 Focusing on Language

■ 教师鼓励学生用英文表达与书籍和阅读相关的短语和句子。

◇ Try translating the following phrases and sentences related to books and reading.

1）一本爱情/悬疑/科幻/冒险/传记/侦探小说	
2）以战前的伦敦为背景	
3）基于真实历史	
4）这本书是有关……	

（续表）

5）跟随着主角的成长展开	
6）故事构思精巧，情节紧凑。	
7）超越时空	
8）追求独立和平等	
9）激发读者去思考、去探究、去实践	
10）这本书可以有多种解读。	
11）好书给读者源源不断的智慧、灵感和启发。	
12）挑战读者已有的偏见	
13）帮助读者形成正确的人生观和世界观	
14）对人性独特的洞见	
15）探讨人类共同的苦难	

☆ *Answers for reference:*

1) a romance novel / suspense thriller / science fiction / adventure story / biography / detective story

2) is set in pre-war London

3) is based on real history

4) The book is about ... / deals with ...

5) follows the character development of the hero

6) The story is well-constructed and the plot is well-knit.

7) transcend space and time

8) pursue independence and equality

9) provoke readers to think, to inquire and to practice

10) The book lends itself to different interpretations.

11) Good books provide readers with sources of continuing wisdom, inspiration and enlightenment.

12) challenge readers' established prejudices

13) help readers form proper outlook on life and the world

14) unique insight into human nature

15) address/explore the shared suffering of mankind

　　该写作话题的语言较为贴近学生的学习生活，教师可以根据学生的实际水平给予适当的语言帮助。如果教师在提纲撰写过程中发现学生的语言困难不大，也可以略去这个环节。

组织布局 Designing the Layout

■ 教师给出参考布局格式，提示学生写初稿时应注意该写作话题的要求：简述著作，并给出推荐理由。

◇ Write the draft with the reference layout shown below. Note that your draft should include introducing the recommended book briefly and giving reasons.

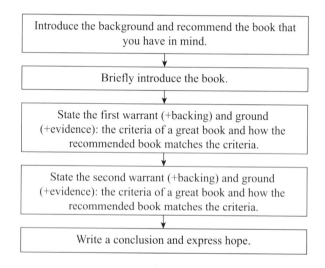

互动评价 Evaluating the Drafts

■ 教师鼓励学生依据评价量表进行自我评价或同伴互评。

◇ Evaluate the drafts in pairs or in groups with the following checklist.

　　（请参见本书理论篇第三章第四节价值型议论文评价清单样例，选取合适的维度，鼓励学生围绕习作初稿开展自评和互评。）

分享范文 Sharing the Samples

■ 教师分享优秀范文，供学生交流、评价、学习。

◇ Read the sample writings of your classmates and learn from them.

Dear club president,

Hearing that our club is going to select 5 great books for all members to read in this academic year, I'd like to recommend a great book—*Pride and Prejudice* written by Jane Austen.

Pride and Prejudice is a classic novel about the social life in the nineteenth-century England, in which the two main characters initially hold prejudice against each other but later find true love.

This book is not simply a love story, but raises the questions of pride, vanity, morality, etc., which makes it a classic. Great books should be the ones that provide insight into the basic questions that humans must face and enable readers to gain wisdom. Through Jane Austen's sarcasm and humour, I am sure all club members can find their own answers to these questions as I do.

Great books should also give readers strength. They allow readers to journey with the characters and see the growth and changes in them. *Pride and Prejudice* is just such a book. The richness of characters will allow readers to easily identify with one of them and find inspiration. After I read it, I feel empowered by Elizabeth Bennet's confidence and independent mind.

Therefore, I am eager to recommend *Pride and Prejudice* to all of the club members. I am sure everyone will benefit from reading it.

◇ Write down what you have learned from this sample writing.

 教师点评

这篇习作结构完整，共分为五段。第一段交代背景，并给出推荐著作，第二段简要介绍该书的内容，第三段和第四段给出理由，最后一段再次重申推荐，并表达对推荐著作的信心。在段落转折中，虽然作者没有用到明确的话语标记词，但我们通过分段和段首句可以看出自然而然的转折。比如，通过第二段段首句 Pride and Prejudice is a classic novel about ... 可以看出作者在描述该著作，通过第三段段首句 This book is not simply ..., but ... 可以看出作者在讲述该著作值得推荐的特点，通过第四段段首句 Great books should also ... 可以看出作者在陈述第二条价值标准。因此，段落过渡合理自然。

从内容上看，作者的价值标准很清晰，且不重复。第一条价值标准提出伟大的著作应该触及全人类都必须面对的基本问题，使读者获得智慧，第二条标准是伟大的著作应该给予读者力量，使读者跟随角色获得成长。与此同时，作者给出的根据也与价值标准相匹配。另外，从该习作可以看出，作者对这本书的内容非常熟悉，还写下了自己阅读时的感受，提升了人格诉求，增强了推荐的可信度。

从语言上看，作者对伟大著作的标准描述清晰准确，比如 provide insight into ...、enable readers to ... 以及 allow readers to ...。此外，作者对推荐著作特点的描述也较为具体，比如作者列举了该著作涉及的人性问题（pride、vanity、morality 等），还写到了角色的丰富性（the richness of characters allows readers to identify with ...），使读者能够感同身受。在谈及读后感时，作者使用的形容词也较为准确，比如 feel empowered、independent mind 等。

尝试相似话题 Suggested Writing Prompts

写作话题	你们班级打算举办"我身边的'成功'人士"主题班会。写一份演讲稿，介绍你身边的"成功"人士，并给出理由。

写作话题 10 勇气标准

学习目标汇总 Learning Objectives

Can-do statements

By the end of this session, students will be able to say:

- I can judge whether the acts in the given cases are courageous or not through group discussion.
- I can generalize about the value criteria of courage.
- I can write an argument analyzing whether Oliver's behaviour is courageous.

Thinking focus	**Expression focus**	**Style focus**
Logos: Value criteria for a philosophical issue	**About courage:** *for an act to be courageous, one must ..., do sth of one's own free will, be foolhardy, be in control of fear*	**Objective and neutral tone:** Using analytical language

准备开始写作 Preparing to Write

在前一个写作话题中，教师带领学生阅读了 *What Is a Great Book?* 这一语篇，鼓励学生结合自己的阅读经历总结心目中"伟大的著作"的标准。可见，对于这类经典的价值论题，教师可以鼓励学生采用归纳法，即从身边的例子去思考和归纳。这类价值论题常常会在小说中出现，比如"什么是美""什么是虚荣""什么是勇气""什么是忠诚"等。教师可以利用教材中的文学作品节选，在适当的时机引导学生开展相关话题的思考。

■ 教师要求学生阅读《高中英语》（新世纪版）高二第二学期第 7 单元语篇 *Oliver Wants More* 并回答问题。

◇ Read the following excerpt from *Oliver Wants More* and answer the following questions.

1）Has Oliver done a foolish thing?

2）Is "Oliver asking for more" a courageous act?

以下为语篇节选：

> Life in the workhouse was very serious indeed. The members of the board of management had ruled that the children should work to earn their living, and that they should be given three meals of thin soup a day, with an onion twice a week and half a cake on Sundays.
>
> The room, in which the boys were fed, was a large stone hall, with a huge pot at one end. Out of this, the master, assisted by one or two women, served out the soup at mealtime. Each boy had one small bowl, and nothing more—except on public holidays, when he had a small piece of bread as well. Never ever did the bowls need washing. The boys polished them with their spoons till they shone again; and when they had performed this operation, they would sit staring at the huge pot, as if they could have eaten that, too.
>
> ...

【课堂再现】

T: So by asking for more, Oliver got beaten by the master. Do you think Oliver has done a foolish thing?

S1: I don't think so.

T: Why?

S1: He had no choice. If he didn't ask for more, other boys might turn against him because he was chosen as the one to represent them.

T: Then do you think Oliver asking for more is a courageous act?

S1: Yes, I think so.

T: Any different opinions?

S2: I don't think Oliver asking for more is courageous. I think he was just afraid of being eaten by the tall boy.

T: I see you have different opinions. So the most important thing is to establish the criteria of courage.

了解写作话题 Understanding the Prompt

写作话题	在读完《雾都孤儿》小说节选 *Oliver Wants More* 之后，你认为"奥利弗想要更多"的行为是有勇气的行为吗？请给出理由。

■ 教师要求学生仔细读题，然后围绕写作话题具体内容提问，确保每个学生都理解写作话题的要求。

◇ Think and answer the following questions.

1）What is the purpose of this writing?

2）Who is the target reader?

3）What tone and voice should be used?

4）Could you use one sentence to sum up what you are going to write?

> I am going to ＿＿＿＿＿＿＿＿＿＿＿＿＿＿＿＿＿＿＿＿＿＿＿
> ＿＿＿＿＿＿＿＿＿＿＿＿＿＿＿＿＿＿＿＿＿＿＿＿＿.

☆ *Answers for reference:*

1) The writing purpose is to make an evaluation of Oliver's act of asking for more.

2) The target reader is probably the English teacher since this writing topic is a piece of homework after reading.

3) The tone should be standard and objective and the voice should be analytical.

4) I am going to analyze an act of a literary figure Oliver Twist and judge whether his act is courageous or not and give the reasons.

搭建思维模型 Constructing the Model

和"伟大的著作"不一样,"勇气"这一话题涉及哲学层面,较为抽象,学生一时间很难找到合适的例子来归纳提炼。因此,教师需要提前做好准备,给予学生足够的案例进行分析,否则学生的讨论容易流于形式。

■ 教师发给学生"这是有勇气的行为吗?"学习任务单,让学生在讨论中完成任务。

◇ Discuss with the group members and finish tasks on the worksheet titled "Is the Act Courageous?"①

Is the Act Courageous?

Tasks:

1. Read each of the following cases and answer YES or NO to the question.

2. Write the criterion by which you decide whether the action is courageous or not.

Cases:

① Near the end of the medical training, William volunteered to take part in a mission that the director said might "involve some dangers". William assumed it was another part of the training. When the plane took the volunteers to a battlefield, William was surprised to see that they were going to take care of the wounded soldiers. Was Williams' willingness to volunteer courageous?

YES/NO _____ Criterion: _____

② Bruce broke his legs while playing basketball and the doctor asked him to rest for three months for full recovery. But before the end of three months, his school mate dared him to a basketball

---

① 任务改编自"OPINIONNAIRE: What is Courage?"(Hillocks G. Teaching Argument Writing, Grades 6–12[M]. Portsmouth, NH: Heinemann, 2011.)

game. Bruce accepted the challenge and broke his legs again. Was Bruce courageous?

YES/NO _____ Criterion: _____

③ Harry was bullied in the class by a group of tall boys. One day, they surrounded him in the corridor. He was so frightened that he didn't know what to do. Out of panic, he pushed one boy to the ground. Was his push courageous?

YES/NO _____ Criterion: _____

④ Emily lost the game "truth or dare", so she had to do what they asked her to do—stand up in class and call the teacher "a pig". She knew if she didn't do that, she would be laughed at by her friends and even be excluded from the social circle. So she did what she was asked to do. Was her act courageous?

YES/NO _____ Criterion: _____

⑤ Lesley worked in a bank. Her father was suddenly in great debt and the family needed money. She knew the bank was full of security cameras. But she managed to take out some money every day without being noticed. Was her act courageous?

YES/NO _____ Criterion: _____

该讨论较为复杂，所花时间可能较长，为了提高小组活动的效率，教师可以鼓励小组成员进行角色分配，以便高效地开展讨论。

以下为角色分配表：

Leader:	Time controller:
"Let's hear from _____ first."	"Isn't it time that we move to the next ..."
"That's interesting, but let's focus on the task."	"We only have_____ minutes left. Let's see if we have a conclusion."
Judge:	**Presenter:**
"Does everybody agree on _____?"	Note down your group's idea.
"I heard you say ... Is that right?"	

■ 教师引导学生在讨论后回答学习任务单上的问题, 并鼓励学生得出勇气的标准。

◇ Answer the teacher's questions regarding the tasks on the worksheet and try to come up with the criteria of courage.

【课堂再现】

(After the discussion)

T: I see you have finished your discussion. Let's analyze it one by one. For the first case, do you think the act is courageous?

S1: No, we don't think so.

T: Why?

S1: Because William doesn't know what he is going to face. He assumed it was part of the training.

T: Good. I see your point. But what did you write in the "criterion" part?

S1: I just wrote "he doesn't know the danger".

T: Can you rewrite your criterion in another way, starting with "for an act to be courageous, ..."? (Writing on the blackboard)

S1: I see. Let me think. For an act to be courageous, the person who is doing the act must be aware of the danger.

T: Good. We can say "For an act to be courageous, the actor must be aware of the danger". (Writing on the blackboard) Then, let's move on to the second case. Peter, what about your group? Do you think Bruce is aware of the danger?

S2: Yes, Bruce must be aware that the challenge may damage his legs again. But in our opinion, this act is not courageous either.

T: Why do you think not?

S2: Because it is not necessary to run the risk of hurting the legs again. And it is not something big like winning an honour for the class. It's simply that somebody dared him. It's silly.

T: I agree. That's a silly decision to sacrifice one's own health for something meaningless. So can you give the criterion for this one?

S2: For an act to be courageous, it must not involve unnecessary risk.

T: That's good. And I want to add one. It must not be foolhardy or reckless, which means 鲁莽的, 不计后果的.（Writing on the blackboard）

S2: Yes, just what we want to say.

T: Then, how about the third case?

S3: We are not sure about this one. Harry is trying to protect himself. He dared to push those who bullied him. It takes some courage.

T: Any group has different opinions?

S3: We think the key lies in "out of panic". He actually didn't know what he was doing. Like what we have discussed before, the actor must be aware of the danger.

T: So what is your group's criterion for this case?

...

【板书演示】

For an act to be courageous, ...	the actor must be aware of the danger.
	it must not involve unnecessary risk.
	it must not be foolhardy/reckless.
	the actor must be clear-headed and in control of the fear.
	it must be something that the actor does of his own free will, not something he is forced to do.
	it must serve a good purpose and not involve any crime.

■ 教师鼓励学生根据讨论结果和自己的想法写出 "勇气" 的定义，包含价值标准、必要解释和例子。

◇ Write a definition of courage（You can use the above criteria to help you or you can come up with more criteria）. The definition should include the criteria and necessary explanation or examples.

> A courageous act is an act in which the actor ... / that involves _____
> _____
> _____
> _____

　　该活动的目的是为学生留出一段自我思考、消化、沉淀的时间，帮助他们梳理并添加有关勇气的标准，这一标准也可以用到最后的习作中。

■ 教师鼓励学生再次讨论并思考奥利弗的行为是否是有勇气的行为，并给出判断标准和根据。

◇ Discuss and evaluate Oliver's act again, i.e. whether asking for more is a courageous act. Give your criteria and grounds.

【课堂再现】

（After the discussion）

T: Now what do you think of Oliver's act.

S1: I don't think it is courageous.

T: Why?

S1: Because asking for more was not his idea. It was the result of a vote. He was actually forced to do so. We have just discussed the criteria: a courageous act must not be forced.

S2: I don't entirely agree. It is true that he was forced to do so, but that doesn't mean he himself didn't want to ask the question. He was starving too.

T: So you think he is courageous?

S2: Yes. He must know everybody was afraid to ask that question, otherwise there would be no vote. But he asked anyway. He was aware of the danger and clear-headed, and what he did was admirable.

T: You both got a point. You can start to produce an outline.

撰写提纲 Producing an Outline

■ 教师鼓励学生将讨论的内容按照图尔敏论证模型的三大要素列成提纲，

并邀请两位学生在黑板上书写提纲。

◇ Produce an outline using the Toulmin model of argumentation.

Claim	Warrants (Criteria)	Grounds + Evidence

■ 教师和学生一起探讨黑板上提纲初稿的修改,确保提纲中有明确的价值标准,并且根据和价值标准相互匹配。同时,教师要帮助学生提升语言表达,并指出学生提纲中明显的语言错误。

◇ Revise the outline with the help of the teacher and try to avoid the mistakes the teacher has mentioned.

☆ *Possible outline:*

Claim	Warrants (Criteria)	Grounds + Evidence
I don't think Oliver asking for more is a courageous act.	For an act to be courageous, the actor must be aware of the danger he might face.	From what the novel says, Oliver doesn't even know what danger he is facing.
	For an act to be courageous, the actor must perform the act of his own free will, not be forced.	Oliver was obviously afraid of being bullied by other boys and was forced to ask for more.

由于该写作话题比较特殊,涉及对小说某个人物的行为展开评价,不带有过多交际性质,大部分语言都能从小说节选中引用,因此教师可以略去"提升效果"和"聚焦语言"环节,直接进入"组织布局"环节。

组织布局 Designing the Layout

■ 教师给出参考布局格式,提示学生写初稿时应注意该写作话题的要求:

判断小说人物行为，并给出理由。

◇ Write the draft with the reference layout shown below. Note that your draft should include evaluating Oliver's act and giving reasons.

After reading *Oliver Wants More*, I (think / don't think) Oliver asking for more is a courageous act.

For an act to be courageous, ... / A courageous act is an act in which ... _____

_____

_____

_____ In the novel, Oliver _____

_____

_____

Besides/Moreover/Furthermore, _____

_____

_____

_____

_____

_____

Therefore, _____

_____

互动评价 Evaluating the Drafts

■ 教师鼓励学生依据评价量表进行自我评价或同伴评价。

◇ Evaluate the drafts in pairs or in groups with the following checklist.

（请参见本书理论篇第三章第四节价值型议论文评价清单样例，选取合适的维度，鼓励学生围绕习作初稿开展自评和互评。）

分享范文 Sharing the Samples

■ 教师分享优秀范文，供学生交流、评价、学习。

◇ Read the sample writings of your classmates and learn from them.

> After reading *Oliver Wants More*, I don't think Oliver asking for more is a courageous act.
>
> For an act to be courageous, the actor must be aware of the danger that he might face. If someone who doesn't know the danger rushes into a dangerous situation, it is not courage, but mere naivety. Only a person who knows the danger but still chooses to act can be called courageous. In the novel, Oliver doesn't seem to know what would happen after he asked for more. When the master asked in a faint voice "What!", Oliver answered "Please, sir, I want some more" again. If he knew he would be locked up and sold, he would not dare ask twice.
>
> Besides, Oliver didn't act out of his desire to help other workhouse boys. Rather, he was selected by votes and might be driven by the fear of being eaten by one tall boy. A courageous act must not be something that one is forced to do. It should arise out of one's own free will to engage in a noble endeavour.
>
> Therefore, I don't regard Oliver's act as a courageous one. Oliver is simply a poor innocent boy who had no choice but to ask for more.

◇ Write down what you have learned from this sample writing.

 教师点评

　　这篇习作较好地完成了写作话题的要求，也就是对小说中人物的行为进行评析。该习作中，作者明确给出自己的评价和理由。两个理由分别围

绕着一条勇气标准来写，中间使用 besides 过渡。最后一段中，作者重申自己的观点，结构合理。

从内容上看，作者明确写出了自己心目中的勇气标准，即保证，所给的根据也能和保证相匹配。第二段中，作者先交代标准，即"一个行为如果要算作有勇气的行为，行为人必须意识到危险的存在"，再分析奥利弗的行为为何与该标准不匹配。第三段中，作者则反过来，先分析人物行为的动机，再给出第二条标准，即"行为人必须主动开展行动，而非被迫"。论证逻辑非常清晰。

从语言上看，习作用词较为准确，从语气中可看出作者对人物行为进行了仔细的分析，比如 in the novel, Oliver doesn't seem to know what would happen ...。在论述过程中，代词和连接词的使用能够确保习作衔接流畅。

尝试相似话题 Suggested Writing Prompts

写作话题	在读完欧亨利的短篇小说《二十年后》〔《高中英语》(沪教版)选择性必修第三册"文学探索 2"〕之后，你认为 Jimmy 能算得上是 Bob 的"好朋友"吗？请给出理由。

第八章　政策型议论文教学案例

写作话题 11　考前焦虑

学习目标汇总 Learning Objectives

Can-do statements

By the end of this session, students will be able to say:

- I can conduct a survey with my group members to find out the size of the problem that exists in my class and its possible causes.
- I can apply the Toulmin Model to produce an outline for an argument of policy.
- I can write a problem-solution essay to analyze a problem in my class.

Thinking focus	Expression focus	Function focus
Logos: The relationship between grounds and warrants in an argument of policy *Pathos:* Using narration or if-clauses to emphasize the size of the problem	**Describing proportion:** *account for / occupy, rank first, followed by, stand as high as, a large percentage of ...*	**Introducing causes:** *is responsible for, ... is to blame, result in* **Introducing solutions:** *to ease the problem, in view of the causes, it is high time that ...*

准备开始写作 Preparing to Write

　　本案例是政策型议论文写作教学的第一个案例。政策型议论文往往围绕问题展开，作者分析问题成因后提出对策。为了让学生更好地理解政策型议论文的写作要点，教师可以引导学生在真实情境下开展写作，鼓励他们发现班级或学校里存在的问题，思考成因并给出解决方案。这种真实的写作任务有助于学生达成交际目的，提升学生写作的成就感。

■ 在本节写作指导课开始前一周，教师告知学生下周的写作任务，即针对班级里存在的问题给班主任写一封建议信。教师让学生自行组队，每组3—4 人。学生须进行头脑风暴，讨论出一个组员想要深入探究的问题，并通过电子平台提交给教师。

◇ Form a group of 3 to 4 members. Brainstorm and choose one problem that you think exists in the class and want to further inquire into. Send it to the teacher.

A problem that you think exists in the class

_____

_____

■ 教师收到学生头脑风暴的结果后，引导学生探究这些问题。

◇ Answer the teacher's questions regarding the problems that students submit.

【课堂再现】

T: I have received the problems that you think exist in our class, like some students sleeping during class, some students shirking their cleaning duty, etc. Then the first thing we need to address here is how to convince your class teacher that this is a serious problem.

S1: I bet the class teacher knows some of the problems. She often reminds us not to do this, not to do that.

T: But once she receives all your letters and sees so many problems, how can she determine which one to deal with first?

S2: I know what you mean. You mean we need some evidence to prove that the problem is urgent and worth paying attention to.

T: Exactly. So in order to get the evidence, what can you do?

S2: We can carry out a survey.

T: Right. Usually a simple questionnaire survey will do. But you need to design the questionnaire carefully. Think about what should be included in the survey. Emma, what do you think?

S3: I think the survey should ask how many students feel that problem exists.

T: Yes. We need to emphasize that the problem is widespread and serious, and deserves the attention of the class teacher, right? Anything else?

S4: I think that depends on what the problem is. Our group wants to talk about the problem that too many students chat during the evening study session. So I want to ask why they chat and what they are chatting about.

T: Good. It is important that you ask around the causes of the problem. Remember we are doing the survey for the writing task next week. So again, remind me of what we are going to write?

S4: We are going to write a letter of suggestion to the class teacher regarding the problems.

T: That's true. So in order to make practical suggestions, we need to know what leads to the problem. You'd better come up with some possible causes, and put them in the questionnaire.

　　这个活动的关键在于让学生理解从发现问题到提出解决方案不是一蹴而就的。为了更好地提出解决方案，作者必须弄清楚问题的普遍性和严重性、问题发生的原因等。调查问卷就是很好的工具，可以帮助学生形成证据意识及探究问题成因的习惯。

■ 教师要求学生在本周内设计好问卷并通过网络平台发放，下周写作课前须得到调查结果。

◇ Design the questionnaire within the week, distribute it via apps and obtain the survey results before the writing class next week.

了解写作话题 Understanding the Prompt

写作话题	请围绕"我们发现的班级问题"写一封信给班主任,描述班级目前存在的一个问题,分析原因,并给出解决方案,说明理由。

■ 教师要求学生仔细读题,然后围绕写作话题具体内容提问,确保每个学生都理解写作话题的要求。

◇ Think and answer the following questions.

1) What is the purpose of this writing?

2) Who is the target reader?

3) What tone and voice should be used?

4) Could you use one sentence to sum up what you are going to write?

I am going to _____

_____.

☆ *Answers for reference:*

1) The writing purpose is to propose some suggestions to the class teacher regarding the problem that exists in the class.

2) The target reader is the class teacher.

3) The tone should be standard and sincere. The voice should be polite and respectful since this is a student trying to offer some constructive suggestions to the teacher.

4) I am going to write a letter of suggestion to inform the class teacher of a serious problem, analyze the causes, give suggestions, and explain the reasons.

搭建思维模型 Constructing the Model

■ 教师让"考前焦虑"小组给出调查数据,并以该组为例,引导学生思考并讨论该问题的解决方案。

◇ Read the survey data given by the group "anxiety before exams". Think and discuss the possible solutions for this group.

【课堂再现】

（ Before the discussion ）

T: So what can you get from the survey data?

S1: Well, the data show that 85% of the students suffer from some kind of anxiety before exams. That's a lot.

T: I agree. It means it is a widespread problem. Then do you think the problem is serious?

S1: I think so. Because it has caused many bad effects, like stomachache.

T: Yes, the data confirmed that. Then if we want to give helpful suggestions, we need to know what caused the anxiety, right? So what do the data suggest?

S2: The data show that the top two causes are that most students are afraid that all their efforts may come to nothing and that they may disappoint teachers and parents. The third one is some students feel they are not adequately prepared for the exam.

T: Good. Now that you have the data at hand, you can think about the possible solutions. Let the discussion begin.

以下是"考前焦虑"小组设计的问卷及调查结果：

Questionnaire

1. 你在考试前会焦虑吗？

   Will you feel anxious before having the exams?

   A. 非常焦虑 extremely   15%

   B. 比较焦虑 sometimes   70%

   C. 比较不焦虑 just so so   12%

   D. 根本不焦虑 not at all   3%

2. 考前焦虑对你有什么影响？（可多选）

   How may anxiety before exams affect you?（ Select one or more answer choices ）

   A. 影响考试发挥 affect exam performance   67%

B. 影响身体健康，比如胃疼、腹泻、睡不着、恶心呕吐、浑身发抖 affect physical health, e.g. stomachache, diarrhea, insomnia, nausea, shaking 60%

C. 无法集中精力复习 cannot concentrate on revising 80%

D. 没什么影响 have no impact on me 8%

3. 你觉得你考试焦虑的原因是什么？（可多选）

Why do you feel anxious?（Select one or more answer choices）

A. 担心考不好，对不起自己的努力 worried that all the efforts come to nothing 82%

B. 怕输给竞争对手 afraid of losing to my rivals 29%

C. 怕让老师和家长失望 afraid of disappointing teachers and parents 56%

D. 觉得复习得不全面 feel not adequately prepared 48%

E. 周围同学都在焦虑，跟风焦虑 just following the trend 23%

【课堂再现】

（After the discussion）

T: So what suggestions does your group come up with?

S1: We analyzed the causes very carefully. We found a strange thing.

T: Is that so? What strange thing?

S1: It is that all of us are worried about some bad consequences, like all the efforts may come to nothing, or we may disappoint teachers and parents. So we think the suggestion should be to ask all the students not to worry about such things.

T: Stop worrying. That is an obvious one. But how to ask people to stop worrying? If I tell you to stop worrying, will you stop immediately?

S1: No. It is not an easy thing to do.

T: So we need more practical and effective solutions. Remember whom we are writing to?

S1: The class teacher.

T: Yes, we are asking the class teacher to help us, right? So be creative. What can a class teacher do? Any other groups have better ideas?

S2: We think all the worrying comes down to one thing—fear of failure. Almost all of us are afraid that we might do badly in the exam, which will disappoint somebody or even disappoint ourselves. But that's not a healthy way to deal with failure.

T: Fear of failure. (Writing on the blackboard) I agree. You dig deeper into the problem. So what does your group propose?

S2: We want to ask the class teacher to hold a class meeting themed "how to deal with failure".

T: (Writing on the blackboard) Why do you think the class meeting will help?

S2: Because the number of students suffering from anxiety is large. A class meeting will be the most efficient way to teach all the students the right attitude towards failure.

T: Good. That's arguing from consequence. A class meeting can bring good consequences, so the policy is worth having. That's the warrant. (Writing on the blackboard) Any group has more suggestions?

S3: We want to ask the class teacher to communicate with our parents.

T: And say what?

S3: One exam doesn't mean everything.

T: I get it. (Writing on the blackboard) To ask parents not to take the score too seriously, right?

S3: Yes. More than half of our classmates choose C, which means most of us care about what our parents and teachers think.

T: (Writing on the blackboard) I see. You hate to disappoint your parents and teachers, right? Then why not ask your class teacher to communicate with other teachers?

S3: Because we think we can do that by ourselves and the class teacher may not have such a big influence on other teachers. But the class teacher can influence our parents' thought.

T: That's practical consideration. Thank you. Now you can produce an outline with the survey data gathered by your own group.

【板书演示】

Grounds (Causes)	Claim of Policy	Warrants
• Fear of failure is main cause of the anxiety.	• Hold a class meeting: "how to deal with failure"	• A class meeting is efficient to teach the right attitude towards failure.
• More than 50% of the students are afraid of disappointing parents and teachers.	• Communicate with parents, asking parents not to take the score too seriously	• Students care about what their parents think. Class teacher has influence on parents.

　　该环节的关键在于通过一个小组的调查结果分析，帮助学生认识到政策型议论文的写作要点：

　　（1）描述问题时，需要指出问题的普遍性和严重性，即为什么该问题值得解决；

　　（2）对原因的分析要深入、透彻（比如分析出 fear of failure 是考前焦虑的主要原因）；

　　（3）提出的解决方案必须是可行的、有效的（不能仅提出诸如 stop worrying 之类的方案）；

　　（4）提出的解决方案需要考虑到政策执行者的权限和执行能力等；

　　（5）保证的写作可以从后果法和原则法去思考。

撰写提纲 Producing an Outline

■ 教师鼓励学生根据自己小组的调查结果，按照图尔敏论证模型的三大要素列成提纲，并邀请两位学生在黑板上书写提纲。

◇ Produce an outline using the Toulmin model of argumentation based on the survey results of your own group.

Grounds (Causes)	Claim of Policy	Warrants

（续表）

Grounds (Causes)	Claim of Policy	Warrants

■ 教师和学生一起探讨黑板上提纲初稿的修改，确保提纲中的主张（提议）是基于根据（原因）提出的，并确保保证能解释前两者之间的关系。同时，教师要帮助学生提升语言表达，并指出学生提纲中明显的语言错误。

◇ Revise the outline with the help of the teacher, make sure the claim is aligned with the grounds and try to avoid the mistakes the teacher has mentioned.

☆ *Possible outline:*

Grounds (Causes)	Claim of Policy	Warrants
The main reason of anxiety is fear of failure.	A class meeting themed "how to cope with failure" should be held.	A class meeting is an efficient way to help all the students to form a proper attitude towards failure and promote healthy competition.
Many students don't feel prepared before exams. Every day is full of classes.	More free self-study sessions should be arranged.	More self-study sessions can provide students with extra time to prepare for exams.

提升效果 Adding the Impact

■ 教师鼓励学生使用叙述、描写或适当假想的手段强调问题的普遍性或严重性，以唤起读者的重视，提升情感诉求。

◇ Use some techniques like narration, description or if-clauses to emphasize the size or seriousness of the problem, increasing the *pathos* of the argument. The following is an example.

e.g. During every evening study session, the classroom is filled with chatting voices, murmuring and giggling, which has made it difficult for many students to concentrate. If the situation continues, we are bound to lag behind other classes.

■ 教师鼓励学生在写作过程中提及自己对问题或解决方案的了解，以提升话语的可信度。

◇ Refer to your own experience with the problem to show that you understand the problem and the proposed solutions well, increasing the credibility of your words.

■ 教师提示学生思考反方可能存在的质疑，并让学生思考如何回应。

◇ Think about the possible objections against the claim and come up with ideas to respond to the objections.

Objections:

_____

_____

Responses:

_____

_____

☆ *Answers for reference:*

Objections:

It may be difficult for the class teacher to ask the Administration Office to add more self-study sessions.

Responses:

It is true. But at least it is worth a try.

聚焦语言 Focusing on Language

■ 教师让学生尝试补全以下有关描述比例的句子，提升句型表达的多样性。

◇ Try completing the following sentences related to describing proportion, increasing the variety of sentence patterns.

1）_____（大约四分之三的同学）think that they are disturbed by the chatting voices during the evening study session.

2）The figure for those who have once slept in class _____ _____（高达75%）.

3）_____（85%的同学）all feel some degree of anxiety before exams _____（而）only 3% don't feel anxious at all.

4）Those who choose "the study load is too much for me" _____ _____（占42%）

5）_____（十分之一的同学）think they need a deskmate.

6）_____（很大比例的同学）hate to disappoint their teachers.

7）The survey results show _____（大量同学）report to have fallen asleep in class once.

8）The number of classmates who choose "cannot concentrate on revising" _____（排第一）at 80%, _____（接下来是）67% of students who say it affects their exam performance.

9）_____（不少同学）regard it as a serious problem.

☆ *Answers for reference:*

1) Approximately/Around three quarters / Three fourths of our classmates

2) stands as high as 75%

3) 85% of classmates; while

4) account for / occupy 42%

5) One in ten classmates

6) a large percentage/proportion of classmates

7) a significant number of classmates

8) ranks first; followed by

9) Quite a few / A good few classmates

组织布局 Designing the Layout

■ 教师给出参考布局格式，提示学生写初稿时应注意该写作话题的要求：陈述问题，分析原因，提出方案，给出理由。

◇ Write the draft with the reference layout shown below. Note that your draft should include stating the problem, analyzing causes, proposing suggestions, and giving reasons.

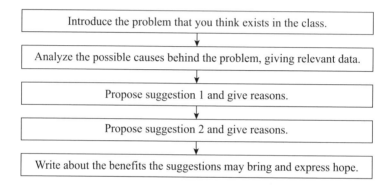

■ 教师给出以下引出问题原因和解决方案的参考句型，为段落转折提供合适的语言参考。

◇ Learn the following sentence patterns to help with the transitions between paragraphs.

引出问题原因	1) _____ （为什么这么多同学存在考试焦虑）？ 2) The survey results show that fear of failure _____ （主要为……负责）the anxiety before exams. 3) _____ （至于原因）, the survey results show ... 4) According to the survey results, _____ （……的主要原因是……） 5) _____ （问题原因明显地呈现在）in our survey results. 6) Based on the data, we think _____ （一部分原因在于）our fear of failure. 7) From what we have learned, it is the fear of failure that _____ （导致）the anxiety.

（续表）

引出 解决 方案	1）Therefore, ＿＿＿＿＿＿＿＿（急需采取努力）to prevent the situation from getting worse. 2）＿＿＿＿＿＿＿＿＿（为了有效缓解问题）, I suggest that ... 3）After analyzing the survey results, ＿＿＿＿＿＿＿＿（我们想要提出以下建议）. 4）＿＿＿＿＿＿＿（鉴于以上原因）, we respectfully ＿＿＿＿＿（提交以下建议）. 5）We believe ＿＿＿＿＿＿（到了……的时候）that we addressed the problem. 6）As far as I am concerned, ＿＿＿＿＿＿＿（最好的解决方案就是）to hold a class meeting.

☆ *Answers for reference:*

引出 问题 起因	1）why do so many classmates have test anxiety 2）is mainly responsible for 3）As to the reasons 4）the main reason why ... is that ... 5）The causes of the problem are clearly shown 6）part of the reasons lies in 7）is to blame for / results in
引出 解决 方案	1）efforts are desperately needed 2）To effectively ease the problem 3）we'd like to make the following suggestions 4）In view of / In light of the causes; submit the following proposals 5）it is high time 6）the best solution is

互动评价 Evaluating the Drafts

■ 教师鼓励学生依据评价量表进行自我评价或同伴互评。

◇ Evaluate the drafts in pairs or in groups with the following checklist.

（请参见本书理论篇第四章第四节政策型议论文评价清单样例，选取合适的维度，鼓励学生围绕习作初稿开展自评与互评。）

分享范文 Sharing the Samples

■ 教师分享优秀范文，供学生交流、评价、学习。

◇ Read the sample writings of your classmates and learn from them.

Dear class teacher,

Recently, we have noticed a problem among many of our classmates, which we think you should know—test anxiety before exams. According to our survey, 85% of students in our class say they feel anxious before exams. From what we have observed, the anxiety has made some students depressed and even led to physical health problems, like stomachache, insomnia, shaking, diarrhea and nausea. Therefore, it is really worthy of concern.

Why do so many classmates have test anxiety? Our survey results show that most students are worried that they might do badly in the coming mid-term exam and their efforts may come to nothing. They are also afraid that they may disappoint the parents and teachers. Another 32% of students are afraid of losing to their rivals in exams. Besides, a large proportion of students choose "I don't feel prepared enough" in the questionnaire.

In view of the causes, we respectfully submit the following proposals. First, we propose that a class meeting themed "how to cope with failure" should be held. It is obvious that the main cause of anxiety is our fear of failure, either afraid of disappointing somebody or afraid of losing. A carefully-designed class meeting can help all of us to form a proper attitude towards failure and promote healthy competition between classmates, thus relieving the anxiety.

Second, we suggest that more free self-study sessions

be arranged. We think the reason why many of us don't feel prepared is that every day is fully packed with classes and we don't have much time to internalize what we have learned. More self-study sessions can offer us extra time to prepare for the coming exams. In this way, fewer students will suffer from anxiety.

If the proposals are put into effect, we believe the test anxiety in our class can be greatly reduced, which will bring benefits to all the classmates.

◇ Write down what you have learned from this sample writing.

 教师点评

这篇政策型议论文结构完整。第一段描述问题，第二段分析原因，第三段和第四段针对原因给出解决方案，并说明了理由，最后一段再次强调了建议采纳后可能带来的美好愿景。段落之间的转折非常自然：引出原因段时，作者用到了一个设问句；引出解决方式段时，作者用 submit the following proposals 直接表明了之后段落的功能。

从内容上看，从问题的发现、原因的分析，到解决方案的提出，逻辑清晰，环环相扣。第一条政策型主张（召开主题班会）对应的正是原因分析中的第一项"学生害怕失败"，而主题班会的召开可以帮助全班同学形成正确对待失败的态度。第二条政策型主张（设置更多的自习课）对应的是第二项原因"觉得没有复习到位"，而自习课可以给予学生更多内化的机会。除了逻辑清晰之外，作者还在情感诉求上下功夫，比如在第一段描述问题的时候描写了考前焦虑的具体症状，以调动读者情感。如果可能的话，作者还可以适当提升人格诉求。

从语言上看，作者的语调和语气把控得较好。首先，语调是真诚的、想解决问题的，作者用到了 really worthy of our concern、the test anxiety can be greatly reduced 等短语和句子。其次，语气流露出对班主任的尊重，用到了

we think you should know、we respectfully submit the proposals 等。此外，作者的英语功底较好，尤其是动宾搭配使用准确，如 cope with failure、form a proper attitude、promote healthy competition、be packed with classes、relieve anxiety 等短语。

写作话题 12 池塘污染

学习目标汇总 Learning Objectives

Can-do statements
By the end of this session, students will be able to say:
• I can analyze the causes of a social issue from the perspectives of various involved parties.
• I can apply the Toulmin Model to produce an outline for an argument of policy, aligning causes with solutions.
• I can write an argument to analyze and solve a social problem.

Thinking focus	Expression focus	Function focus
Logos: The relationship between grounds and warrants in an argument of policy	**About pond pollution:** *suffer from years of neglect, discharge polluted water, give off bad smell*	**Expressing anticipation:** *I would appreciate it if ..., take my proposals seriously, I expect to see ...*
Pathos: Using narration, description or if-clauses to emphasize the size of the problem	**About estate maintenance:** *lay down regulations, launch a publicity campaign, set up signs*	

准备开始写作 Preparing to Write

　　在上一个案例中，教师启发学生思考和探究班级里存在的问题，该写作话题最为贴近学生生活，适合教师首次开展政策型议论文教学。然而，在高中阶段的学习中，学生还会广泛接触有关社会问题的任务型写作话题。考虑到学生可能没有办法通过开展问卷调查去探究这些问题的本源，教师可以引导学生回顾之前在事实型议论文中所学的因果论证。

■ 教师带领学生回顾事实型议论文中所学的因果论证。

◇ Review what has been learned in the writing of causal arguments.

【课堂再现】

T: Today we are going to write on new topic of the argument of policy. In the previous lesson, we have learned how important it is to analyze the causes behind a problem. Remember? We did a survey to find out the causes of a problem in the class. But there are still some writing topics that deal with social problems. How do we analyze the causes for such social problems?

S1: We can make some reasonable inferences.

T: Yes. Making inferences is important. We can try to find out the correlation between different elements. Actually, we have talked about how to make a causal argument before. Remember the argument about the popularity of mystery boxes, Lisa?

S1: Yes, I remember that topic.

T: Do you remember the causes we have found out about their popularity?

S1: Well, the mysterious nature of the boxes is one reason and the students' excitement about what's in the box is another reason. And other reasons ... I don't remember them all.

T: The two reasons are enough. The first reason is about the boxes themselves and the second reason is about the consumers, right? So from that writing topic, we have learned that to identify the causes of a problem or a phenomenon, we may analyze the different parties responsible for this problem or phenomenon. The same is true of an argument of policy.

了解写作话题 Understanding the Prompt

写作话题	最近，你们小区的池塘受到污染，飘出阵阵臭味。写一封信给居委会，反映这一情况，分析原因，并给出合理建议，说明理由。

■ 教师要求学生仔细读题，然后围绕写作话题具体内容提问，确保每个学生都理解写作话题的要求。

◇ Think and answer the following questions.

1）What is the purpose of this writing?

2）Who is the target reader?

3）What tone and voice should be used?

4）Could you use one sentence to sum up what you are going to write?

I am going to _____
_____ .

☆ *Answers for reference:*

1) The writing purpose is to propose some suggestions to the residents' committee regarding the pond in the neighbourhood.

2) The target reader is the residents' committee.

3) The tone should be formal. The voice should be serious and helpful since this is a letter from a teenager resident to report a serious problem to the residents' committee and try to offer constructive suggestions.

4) I am going to write a letter of suggestion to inform the residents' committee of the problem in the neighbourhood, analyze the causes, give suggestions, and explain the reasons.

搭建思维模型 Constructing the Model

■ 教师引导学生开拓思路，作出原因推理。

◇ Brainstorm and think about how to make inferences about causes.

【课堂再现】

T: First, let's focus on the cause analysis. (Writing on the blackboard) Based on what we have reviewed about causal argument, who do you suppose are the different parties responsible for the pollution of the pond, Nigel?

S1: The pond is inside the housing estate, so the residents themselves must be responsible.

T: Yes, the residents. (Writing on the blackboard) Who else or what else?

S2: I think the lack of supervision by the residents' committee is another reason.

T: I agree. The resident's committee itself. Anybody has more ideas to add?

S3: I think maybe it's just that the pond has been dug for a long time and the water just needs changing.

T: I see. That's a reasonable inference. Now you can have a discussion with your group members on the causes of and solutions to the problem. I believe you will come up with more ideas after the discussion.

【板书演示】

Cause Analysis

What parties are responsible?

Residents | The residents' committee | The water needs changing

---

■ 教师引导学生讨论并思考池塘污染的原因和解决方式。

◇ Think and discuss the causes of and solutions to the pollution of the pond with the group members.

【课堂再现】

(After the discussion)

T: So what does your group think are the causes of the pollution?

S1: We think the bad smell might be caused by the dead fish bodies and certain algae in the pond.

T: (Writing what S1 says on the blackboard) Why do you connect the bad smell with the fish bodies and algae?

S1: Well, it is common knowledge that dead fish bodies smell bad and algae may have some kind of chemical reactions that will cause the smell.

T: That's good. What you said is actually the warrant for the causal claim. (Writing on the blackboard) So based on this cause, what do you propose the residents' committee should do?

S1: We think the residents' committee should employ some workers to clear the dead fish bodies and the algae.

T: (Writing on the blackboard) That's a reasonable solution. Once the source of pollution is cleared, the smell will be gone. That brings good consequences, right?

S1: Yes, arguing from consequence.

T: So you've got your claim, grounds and warrants. (Writing on the blackboard) That is the first suggestion. Any other suggestions? Let's hear from Sam's group.

...

该课堂对话的关键是让学生意识到以下几点：

（1）政策型主张的提出通常需要建立在原因分析的基础上；

（2）原因分析本身是一个事实型议论，需要得到进一步证明。

【板书演示】

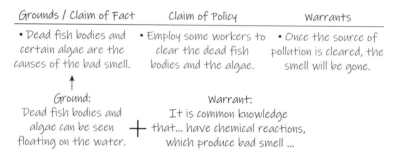

Grounds / Claim of Fact	Claim of Policy	Warrants
• Dead fish bodies and certain algae are the causes of the bad smell.	• Employ some workers to clear the dead fish bodies and the algae.	• Once the source of pollution is cleared, the smell will be gone.

Ground:
Dead fish bodies and algae can be seen floating on the water.

Warrant:
It is common knowledge that... have chemical reactions, which produce bad smell ...

撰写提纲 Producing an Outline

■ 教师鼓励学生将讨论的内容按照图尔敏论证模型的三大要素列成提纲，同时要求学生进一步分析问题的成因。教师邀请两位学生在黑板上书写提纲。

◇ Produce an outline using the Toulmin model of argumentation. Note that the causes of the problem need further analysis.

Grounds / Claim of Fact		Claim of Policy	Warrants
	G:		
	W:		
	G:		
	W:		
	G:		
	W:		

■ 教师和学生一起探讨黑板上提纲初稿的修改，确保提纲中的主张（提议）是基于根据（原因）提出的，并确保保证能解释前两者之间的关系。同时，教师要帮助学生提升语言表达，并指出提纲中明显的语言错误。

◇ Revise the outline with the help of the teacher, make sure the claim is aligned with the grounds and try to avoid the mistakes the teacher has mentioned.

☆ *Possible outline:*

Grounds / Claim of Fact		Claim of Policy	Warrants
The main cause of the smell is the residents throwing things however they like.	G: The household waste is seen floating on the river.	... should launch a publicity campaign to educate the residents not to throw things in the pond.	Publicity campaign raises people's awareness.
	W: Spoiled household waste gives off bad smell.		
The smelly water in the nearby river is the second cause of the pond pollution.	G: The river is connected to our pond.	... should contact the local authorities responsible for river management.	The river can only be treated under the authority of the local government.
	W: It is common knowledge that water flows freely.		

提升效果 Adding the Impact

■ 教师提醒学生可以使用叙述、描写或适当假想的手段强调问题的普遍性或严重性，以唤起读者的重视，提升情感诉求。

◇ Review the techniques used to emphasize the extent or seriousness of the problem, increasing the *pathos* of the argument.

【课堂再现】

T: What is the problem mentioned in the writing topic? (Writing on the blackboard)

S1: The pond is polluted and gives off a bad smell.

T: Yes. But is that enough to catch the attention of the residents' committee? Remember what we have learned in the previous writing topic?

S1: I know. We should also show the seriousness of the problem.

T: Exactly. We need to tell the reader why the problem is worth our efforts, right? (Writing on the blackboard) Do you remember how to do that?

S1: Yes, we can use narration, description or if-clauses.

T: (Writing on the blackboard) Right. So in this writing topic, how can you apply the three methods?

S1: Like we can describe how bad the smell is.

T: Good. Anything else, Robin?

S2: We can allow the readers to visualize the situation of the pond, like how the rubbish piles up, etc.

T: Very good. "Show not tell", remember? (Writing on the blackboard) Use your imagination to show the readers how polluted the pond is. Anything else?

S3: We can also use narration, like briefly telling a story about how the pond is polluted. For example, people throw all kinds of things to feed the fish.

T: I agree. That's an effective way to arouse readers' imagination.

S3: We can also use if-clauses to emphasize the bad consequences that the pollution might lead to, like the bad smell may harm the residents' health.

T: Great. I think you all get the point.

【板书演示】

Seriousness of the Problem

Why is the problem worth the efforts?

narration, description (show not tell), if-clauses

聚焦语言 Focusing on Language

■ 教师鼓励学生用英文表达与池塘污染和小区管理相关的短语和句子。

◇ Try translating the following phrases and sentences related to pond pollution and estate maintenance.

1）池塘几年以来疏于管理。	
2）与工厂排放的污水有关	
3）腐败的食物和腐烂的落叶散发出难闻的味道。	
4）充足的阳光和营养令池塘内的藻类大量生长。	
5）随意往池塘里扔垃圾	
6）在池塘边设立标识牌	
7）多种植吸收池塘内多余营养的植物	
8）制定池塘管理条例，设立严格的奖惩制度	
9）指派专人在池塘边监督	
10）招募专业团队来处理污水	
11）开展小区宣传活动	
12）与有关部门/当局沟通	

☆ *Answers for reference:*

1) The pond suffers from years of neglect.

2) be related to the sewage / polluted water discharged from factories

3) Spoiled food and decayed leaves give off bad smell.

4) Sufficient sunlight and nutrients make the algae bloom quickly in the pond.

5) throw rubbish into the pond however they like / as they want

6) set up signs beside the pond

7) grow more plants that absorb extra nutrients in the pond

8) lay down the regulations on pond management, establish a strict system of rewards and punishment / impose penalties on those who break the regulations

9) assign staff members to supervise around the pond

10) hire professional team to treat the polluted water

11) launch a publicity campaign in the neighbourhood

12) communicate with the department concerned / the local authorities

　　学生在写作中常常会使用中文的习惯表达, 比如"加强池塘的管理"等, 如果将这些短语直译成英文 strengthen the management of the pond 显得十分生硬。这时, 教师可以指导学生采用意译, 比如 more emphasis should be put on the management of the pond。当然, 更重要的是, 教师应提示学生英文写作的特点是倾向于具体的表达, 要鼓励学生进一步思考"加强管理"的具体做法, 包括指派专人在池塘边监督, 在池塘边设立标志牌, 或在小区设立奖惩制度等, 而不是泛泛而论。

组织布局 Designing the Layout

■ 教师给出参考布局格式, 提示学生写初稿时应注意该写作话题的要求: 陈述问题, 分析原因, 提出方案, 给出理由。

◇ Write the draft with the reference layout shown below. Note that your draft should include stating the problem, analyzing causes, proposing suggestions, and giving reasons.

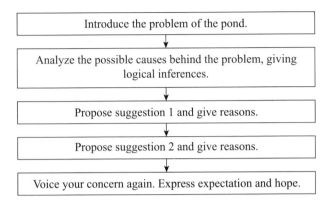

Introduce the problem of the pond.

↓

Analyze the possible causes behind the problem, giving logical inferences.

↓

Propose suggestion 1 and give reasons.

↓

Propose suggestion 2 and give reasons.

↓

Voice your concern again. Express expectation and hope.

在前一个政策型写作话题中，笔者已给出了有关段落转折（引出问题原因和解决方案）的参考句型。本写作话题不再重复这部分内容。

■ 教师让学生补全句子，并为建议信写一个合适的结尾段。

◇ Add an ending by making the following sentences complete, using the words in the brackets.

期盼采纳	1）_____ if you could take my proposal into consideration.（appreciate） 2）I sincerely hope my suggestions can catch your attention and you can _____.（thought） 3）Modest as my reasoning may seem, I believe it makes sense. I hope you will _____ when you discuss the issue.（consider） 4）My plan may still leave plenty to be desired, but I genuinely hope you can _____.（seriously）
表达期望	1）With joint efforts, _____ that the pollution can be resolved.（convinced） 2）_____ that by working together, we will be able to eliminate pollution.（confident） 3）_____ the day when the residents in the neighbourhood can breathe clear air again.（expect）

☆ *Answers for reference:*

期盼采纳	1）I would really appreciate it 2）give them some serious thought

（续表）

期盼 采纳	3) consider my ideas 4) take my proposals seriously
表达 期望	1) I am convinced 2) I am confident 3) I expect to see

互动评价 Evaluating the Drafts

■ 教师鼓励学生依据评价量表进行自我评价或同伴互评。

◇ Evaluate the drafts in pairs or in groups with the following checklist.

（请参见本书理论篇第四章第四节政策型议论文评价清单样例，选取合适的维度，鼓励学生围绕习作初稿开展自评与互评。）

分享范文 Sharing the Samples

■ 教师分享优秀范文，供学生交流、评价、学习。

◇ Read the sample writings of your classmates and learn from them.

Dear residents' committee,

　　I am writing to draw your attention to the situation of the pond in our neighbourhood. I used to walk around the pond after dinner because of its fine scenery. However, recently, whenever I walk past the pond, I cannot help but hold my breath because of the disgusting smell. I believe it will not only lower the property value but also threaten the physical well-being of the residents.

　　Part of the reasons lies in the rubbish and possibly some dead fish bodies in the pond. Although we cannot clearly see

---

what is beneath the dirty water, it is obvious that there are many bottles and yoghurt boxes floating around. It is difficult for fish to live in such an environment. Besides, I know the pond is connected to a river nearby. From my observation, the river has been polluted recently and the oil on the river has gradually flowed to our pond. So the pollution of the river is partly to blame.

In light of the causes, I think it is high time that you figured out some ways to address the problem. First, I suggest you employ some cleaners to remove the rubbish and dead fish bodies from the pond. Signs should also be set up beside the pond to arouse people's awareness of protecting the pond. Only when everyone takes action can the problem be solved. Second, it is advisable that you contact the local authorities responsible for the river management. It is important that they don't forget our pond when they treat the polluted river.

I sincerely hope my letter can catch your attention and effective measures can be taken. With joint efforts, I am confident that the pond will still be the jewel of our neighbourhood.

◇ Write down what you have learned from this sample writing.

教师点评

这篇政策型议论文结构完整，完成了写作话题的要求。第一段描述问题，第二段分析原因，第三段给出两个解决方案，并说明理由，最后一段表达了对居委会的期望以及对池塘治理的信心。段落转折自然流畅，先通过 part of the reasons 引出原因，再通过 in light of the causes, I think it is high time ... 引出解决方式，使读者较为容易地捕捉作者的观点。此外，习作的开头结尾相互呼应，第一段写明来信目的时用到 draw your attention to ... 最后一段作出总结时用到 hope ... can catch your attention，希望对方能够关注自己的来信。

从内容上看，作者描述问题的方式很好地抓住了读者的眼球，不仅使用叙述和描写的手段，让读者脑海中充满画面感，还对池塘污染不解决可能带来的后果作出假设，充分体现出问题的严重性。在原因分析部分，作者对池塘臭味的来源作出了合理的推断，将各种要素之间的关联解释得非常清楚。在提出建议部分，作者给出的两个建议分别针对第二段分析得出的两个原因，逻辑清晰。以第一个原因（池塘垃圾问题）为例，作者不仅给出了现有垃圾的处理建议，还给出了如何预防未来池塘出现垃圾的建议。

从语言上看，作者对语言的运用较为纯熟。描述问题时，作者用到了 cannot help but ...、lower the property value、threaten the well-being 等；提出建议时，作者用到了 figure out ways、address the problem、employ some cleaners、remove the rubbish、set up signs、arouse sb's awareness、contact the local authorities、treat the polluted river 等常见动宾搭配，值得同伴学习。

尝试相似话题 Suggested Writing Prompts

写作话题	最近，你们小区常出现高空抛物（high-rise littering）现象。写一封信给居委会，反映这一情况，分析原因，并给出合理建议，说明理由。

写作话题 13　友情困境

学习目标汇总 Learning Objectives

Can-do statements

By the end of this session, students will be able to say:

- I can analyze where the real troubles lie in a "trouble-type" problem.
- I can apply the Toulmin Model to produce an outline for an argument of policy, aligning troubles with solutions.
- I can write an argument of policy to respond to others' troubles and provide solutions.

Thinking focus	**Expression focus**	**Style focus**
Logos: The relationship between grounds and warrants in an argument of policy *Pathos:* Expressing empathy	**About friction with friends:** *inevitable conflicts, carry a grudge, make the first move, listen to others' perspective*	**Comforting and supportive tone:** Using conversational language

准备开始写作 Preparing to Write

前两个政策型写作话题（考前焦虑和池塘污染）有一个共同之处，就是这两个问题都是可逆的，也就是说，解决这两个问题是为了使问题不再发生（考前不再焦虑、池塘不再被污染）。然而在日常生活中，我们碰到的许多问题是不可逆的，比如超市已积压了大量临期食品，某人已和朋友产生了冲突。这些问题更偏向于"困境应对型"，而不是常规意义上的"问题解决型"。对于"困境应对型"问题，原因分析的意义不大，作者应直接提出应对方案。关键在于要分析出这些问题为何会成为问题，即可能给当事人造成怎样的困扰。教师可以在导入时借助日常生活中的情境帮助学生明确这一点。

■ 教师以生活中的例子引导学生思考如何解决"困境应对型"问题。

◇ Think about how to find solutions to the "trouble-type" problem and answer the teacher's questions.

【课堂再现】

T: In previous two arguments of policy, we have learned to offer suggestions to some problems. Do you remember how to do that?

S1: Yes, we tried to identify the causes of the problem and give suggestions accordingly.

T: That's true. The cause analysis is an important part. But there are still some problems in real life that don't involve cause analysis. For example, suppose you are a businessman who owns a grocery store. One day, you suddenly find that dozens of products are near the expiration date, which means the end of the shelf life (快过期了). How would you deal with those products?

S1: I may lower the prices of those products so that more customers will buy them.

T: That's good. You wouldn't look for the causes, right? You want immediate solutions.

S1: Yes.

T: So to find solutions to such troubles, we should first analyze where the trouble lies. In this case, why do you think the near-expired products bring you trouble?

S2: Because I might lose money if I can't sell them.

T: OK. That's a big trouble. (Writing on the blackboard) Anything else? What if "I" don't care about the money? Can "I" just dump the products when they have expired?

S3: No, I wouldn't just dump them. It would lead to huge waste. If I can't sell them, I think I will give them out for free.

T: You see? The second solution is here. (Writing on the blackboard) Based on our analysis, the near-expired products will bring two troubles: one is the loss of money and the other is that they may result in huge waste of resources. So we can give two suggestions: one is to lower the prices, and the second is to give out some of the products for free, maybe donating them to an orphanage, right? (Writing on the blackboard)

S3: Yes.

T: So before we try to give solutions to such a trouble, we should first find out why it becomes the trouble in the first place.

【板书演示】

Troubles	Solutions
may lose money if they aren't sold	lower the prices of those products
may lead to huge waste	give some of them out for free

了解写作话题 Understanding the Prompt

写作 话题	王婷最好的朋友摔碎了她的手表，而这个手表是王婷奶奶送给她的生日礼物。王婷不知道该怎么办，写信向校报"烦恼热线"栏目求助。假设你是校报编辑，写一封回信给王婷，提出你的建议和理由。

■ 教师要求学生仔细读题，然后围绕写作话题具体内容提问，确保每个学生都理解写作话题的要求。

◇ Think and answer the following questions.

1) What is the purpose of this writing?

2) What is your identity as the writer?

3) Who is the target reader?

4) What tone and voice should be used?

5) Could you use one sentence to sum up what you are going to write?

I am going to _____

_____.

☆ *Answers for reference:*

1) The writing purpose is to help Wang Ting to deal with her trouble.

2) "I" am an editor of the school newspaper.

3) The target reader is Wang Ting. Other readers of the newspaper may be the target readers as well.

4) The tone should be friendly and supportive. The voice should be like a patient, encouraging, and friend-like editor who is trying to help Wang Ting analyze and solve the trouble.

5) I am going to write a letter to Wang Ting to offer suggestions to her trouble.

搭建思维模型 Constructing the Model

■ 教师启发学生思考从哪些角度提出建议。

◇ Think about from what aspects the suggestions can be made and answer the teacher's questions.

【课堂再现】

T: After reading the topic, can you see why the watch incident becomes trouble for Wang Ting?

S1: Well, I think she loves the watch very much because this watch is a birthday gift from her grandmother.

T: I agree. The watch must have some emotional value for her. Then again, why does the incident trouble her?

S1: I think when someone breaks something I love, I would be unhappy.

T: (Writing on the blackboard) Right, being unhappy is one trouble. Anything else? If she is just upset and unhappy, do you think she will write to the school newspaper for help?

S2: I think Wang Ting blames her best friend in her heart, but she doesn't want to tell her that face to face. She was afraid the watch will ruin their friendship.

T: Yes, that's an important point. (Writing on the blackboard) What would you suggest Wang Ting do?

S2: I think if this is an accident and her friend has apologized sincerely, she should try to accept the apology and forgive her.

T: (Writing on the blackboard) Why do you think she should forgive her?

S2: Well, having a beautiful friendship is something valuable. It should not end because of an accident.

T: Right, friendship is something to be treasured. That's a principle, arguing from principles, right?

S2: Yes.

T: So we have the warrant. (Writing on the blackboard) Now it is time for you to have a discussion. Try to find more about Wang Ting's troubles, and give more useful suggestions.

【板书演示】

Grounds (Troubles)	Claim (Solutions)	Warrants
• be unhappy when a loved watch is broken	• ... (you can give solutions here)	• ...
• doesn't want to ruin the friendship with her best friend	• try to accept the apology and forgive her best friend	• Friendship is something to be treasured.

■ 教师引导学生开展讨论, 从多个角度对王婷提出建议。

◇ Discuss with the group members and come up with more suggestions for Want Ting.

撰写提纲 Producing an Outline

■ 教师鼓励学生将讨论的内容按照图尔敏论证模型的三大要素列成提纲, 并邀请两位学生在黑板上书写提纲。

◇ Produce an outline using the Toulmin model of argumentation.

Grounds (Troubles)	Claim (Solutions)	Warrants

（续表）

Grounds (Troubles)	Claim (Solutions)	Warrants

■ 教师和学生一起探讨黑板上提纲初稿的修改，确保提纲中的主张（提议）是基于根据（困境）提出的，并确保保证能解释前两者之间的关系。同时，教师要帮助学生提升语言表达，并指出提纲中明显的语言错误。

◇ Revise the outline with the help of the teacher, make sure the claim is aligned with the grounds and try to avoid the mistakes the teacher has mentioned.

☆ *Possible outline:*

Grounds (Troubles)	Claim (Solutions)	Warrants
... worry that grandmother will find out and be upset	talk to your grandmother and she will surely understand	Communication is the best way to lighten the burden of the heart.
... sad that you can never wear the watch anymore	change your mindset about the loss of things	Nothing stays forever in life. Focus on the present.

提升效果 Adding the Impact

■ 教师引导学生表达情感上的同理心，可以在回信中表示已经了解王婷信中所说情况或提及自己的相似经历，以提升情感诉求和人格诉求。

◇ Express empathy by showing that you understand Wang Ting's situation or mentioning your own experiences, increasing *pathos* and *ethos* of the argument. The following are some examples.

e.g.

Showing understanding of the situation	• After reading your letter, I know you must be going through a hard time. The watch ... • I received your letter and it seems that you are troubled by ...

（续表）

Mentioning your own experiences	• It is natural that you are at a loss what to do. Honestly, I was once in a similar situation like you. • The same thing happened to me once. I was so upset that I shouted at my best friend.

聚焦语言 Focusing on Language

■ 教师鼓励学生用英文表达与友情相关的短语和句子。

◇ Try translating the following phrases and sentences related to friendship.

1）生闷气只会影响你的身体健康。	
2）好朋友来之不易。	
3）一段美好的友谊需要好好地培养和维持。	
4）友情是人生幸福最大的影响因素之一。	
5）没有人是完美的，有时冲突不可避免。	
6）弄清楚这个不愉快事件冲突的来源	
7）选一个双方都方便的地方来真诚地交心	
8）主动找朋友交谈	
9）沟通是促进理解、改善关系最好的方法。	
10）不要急于下结论。	
11）真诚地告诉朋友你的感受	
12）倾听朋友对这件事的思考角度	

☆ *Answers for reference:*

1) Carrying a grudge can only affect your physical well-being.

2) A good friend is hard to come by.

3) A beautiful friendship needs cultivating and maintaining.

4) Friendship is one of the biggest influences of happiness in our lives.

5) Nobody is perfect, and sometimes conflicts are inevitable.

6) clarify what is the source of conflict in this unpleasant incident

7) arrange a place that is mutually agreeable and convenient to have a sincere conversation

8) make the first move to start a conversation with your friend

9) Communication is the best way to facilitate understanding and improve relationship.

10) Don't rush to any conclusions straight away.

11) genuinely share how you feel with your friend

12) listen to your friend's perspective on what happened

组织布局 Designing the Layout

■ 教师给出参考布局格式，提示学生写初稿时应注意该写作话题的要求：陈述问题，提出方案，给出理由。

◇ Write the draft with the reference layout shown below. Note that your draft should include stating the problem, proposing suggestions, and giving reasons.

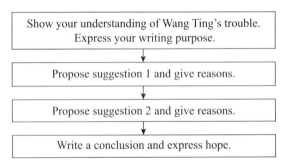

互动评价 Evaluating the Drafts

■ 教师鼓励学生依据评价量表进行自我评价或同伴互评。

◇ Evaluate the drafts in pairs or in groups with the following checklist.

（请参见本书理论篇第四章第四节政策型议论文评价清单样例，选取合适的维度，鼓励学生围绕习作初稿开展自评与互评。）

分享范文 Sharing the Samples

■ 教师分享优秀范文，供学生交流、评价、学习。
◇ Read the sample writings of your classmates and learn from them.

Dear Wang Ting,

After reading your letter, I have learned what troubles you. The watch is a birthday gift from your grandmother, which clearly has emotional value to you. But the person who broke it is your best friend, and you clearly don't want that to ruin your friendship. Honestly, I was once in a similar situation like you, so I hope my suggestions can be of some help to you.

First, if your friend broke the watch accidentally and apologized to you, the best solution is to accept her apology and try to forgive her. After all, having a strong friendship with someone that you grow up with can be more valuable than any piece of jewelry. Without forgiveness, you can never nurture any relationship. However, if your friend broke the watch on purpose, maybe you should reconsider your friendship with her.

Second, you must be unhappy because you are unable to wear the watch any more, but I suggest you change your mindset. The important thing is not the watch, but the memories and connections between your grandmother and you, which I am sure still remain. Remember nothing is going to stay in your life forever. You have to learn to accept the loss of loved things or even loved ones, and hold on to what is important right now, like your friendship.

I hope you will free yourself from this unhappy incident and focus on the happy moments in your friendship. Live in the moment.

◇ Write down what you have learned from this sample writing.

 教师点评

　　这篇政策型议论文结构完整，完成了写作话题的要求。第一段表达了对王婷烦恼的理解，并说明来信理由，第二段和第三段分别给出两个解决方案，最后一段表达了祝愿和希望。作者使用了 After reading your letter、First、Second 和 I hope... 等段落转折语，过渡自然流畅。

　　从内容上看，作者对王婷的困境进行了合理的分析，第一段就点出了她困惑的主要内容，即一方面心痛于手表的毁坏，另一方面又不想破坏友情。并且，作者还表示自己曾有过类似的处境，提升了情感诉求和人格诉求。接下来，在建议提出的过程中，作者逻辑思路清晰。首先，针对不想破坏友情这一条，作者建议王婷原谅朋友，给出的保证是友情难得，而原谅是维护友情的必经之路；其次，作者点出王婷对手表毁坏的不舍，建议她转换思维，给出的保证是手表坏了不代表记忆没了，人应该向前看。

　　从语言上看，作者所用词汇都较为精准：在开篇时，用到了 has emotional value to you、ruin your relationship，点明了王婷心中的困惑所在；在提出建议时，使用了 the best solution is to ... 以及 I suggest that ... 等提建议的相关句型，在描述具体建议时所用的动宾结构也表意准确，如 try to forgive her、change your mindset、memories and connections remain。此外，整篇习作的语气体现出一个耐心的、善于开导人的校报编辑形象，比如为了使语言更柔和，作者使用了 honestly、after all、maybe、must be、which I am sure、you have to 等。

尝试相似话题 Suggested Writing Prompts

写作话题	学校图书馆打算购买一批新书，正在考虑如何处理旧书。写一封信给图书馆管理员，提出你的建议和理由。

写作话题 14　募捐策划

学习目标汇总 Learning Objectives

Can-do statements

By the end of this session, students will be able to say:

- I can analyze the needs of those who request proposals.
- I can apply the Toulmin Model to produce an outline for an argument of policy, aligning needs with solutions.
- I can write a proposal for a school fundraising day with clear reasoning.

Thinking focus	Expression focus	Style focus
Logos: The relationship between grounds and warrants in proposal writing *Pathos:* Using detailed description and visualization techniques	**About fundraising activities:** *bring unwanted secondhand items for sale, sell tickets to the talent show, collect student artworks*	**Positive and supportive tone**

准备开始写作 Preparing to Write

　　前三个政策型议论文写作案例涉及的"政策"都属于笼统建议,比如建议班主任开一个班会、建议居委会找专人清理垃圾等,但班会怎么开、垃圾如何清理就属于另一种类型的政策型议论,即策划书,涉及具体政策的提出。之前,针对"问题解决型"议论文,我们作了原因分析(cause analysis);针对"困境应对型"议论文,我们作了"烦恼分析"(trouble analysis)。而对于策划书,作者必须了解待策划活动各参与方的需求,也就是要进行需求分析(need analysis),这样才能设计出好的活动方案,教师可以在导入时帮助学生明确这一点。

■ 教师以身边的例子引导学生思考如何写策划书。

◇ Think about how to write an activity plan and answer the teacher's questions.

【课堂再现】

T: Today, we are going to write on a new type of argument of policy—activity plan. Charles, as monitor of the class, you often take on the task of planning a class meeting, right?

S1: Yes.

T: Could you tell us how you usually make a plan? What is the first step?

S1: Well, I have to know what the class meeting is about, the theme of the class meeting.

T: OK. How about the one we talked about in previous writing lessons, "How to deal with failure"?

S1: Then first, I have to know what my classmates want from the class meeting.

T: Like what?

S1: Like ... like they want to find ways to relax themselves when meeting with possible failures.

T: (Writing what S1 says on the blackboard) Good. You have to know what your classmates want or need, right? That is, to make a good activity plan, you have to do "need analysis" first. (Writing on the blackboard) Then you can plan the activity according to your classmates' needs, right?

S1: Yes. And sometimes, I also need to consider what the class teacher wants. I think the class teacher wants us to understand that failure doesn't equal lack of ability and so on.

T: I see. You need to consider the needs from everyone involved in the class meeting. (Writing on the blackboard) Then, could you tell me what kind of activities will be disliked by your classmates? In other words, what they don't need?

S1: I would say my classmates don't like preaching from the class teacher. Whenever we plan a class meeting, we will try to make the activities fun as well as educational.

T: (Writing what S1 says on the blackboard) I see. So bear in mind, when you propose a plan, you should first think about what everyone wants or needs from the activity. Also, you should think about what they don't want or don't need, which is what you should avoid when proposing a plan.

【板书演示】

Need Analysis

YES   NO

find ways to relax themselves

failure doesn't equal lack of ability   No preaching from the class teacher

了解写作话题 Understanding the Prompt

写作话题	你们学校和社区孤儿院是结对单位，最近学校打算发起"孤儿募捐日"（a fundraising day for orphans）活动。作为学生会的一员，写一份活动策划书供校方参考，提出募捐日当天活动的详细安排，并给出理由。

■ 教师要求学生仔细读题，然后围绕写作话题具体内容提问，确保每个学生都理解写作话题的要求。

◇ Think and answer the following questions.

1）What is the purpose of this writing?

2）What is your identity as the writer?

3）Who is the target reader?

4）What tone and voice should be used?

5）Could you use one sentence to sum up what you are going to write?

I am going to _____

_____.

☆ *Answers for reference:*

1) The writing purpose is to offer a possible plan for the fundraising day.

2) "I" am a member of the Student Union.

3) The target reader is the school authorities. Other members of the Student Union may be the target readers as well.

4) The tone should be standard. The voice should sound like a resourceful and cooperative member of the Student Union.

5) I am going to write an activity plan to the school authorities, introduce the activities I want to design and give reasons.

搭建思维模型 Constructing the Model

■ 教师启发学生思考募捐活动的各方有怎样的需求。

◇ Think about the needs of all parties involved in the fundraising activities.

【课堂再现】

T: After reading the topic, what do you think is the purpose of the fundraising activities? What does everyone want or need from the activities?

S1: I think as the name suggests, the school needs to raise as much money as possible for the orphans.

T: Yes, that's obviously the biggest need. (Writing on the blackboard) Anything else? How about the director of the orphanage?

S2: I think he/she wants to know what the school has done for the orphanage.

S3: Right. And since this is a kind deed and has some social influence, the school will want to publicize it.

T: (Writing on the blackboard) Yes, I agree. Then what about students? What do they need?

S3: Last year, when I donated to earthquake victims, I received a certificate. I think for this fundraising day, students will also want something to commemorate the important event, like a souvenir.

T: (Writing on the blackboard) Good. So much for the "YES" part. What about the "NO" part? What should be avoided when you design the activities?

S4: I think the students don't want to be forced to give money. We want the activities to be fun.

T: Right, that's an important point. Now you can go on analyzing the needs with your group members and come up with as many activities as possible based on the needs.

【板书演示】

Need Analysis

YES	NO
School: raise as much money as possible	not forced to give money
School: publicize the good deeds	
Orphanage: know what the school did	...
Students: a certificate or a souvenir	

...

■ 教师引导学生讨论并思考募捐日可能的活动方案。

◇ Discuss with the group members and come up with as many ideas for the fundraising day as possible.

【课堂再现】

（After the discussion）

T: So what activities does your group come up with?

S1: We think at the beginning of the fundraising event, an opening speech should be given by the school headmaster.

T:（Writing on the blackboard）Why an opening speech?

S1: According to our need analysis, the school wants to publicize the big event, and the director of the orphanage also wants to know how the fundraising is going. So we think the school should invite the director of the orphanage and some journalists. Then the headmaster can give an opening speech to welcome everyone and call on everyone to donate.

T: Good. An opening speech is an inspiring way to welcome all the friends and publicize the event. That's arguing from consequences.（Writing on the blackboard）So we have the ground and the warrant. Then after the opening speech, what activity would you like to plan?

S1: We think in order to collect as much money as possible, each class in the school should contribute. So a talent show competition is a good idea. Each class prepares a performance and the class that attracts the biggest sum of donations wins.

T: That's interesting. Indeed, students all want their own class to win, right? That's arguing from principles. So we have the warrant. (Writing on the blackboard) Now you can try putting your ideas into an outline. I am sure each group has come up with some unique activities. Also bear in mind that the activities you propose should be feasible.

【板书演示】

Grounds (Needs)	Claim of Policy	Warrants
• publicize the event ...	• An opening speech should be given by ...	• A speech is the most inspiring way to welcome friends and convey the meaning of the event.
• collect as much money as possible for the orphans	• A talent show competition should be held.	• Students all want their own class to win, so the rule of the competition makes sure that each class contributes.

撰写提纲 Producing an Outline

■ 教师鼓励学生将讨论的内容按照图尔敏论证模型的三大要素列成提纲，并邀请两位学生在黑板上书写提纲。

◇ Produce an outline using the Toulmin model of argumentation.

Grounds (Needs)	Claim (Activities)	Warrants

■ 教师和学生一起探讨黑板上提纲初稿的修改，确保提纲中的主张（活动提议）是基于根据（需求）提出的，并确保保证能解释前两者之间的关系。同时，教师要帮助学生提升语言表达，并指出提纲中明显的语言错误。

◇ Revise the outline with the help of the teacher, make sure the claim is aligned with the grounds and try to avoid the mistakes the teacher has mentioned.

☆ *Possible outline:*

Grounds (Needs)	Claim (Activities)	Warrants
publicize the event ...	An opening speech should be given.	A speech is the most inspiring way to call on everyone to donate.
The school collects as much money as possible & students want something to commemorate the event	A charity sale should be held and the buyer receives a souvenir.	Selling second-hand items is a common and effective way to bring in donation.
	A contest for teachers should be held (students support their favourite teacher by donating).	Students love to see their teachers compete and support their teachers with money.
Orphans need to know our love for them.	Card-sending ceremony should be held.	The hand-made card is a heartwarming gesture from the students to convey their love.

提升效果 Adding the Impact

■ 教师鼓励学生尽量详细描述所提议的活动，以增加画面感，调动读者的想象力，提升议论的情感诉求。

◇ Describe the proposed activities in detail and allow the readers to visualize the activities, increasing the *pathos* of the argument. The following is an example.

e.g. The activity is called "Skills Auction". Every class prepares at least three sets of skills or services (like solving math problems or cleaning windows) and displays them on the auction stage. Other classes or teachers can bid for the skills or services, which go to the highest bidder.

聚焦语言 Focusing on Language

■ 教师鼓励学生用英文表达与校园募捐活动相关的短语和句子。

◇ Try translating the following phrases and sentences related to school fundraising event.

1）鼓励学生把自己不再需要的二手物品带来出售	
2）获胜的班级可以得到一个月不用穿校服的奖励。	
3）售卖"才艺秀"门票并邀请家长参与	
4）家中自制的饮料和点心	
5）邀请校友表演节目并参与捐赠	
6）收集全校学生的画作和艺术品组成艺术画廊，老师和学生可以竞拍艺术画廊中的作品	
7）参与该活动的同学都将获得神秘大奖。	
8）准备一组智力竞猜题，并将参与者分成几个队伍	
9）学生可以锻炼领导力，加强团队合作，提升创新力和自信。	

☆ *Answers for reference:*

1) encourage students to bring unwanted second-hand items for sale

2) The class that wins can receive a prize of wearing their own clothes for a month.

3) sell tickets to the talent show and invite parents to attend

4) homemade drinks and refreshments

5) invite the alumni to give performances and take part in the donation

6) collect the drawings and artworks from all the students to form an art gallery. Teachers and students can bid on the works in the gallery.

7) The students that participate in this activity will receive a big mystery prize.

8) prepare a list of quiz questions and divide the participants into several teams

9) Students can practise leadership skills, strengthen teamwork, enhance creativity and boost confidence.

组织布局 Designing the Layout

■ 教师给出参考布局格式,提示学生写初稿时应注意该写作话题的要求:提出募捐日当天活动的详细安排,并给出理由。

◇ Write the draft with the reference layout shown below. Note that your draft should include your suggestions for the fundraising day activities and the reasons for suggesting them.

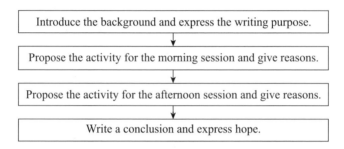

互动评价 Evaluating the Drafts

■ 教师鼓励学生依据评价量表进行自我评价或同伴互评。

◇ Evaluate the drafts in pairs or in groups with the following checklist.

（请参见本书理论篇第四章第四节政策型议论文评价清单样例,选取合适的维度,鼓励学生围绕习作初稿开展自评与互评。）

分享范文 Sharing the Samples

■ 教师分享优秀范文,供学生交流、评价、学习。

◇ Read the sample writings of your classmates and learn from them.

> Hearing that a fundraising event for orphans is going to be held by our school soon, I have come up with some ideas and I'd like to share with you. The following is my plan.

As the fundraising is a big event in the local community, I suggest that the school invite the director of the orphanage and give an opening speech at the beginning of the day. The speech will serve as a welcome to everyone and a way to communicate our love to the orphans.

After the opening speech, I propose an activity called "Teacher Charity Game", in which the teachers compete with each other on certain competitions or sports games. Students can support their favourite teacher by scanning the QR code and donating money. I am sure this activity will generate great excitement among students because we are all eager to see our teachers' performance.

In the afternoon, there will be a "Garden Party" for all students to participate in. For the party, each class in the school prepares a challenge in their stall, which aims to drive students to reach into their pockets and donate. All students have to take at least 10 challenges before getting a souvenir box. The class which receives the largest sum of donations wins a mystery prize. In this way, every class will rack their brains in order to win the big prize.

At the end of the day, a closing ceremony should be held. The headmaster can give a concluding remark on the day and if possible, share with everyone the sum of money raised during the day. This will increase students' sense of achievement and also make the event more meaningful.

The above is my plan. If you are interested in my idea, please let me know. I can offer more details. I wish the fundraising day a complete success.

◇ Write down what you have learned from this sample writing.

 **教师点评**

这份策划书结构完整，完成了写作话题的要求。第一段说明了背景和来信目的，第二段到第五段按照时间顺序分别给出四个活动提议，涵盖了一天的活动内容，最后一段表达了诚意和期待。作者使用了时间标记词（at the beginning of the day, after the opening speech, in the afternoon, at the end of the day）来标记段落之间的转折，使整篇习作流畅自然。

从内容上看，作者设计的活动针对性强，可见其对活动的需求分析很清晰，比如第一个活动"开幕演讲"就是针对"the fundraising is a big event in the local community"这一需求而设计的，之后的两个活动虽然未写明所针对的需求，但从作者的描述和分析中可以看出，这两个活动都能有效引起学生的兴趣，从而鼓励他们进行捐赠。同时，每个活动开展的合理性都在保证中予以说明，逻辑清晰。此外，作者在描述活动时具体说明了活动的操作，让读者脑海中有画面感，提升了议论的情感诉求。

从语言上看，作者提出四个活动所用的句型都不一样，如 As ..., I suggest that; After ..., I propose ...; In the afternoon, there will be ...; at the end of the day, ... should be ...。在用词方面，作者使用的动宾短语搭配准确且地道，如 invite the director、serve as a welcome、scan the QR code、generate excitement、win a prize、rack their brains 等。在语调方面，作者在开篇用到了分词作状语，表述"the following is my plan"较为正式。在结尾时，作者作出较为正式的总结，提出期望的句子也很有礼貌。在语气方面，从作者的活动创意可以看出其足智多谋，并且在最后一段，作者提出与校方进一步合作的意愿，其乐于合作的形象也跃然纸上。

尝试相似话题 Suggested Writing Prompts

写作话题	学校打算开展"美丽校园日"（Cleaner Campus Day）活动。作为学生会的一员，写一份活动策划书供校方参考，提出"美丽校园日"当天活动的详细安排，并给出理由。

第九章　驳论文教学案例

写作话题 15　方案讨论

学习目标汇总 Learning Objectives

Can-do statements

By the end of this session, students will be able to say:

- I can understand the two steps of developing counter-argument, attacking the original argument and stating my own claim.
- I can apply the Toulmin Model to come up with an attacking strategy.
- I can write a counter-argument to express my objection and raise suggestions.

Thinking focus	Expression focus	Function focus
Logos: Ways of developing counter-argument *Ethos:* Establishing understanding and familiarity of the issue	**About the design of newspapers:** *publication schedule, well-received among students, print copies*	**Introducing areas for improvement:** *I don't think it reasonable, my main opposition to the plan is ..., ... leave much to be desired* **Introducing alternative suggestions:** *If I were to design the sections, I propose that ...*

准备开始写作 Preparing to Write

日常生活中，除了提出正向建议之外，人们也会遇到反对意见，比如当某团体为某一方案征求意见时，我们可能需要提出不同的看法，这就涉及驳论文写作（counter-argument）。根据理论篇第五章的分析，驳论文一般由两部分组成：首先指出对方观点错误的实质，继而提出自己的观点并加以论证。而指出对方观点错误的前提是要分析对方观点中的漏洞，也就是分析对方观点中的根据和保证，再针对根据或保证进行合理的质疑，教师可以在导入活动中帮助学生明确这一点。

■ 教师以身边的例子引导学生思考如何开展驳论文写作。

◇ Answer the teacher's questions and think about how to write a counter-argument.

【课堂再现】

T: Having learned so much about arguments, today we are going to write a piece of counter-argument. (Writing on the blackboard) Do you know what a counter-argument is?

All: No.

T: Well, suppose the school is going to introduce a monthly exam policy, will you support the policy?

S1: No, definitely not.

T: Then you want to write a letter to the school authorities to express your objection against this policy. That's a counter-argument. Here, "counter-" means "opposing something". Understand?

S1: I see.

T: So if you are going to write this counter-argument, objecting to the policy of the monthly exams, where would you start?

S2: Well, we already have the mid-term and the final. If we are going to have monthly exams, the exams will be too many for us to bear.

T: But more exams can urge you to study more and help you improve your grades. (Writing on the blackboard) How would you argue against that?

S2: Well, it is not true. More exams don't necessarily mean good grades. And it might even bring the opposite effect. Some students might be more anxious and give up studying entirely.

T: Good. Actually, you are attacking the ground of the argument. (Writing on the blackboard) Also let me give you a hint. You can also attack the warrant. So can someone tell me the warrant for the argument? Does it argue from consequences or principles?

S3: Consequences. It assumes that improved grades can benefit students.

T: Good. (Writing on the blackboard) It assumes improved grades can bring good consequences by helping students get admitted to better universities, right? So do you think you can attack the warrant?

S3: I think it's hard to attack the warrant since it is a bit like common sense. But I want to say students can also benefit without monthly exams because we will have less pressure.

T: You have mentioned something very important. If we can't attack the warrant, we can accept the warrant and bring in a new point. (Writing on the blackboard) That is, less pressure also benefits students. Now you are actually comparing the two and see which one brings greater benefits to students. You see that?

S3: I get it. Obviously healthy body is more important than good grades.

T: Right, you can put that in your writing. So when writing a counter-argument, you should first identify the flaws in the original argument and the flaws might be with the ground or with the warrant. Then, attack the flaws directly. If you cannot find any flaws, you can offer a new perspective that outweighs the argument of the other side, like what we did just now—a healthy body is more important than academic achievements. After that, you can state your own claim and support it. (Writing on the blackboard)

【板书演示】

Argument	Counter-argument
Claim: We should have monthly exams.	1. Attacking (1) Attacking the ground More exams don't mean good grades.

（续表）

Argument	Counter-argument
Ground: Monthly exams can help improve students' grades by urging them to study more. Warrant: Improved grades will benefit students by helping them get into better universities.	(2) Accepting the warrant and introducing a new point It is true that … But less pressure also benefits students. 2. Stating your own claim We shouldn't have monthly exams. Ground: No monthly exams can relieve students' anxiety. Warrant: A healthy body weighs more than anything.

不论师生对话如何展开，该环节的关键是让学生意识到以下几点：

（1）什么是驳论文写作；

（2）驳论文写作的第一步是找出对方观点中的漏洞，可以质疑根据，也可以质疑保证；

（3）如果对方的根据和保证中确实有漏洞，可直接指出；如果没有，可先承认对方观点的合理性，然后从一个新的角度驳斥对方。

了解写作话题 Understanding the Prompt

写作话题	学生会打算成立一个英语报社，定期发行英语校报（目前的计划如下所示），并向全校同学征求意见。写一封信给学生会，提出你的意见和建议，并给出理由。	
	主要版面	时事头条（Current Events）、娱乐新闻（Entertainment News）、好书导读（Book Guide）、校园生活（Campus Life）、备考专练（Test Prep）
	发行时间	每周五
	发行量	每班 5 张

■ 教师要求学生仔细读题，然后围绕写作话题具体内容提问，确保每个学生都理解写作话题的要求。

◇ Think and answer the following questions.

1）What is the purpose of this writing?

2）Who is the target reader?

3）What tone and voice should be used?

4）Could you use one sentence to sum up what you are going to write?

I am going to _____

_____.

☆ *Answers for reference:*

1) The writing purpose is to offer suggestions on how to improve the launch plan of the school English newspaper.

2) The target reader is the member of the Student Union who is in charge of launching the English newspaper.

3) The tone should be standard. The voice should sound like a student who is genuinely concerned about the future of the newspaper.

4) I am going to write a letter of suggestion to the Student Union to help improve the launch plan of the school English newspaper.

搭建思维模型 Constructing the Model

■ 教师启发学生思考英语校报方案中不合理的地方，并提出合理的改进建议。

◇ Think about the areas for improvement and propose alternative plans for the launch of the school English newspaper.

【课堂再现】

T: After reading the plan, what areas do you think need to be improved?

S1: I think the Entertainment News section should be removed.

T: Why?

S1: Because students will talk about the celebrities even more, which might distract us from studies.

T: But why do you think they added this section in the first place?

S1: Maybe they think the section can offer students some interesting stories about celebrities, which can help us relax.

T: Yes, the relaxation can benefit students who are already burdened with the academic load, right? So we have the ground and the warrant of the original argument. (Writing on the blackboard) Then how can we attack them? Remember we can improve the power of the counter-argument by attacking the ground or the warrant of the original argument.

S2: I think I want to attack the warrant. This kind of relaxation doesn't benefit students. On the contrary, too much gossip about celebrities may distract students.

T: Good. So do you have any suggestion to replace the section?

S2: Let me think.

S3: I have an idea. I believe the newspaper can publish some news about technology.

T: Why?

S3: Technology is innovating so rapidly today, so this section can give students information about the cutting-edge technology.

T: (Writing on the blackboard) But how can it benefit students?

S3: It can broaden students' horizon and even motivate their study in the science subjects.

T: Good. (Writing on the blackboard) So we have one counter-argument. Now you can discuss with your deskmates and find more areas for improvement.

【板书演示】

Areas for improvement	Counter-argument
The Entertainment News section Ground: Entertainment news offers some interesting stories about celebrities, which can help students relax. Warrant: Relaxation can benefit students ...	1. Attacking the warrant Two much gossip will not benefit students, but cause distraction. 2. Stating your own claim We can add Technology News section. Ground: Technology innovates rapidly, and the section can give info about cutting-edge technology. Warrant: broaden the horizon ...

撰写提纲 Producing an Outline

■ 教师鼓励学生将正反双方的观点列成提纲，并邀请两位学生在黑板上书写提纲。

◇ Produce an outline covering "Areas for Improvement" and "Counter-argument".

Areas for improvement	Counter-argument
Ground: Warrant:	1. Attacking the ground/warrant (or accepting the warrant and introducing a new point) 2. Stating your own Claim Ground: Warrant:

■ 教师和学生一起探讨黑板上提纲初稿的修改，确保相反意见提出的合理性。同时，教师要帮助学生提升语言表达，并指出提纲中明显的语言错误。

◇ Revise the outline with the help of the teacher, make sure the counter-argument is reasonable and try to avoid the mistakes the teacher has mentioned.

☆ *Possible outline:*

Areas for improvement	Counter-argument
The Test Prep section Ground: Test Prep section provides more exercises for students. Warrant: help students improve their grades	1. Accepting the warrant and introducing a new point Although it can help students improve grades, it adds to their burden. 2. Stating your own claim We can add Career Planning section. Ground: offer career info and advice Warrant: benefit students who have no idea what to do in the future

（续表）

Areas for improvement	Counter-argument
The number of copies is low. Ground: The budget is limited. Warrant: The school newspaper is free of charge and not for profit.	1. Accepting the ground and introducing a new point Although it's true that the budget is limited, the newspaper cannot achieve its intended purpose. 2. Stating your own claim We can increase the print copies for each class by obtaining funds. Ground: The main cause for the limited copies is lack of funds. Warrant: ... reach a larger audience and achieve the purpose

提升效果 Adding the Impact

■ 教师鼓励学生尽量表现出对周围同学关于校报需求的了解，提升话语的可信度。

◇ Show your understanding of students' concern and needs about the school English newspaper, increasing the *ethos* of the argument. The following is an example.

e.g. I know most of my classmates are eagerly anticipating the launch of the new English newspaper and many of them will have English articles published on it. Therefore, they will each wish to obtain a copy of the English newspaper.

聚焦语言 Focusing on Language

■ 从词到句：教师让学生通过翻译补全下列句子，来丰富有关改进建议的表达。

◇ From words to sentences: Try making the following sentences about alternative suggestions complete by translating the Chinese into English.

1) _____ （如果我来设计报纸版面），I _____ （将替换）"Entertainment News" with "Technology News".

2）_____（如果英语校报想要实现预定的
目标），_____（我提议）that the newspaper should be
made available to each of the students.

3）_____（为了使报纸的影响力最
大化），I _____（建议更改出版时间）to
a different day.

4）_____（因此），I suggest removing Test Prep section.

☆ *Answers for reference:*

1）If I were to design the sections / Were it left to me to design the
sections; would replace

2）If the school English newspaper is to achieve its intended purpose; I
propose

3）In order to maximize the impact of the newspaper; I suggest changing
the publication day

4）Therefore

■ 从句到段：教师让学生尝试将提纲内容连接起来，写成一段话。

◇ From sentences to paragraphs: Try connecting different parts of the outline
to form a short paragraph.

The number of copies is low. Ground: The budget is limited. Warrant: The school newspaper is free of charge and not for profit.	1. Accepting the ground and introducing a new point Although it's true that the budget is limited, the newspaper cannot achieve its intended purpose. 2. Stating your own claim We can increase the print copies for each class by obtaining funds. Ground: The main cause for the limited copies is lack of funds. Warrant: ... reach a larger audience and achieve the purpose

_____

_____

_____

_____

_____

☆ *Answers for reference:*

I understand that the budget is limited, so you can only afford to print five copies for each class. However, such a limited number will not help the newspaper achieve its intended purpose. Therefore, I suggest increasing the number of copies by raising funds from outside the school. In this way, the new English newspaper can reach a larger audience.

Other ways of accepting the original argument and introducing a new point besides "I understand ...":

- While it is true that the budget is limited, the number of five copies is simply unacceptable.
- Although it is intended to save money for the school, such a small number may fail to bring benefit to a large group of students.
- The limited copy is understandable since the newspaper is not for profit, but the number of five copies is too small to make a meaningful impact.
- I assume you want to run the newspaper at the lowest cost. Nevertheless, with only five copies per class, the newspaper's influence will be minimal.

组织布局 Designing the Layout

■ 教师给出参考布局格式，提示学生写初稿时应注意该写作话题的要求：对英语校报发行计划提出意见和建议，并给出理由。

◇ Write the draft with the reference layout shown below. Note that your draft should include offering suggestions for the launch plan of the school English newspaper and the reasons for suggesting them.

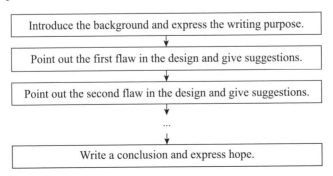

Introduce the background and express the writing purpose.
↓
Point out the first flaw in the design and give suggestions.
↓
Point out the second flaw in the design and give suggestions.
↓
...
Write a conclusion and express hope.

■ 教师给出以下开头段落的句型，为学生提供合适的语言参考。

◇ Try making the following sentences complete by translating the Chinese into English to introduce the background and the purpose of writing.

交代背景	1）_____（我很激动）to hear that an English newspaper will be launched in our school. 2）The news that a school English newspaper is going to be launched _____（确实使我们很兴奋）. 3）The plan for the school English newspaper _____（引发了热烈讨论/争论）among my classmates. 4）Since the release of the plan for the launch of the English newspaper, my classmates _____（加入了对此热烈的讨论中）.
表明目的	1）Hearing you are seeking for suggestions on the plan, I _____（迫不及待给你写信）. 2）Having reviewed the plan, I believe _____（要做出一些调整）to improve its popularity among students. 3）As you are collecting feedback on the plan, I _____（想提出一些建议）. 4）I am writing to _____（给出一些有关该计划必要的微调建议）.

☆ *Answers for reference:*

交代背景	1) I am excited/thrilled 2) does excite each and every one of us 3) have sparked heated debates / generated great controversy / has given rise to heated arguments 4) have engaged / joined in spirited/passionate conversations about it
表明目的	1) can't wait to write to you 2) some adjustments should be made 3) would like to put forward my suggestions 4) offer my suggestions on some necessary modifications to the plan

■ 教师给出以下引出需改进地方的句型，为段落转折提供合适的语言参考。

◇ Learn the following sentence patterns to help with the transitions between paragraphs.

引出 需改 进地 方	1）As far as I am concerned, ＿＿＿＿＿＿＿＿（我认为是不合理的）to include Entertainment News column. 2）＿＿＿＿＿＿＿＿（我对该方案主要的反对）is the publishing day of each week. 3）In my opinion, the design of the columns ＿＿＿＿＿＿＿＿（需要重新考虑）. 4）＿＿＿＿＿＿＿＿（就……而言）the design of the columns, the majority of students think it ＿＿＿＿＿＿＿＿（有很大提升空间）. 5）＿＿＿＿＿＿＿＿（当提及）the publication day, Friday ＿＿＿＿＿＿＿＿＿＿＿＿（不合适）. 6）＿＿＿＿＿＿＿＿（至于）the number of copies distributed to each class, I ＿＿＿＿＿＿＿＿（我觉得是不够的）.

☆ *Answers for reference:*

1) I don't think it reasonable

2) My main opposition/objection to the plan

3) calls for reconsideration

4) In terms of; leaves much/plenty to be desired

5) When it comes to; is not appropriate / is a poor decision

6) As to / As regards; find it insufficient

互动评价 Evaluating the Drafts

■ 教师鼓励学生依据评价量表进行自我评价或同伴互评。

◇ Evaluate the drafts in pairs or in groups with the following checklist.

Aspects		Guiding questions	√ / ×
Organization	Introduction and conclusion	• Does the writing have an opening and closing statement?	
	Transitions	• Does the writing use transitions to get from one paragraph to the next?	
	Paragraph unity	• Does each paragraph address one point?	

（续表）

Aspects		Guiding questions	√ / ×
Content	*Logos*	• Does the writing identify the flaws of the original argument? • Does the writing present an alternative that is logically stronger than the original one? • Is the alternative plan supported by the ground and warrant?	
	Ethos	• Does the author show his/her understanding of students' concern and needs for the school English newspaper?	
Language	Word choice and sentence variety	• Does the author use precise vocabulary and varied sentence patterns to attack the point of the other side and propose suggestions?	
	Cohesion and coherence	• Does the writing use proper connectives and clauses to create coherence within a paragraph?	
	Tone and voice	• Does the author sound like a student who is concerned about the future of the newspaper?	
	Convention/ CUPS	• Are there errors in capitalization, usage, punctuation, and spelling (CUPS)?	

分享范文 Sharing the Samples

■ 教师分享优秀范文，供学生交流、评价、学习。

◇ Read the sample writings of your classmates and learn from them.

> Dear Student Union,
>   The news that a school English newspaper will be launched

excites me greatly. But having reviewed the proposed plan, I believe some adjustments should be made to help the newspaper become better-received among students.

The design of the columns, in my opinion, leaves much to be desired. I highly doubt the necessity of including "Test Prep" column in the school English newspaper. Although it is intended to help students with their grades, it only serves to add to students' study load. If I were to design the column, I would replace "Test Prep" with "Career Planning". I know that a large number of my classmates have no idea what they truly want to become in the future. That will cause significant difficulties when we apply for college majors. With "Career Planning" section, we will gain a better understanding of the qualities required for different jobs and figure out our life goals. Therefore, "Career Planning" is much more meaningful than "Test Prep".

As to the publication schedule, I believe Friday is a poor decision. I assume you want students to make use of their weekends to read the newspaper since we have more spare time then. However, only five newspapers are distributed to each class, so this advantage is only available to five students. Therefore, I suggest moving the publication day to Monday, when all students in the class can have a full week to read the newspaper.

The above are my suggestions for the adjustments. I would really appreciate it if you could take my proposal into consideration. Wish the launch of the newspaper a great success.

◇ Write down what you have learned from this sample writing.

教师点评

这篇习作针对英语校报的发行计划给出了合理的意见和建议。习作结构完整，第一段交代了写作背景和来信目的，第二段和第三段分别指出方案的不足之处，并给出替代建议，最后一段总结了上文，并表达了对方案采纳的希望。第二段和第三段开头分别用到了 in my opinion 和 As to 作为转折，使读者能够较为容易地看出作者的写作意图，跟上作者的思路。

从内容上看，作者对现有方案的不合理之处有着明确的认知。对于两点不合理的地方，作者均采用了"先理解现有方案的意图，再提出新角度"的方法，对现有方案中的不足之处进行回击。在提出替代方案时，作者也给予了足够的根据和保证进行支撑。尤其是第二段提出的替代方案"职业规划"（career planning），其根据部分对学生的需求进行了较为详细的分析，并通过 I know that a large number of my classmates 提升了人格诉求，使读者相信这个提议是有效的。

从语言上看，作者在表达同一含义时使用了不同的句型。在引出方案中需要改进的地方时，作者分别用到了 sth leaves much to be desired 和 sth is a poor decision；在指出方案的不合理之处时，分别用到了 Although it is intended to ... 和 I assume that ...；在提出替代方案时，作者分别使用了 If I were to design the column, I would replace ... 以及 Therefore, I suggest moving ... 等，可见作者对句型的掌握程度。在语气语调方面，作者通过 excites me greatly、become better-received 和 With "Career Planning" section, we will gain ... 及 wish the launch of the newspaper a great success 等短语和句子呈现出一个热心校报发行的学生形象，读起来亲切自然。

尝试相似话题 Suggested Writing Prompts

写作话题	你得知你们学校附近将新建一个大型游乐场（amusement park），你感到十分不满。写一封信给有关部门，提出你的抗议，并给出理由。

结语

本书的理论篇和实践篇系统性地呈现了本套高中英语议论文写作教学课程的设计和实施，其整体思路为基于课标、立足教材、体现单元、重视情境。本课程构建了高中英语议论文写作的专项单元，融合国内多版本教材的议论语篇，充分链接学生生活，挖掘课程资源。在实施层面，本课程注重营造真实交际语境，确保教学活动贴近学生的实际生活经验与认知水平，以思维品质培养为抓手，以教学评一体化为导向，引导学生开展深度学习，并锻炼学生的问题解决能力。

一、高中英语议论文写作课程资源开发

本书上篇介绍了高中英语议论文写作的相关知识，下篇通过 15 个详细的教学案例呈现了如何序列化地开展高中英语议论文写作教学。在课程实施中，最关键的一个环节莫过于课程资源的开发。《普通高中英语课程标准》中提出"指向学生学科核心素养发展的英语教学应以主题意义为引领，以语篇为依托"[1]，语篇就是课程资源的重要组成部分，所有教学几乎都围绕语篇展开，可见课程资源的重要性。对英语教师来说，课程资源的开发也是日常教学积累的重要一环，既是理论体系的具体化，又体现了对教学实践经验的归纳和梳理。

课程资源根据功能特点，可以划分为素材性资源和条件性资源两大类。素材性资源的特点是作用于课程，并且能够成为课程的素材或来源，它是学生学习和收获的对象，比如教材、参考书等。而条件性资源的特点是作用于课程但并非形成课程本身的直接来源，不是学生学习和收获的直接对象，但它在很大程度上决定着课程的实施范围和水平，比如场地、设

---

[1] 中华人民共和国教育部.普通高中英语课程标准（2017 年版 2020 年修订）［M］.北京：人民教育出版社，2020：8.

备等。① 下面笔者将介绍开发高中英语议论文写作课程素材性资源可采用的几种方式。

（一）梳理教材语篇，搭建层次体系

为了使课程内容更具层次性和序列性，笔者在课程开发时浏览了国内五套高中英语教材——《英语》（沪教版）、《英语》（沪外教版）、《英语》（外研社版）、《英语》（牛津上海版）、《英语》（新世纪版），并按照事实型、价值型、政策型议论文及驳论文的分类对五套教材中的语篇进行了梳理，具体如下所示。需要注意的是，表格中提到的部分语篇并非全篇都属于议论文体裁，有的语篇只是部分语段或部分语句涉及议论。

1. 事实型议论文

教材版本	教材分册	单元	板块	语篇题目
沪教版	必修二	Unit 2	Writing	What are the arguments for and against school uniforms?
	选必二	Unit 2	Writing	The advantages and disadvantages of constant connection
沪外教版	选必三	Unit 4	Reading A	The Villain in the Atmosphere
外研社版	必修二	Unit 3	Understanding Ideas	A game for the world
	必修二	Unit 4	Developing Ideas	Good book, bad movie?
	选必一	Unit 4	Developing Ideas	Art and technology
	选必三	Unit 4	Understanding Ideas	Artificial Intelligence: A real threat?

---

① 吴刚平. 中小学课程资源开发和利用的若干问题探讨［J］. 全球教育展望，2009（3）：19-24.

2. 价值型议论文

教材版本	教材分册	单元	板块	语篇题目
沪教版	选必一	Unit 2	Writing	Support a charity
	选必三	Unit 1	Reading and Interaction	Making school meaningful
	选必四	Unit 2	Writing	Older people have a better quality of life than younger people
沪外教版	必修二	Unit 2	Reading A	Zoos: Cruel or Caring?
	必修三	Unit 4	Speaking and Writing	Sharing Views on Online and Traditional Classroom Learning
外研社版	必修一	Unit 2	Understanding Ideas	Neither pine nor apple in pineapple
	必修二	Unit 3	Using Language	DX sports watch
	必修二	Unit 6	Developing Ideas	What's really green?
	选必二	Unit 5	Developing Ideas	Why Shennongjia?
	选必四	Unit 1	Developing Ideas	Writing an application letter
牛津上海版	高一下	Unit 6	Reading	Point of view
	高二上	Unit 2	Reading	Tutorial centers
	高二下	Unit 1	Reading	What is beauty?
新世纪版	高三上	Unit 5	Additional Reading	What Is a Great Book?
	高三下	Unit 5	Additional Reading	A Successful Person in the 21st Century

3. 政策型议论文

教材版本	教材分册	单元	板块	语篇题目
沪教版	必修三	Unit 3	Writing	Dear teen tired of teasing

（续表）

教材版本	教材分册	单元	板块	语篇题目
沪教版	选必三	Unit 2	Cultural focus	Saved or stolen?
	选必三	Unit 3	Writing	The value of life
	选必四	Unit 3	Writing	Should people switch to a vegetarian diet?
沪外教版	必修二	Unit 2	Speaking and Writing	Feeding Homeless Cats
	必修三	Unit 3	Speaking and Writing	Leading a Healthy Life
	选必三	Unit 1	Writing	Writing a letter of advice on how to deal with a problem
	选必三	Unit 4	Writing	Writing a proposal letter for the Green Club
	选必四	Unit 3	Writing	Should historical buildings in the city be reconstructed or removed?
外研社版	选必二	Unit 6	Developing Ideas	Plan B: life on Mars?
	选必四	Unit 2	Understanding Ideas	Tuesdays with Morrie
新世纪版	高三上	Unit 4	Reading	One Person Can Make a Difference for Peace

4. 驳论文

教材版本	教材分册	单元	板块	语篇题目
沪教版	选必四	Unit 2	Writing	Older people have a better quality of life than younger people
沪外教版	选必二	Unit 2	Writing	Is English the Only Foreign Language Worth Learning?
牛津上海版	高三上	Unit 2	Reading	A woman's place is in the home?

从上表可以看出，高中英语教材中有不少语篇与议论文体相关，涵盖了必修和选择性必修课程。教师可以充分利用这些语篇资源，以议论文写作教学为实践内容，帮助学生学会客观理解、识别并提炼他人的观点和态度，分析人物和事件背后的隐含假设，有依据地开展反思和评价，并主动发表自身观点，发现、分析和解决问题，提升整体思维品质。

（二）积累课堂生成，调动交往资源

素材性资源还可以进一步分为外在物化载体和内在生命化载体：前者指承载课程知识、技能和其他信息的课程标准、教材、参考书、练习册、考试卷等文本以及相应的音像资料等，后者指的是师生在交往中形成的经验、感受、理解、创意、问题、困惑、方法、情感、态度、价值观等。[①]

在高中英语议论文写作课程资源开发的过程中，除了教材等外在物化载体资源，教师还应该着眼于内在生命化载体资源的调动。内在生命化载体资源往往来自师生交往、生生讨论碰撞出的信息。教师可以将学生在头脑风暴中的困惑、在黑板上书写的提纲、小组讨论得出的调查问卷、师生对话中出现的金句、共同探讨出的评价清单等积累下来，作为宝贵的生成性资源，用于下一步、下一节或下一届的课堂教学。比如写作话题11，为了让学生理解政策型议论文中"问题发现"的重要性，笔者设计了一个探究型任务，即让学生自由分组探讨班级中存在的真实问题。学生通过小组讨论找出了班级内部的很多问题。接下来，笔者鼓励各小组按照自己的假设设计调查问卷。随后，笔者再组织各小组进行交流，并实施问卷的发放、回收和数据统计。就这样，课程资源随着师生和生生的互动自然产生。事实上，这类通过课堂讨论、探究型活动、师生对话等形成的内在生命化载体资源恰恰是写作教学的灵魂所在，体现了师生之间、生生之间"活生生"的意义和情感交流。它与考试无关，与标准答案无关，是学生自发寻找真相、讨论解决方案、表达观点的过程。

因此，教师要注重内在生命化载体资源的建设和积累。在建设的过程中，教师不再是资源的提供者，而是资源的组织者、管理者、倾听者、处理者。并且，这类资源是动态的，和教材中的静态资源形成天然互补，更受学

[①] 吴刚平.中小学课程资源开发和利用的若干问题探讨[J].全球教育展望，2009（3）：19–24.

生欢迎，促使课程资源从浅表走向深刻，从无生命的教材走向有生命的人，体现课程资源的无限生机和丰富内涵，彰显写作教学的真正价值。

（三）重视学生生活，创设熟悉语境

写作是一种重要的交际模式，着眼于真实生活，最终也回归到生活。根据现代认知理论，认知主体不可能脱离其认知环境。在写作过程中，学生是认知主体，不可能超脱其周围的环境对自身的塑造[①]。设计符合学生认知环境的话题，也就是贴近学生生活的话题，能够帮助学生快速融入情境，让学生有话可说，有思想可表达，加深师生之间的交流。

因此，教师在开发课程资源时，还需要多关注学生在社会生活中的体验，不断挖掘生活素材，整合进自己的教学中，比如学生集体参与的校园活动、学生比较喜欢去的校外场所、学生关注的时事话题，甚至学生每天的衣食起居等，都有可能成为课程资源中宝贵的一部分。越贴近学生日常生活的写作话题，越能调动学生写作的积极性。

笔者在实施整个高中英语议论文写作课程的过程中，十分关注通过学生的生活体验来创设情境。比如写作话题6，为了让学生明白价值标准和选择对象的关系，笔者在课堂开始时就引出学生中午在食堂选菜的场景，引导学生思考选择或不选择某个菜的理由，从而顺利引出相关概念。在写作话题7中，笔者为了让学生更好地理解推荐信的本质，借助学生校园政治生活中的真实场景，即学生会主席换届选举，让学生在班级范围内推荐心目中的学生会主席候选人，学生果然很快进入写作构思状态。在写作话题10中，笔者为了激发学生对"什么是勇气"话题的思考，提供了五个生活中的情境，让学生进行讨论和判断，学生顿时兴趣盎然。在写作话题15中，笔者为了让学生更好地理解驳论文的概念，设计了学校准备增加月考项目的场景，使学生很快就理解了驳论文的要素构成。

写作需要素材和灵感支持，对于熟悉或喜欢的话题，写作者自然会产生更多的想法和灵感。源于学生生活的课程资源更遵循学生的心理发展特点，对思维开发大有裨益。与此同时，在贴近生活的讨论中，师生之间、生生之间能产生更多的思维碰撞，所得出的结论也能直接用于解决现实生活中的问题，从而真正达到写作交际目的。因此，教师在开发课程资源时，要

---

① 曲卫国. 微观层面的批判性思维和写作程序训练［J］. 中国外语，2006（2）：47-50.

学会从学生的生活中发现素材，将这些素材转化为写作的话题情境或师生对话的背景资源。

（四）利用多模态资源，丰富学生体验

《普通高中英语课程标准》强调，学校应鼓励有条件、有较强学科知识和教学能力的本校英语教师，充分利用校内外资源开发校本课程。[①] 就英语学习而言，大多数中国学生的学习资源并不充分。英语语料更新速度快，而英语教材编写周期长，更新慢，且受媒介形式所限，教材中非文字材料所占比例偏低。因此，英语教师一定要敢于突破教材的限制，合理构建课程资源的结构和功能[②]。

笔者在创设高中英语议论文写作课程资源的过程中，注重长期积累，努力寻找教材之外的非文字资源作为情境创设的媒介。比如在写作话题1中，笔者利用 *Crime and Puzzlement* [③] 一书中的侦探破案漫画引入图尔敏论证模型的三大基础要素。从课堂观察中可以发现，学生们在小组讨论中情绪高涨，即便平时对写作不那么感兴趣的学生都能沉浸其中，认真思考案件侦破的逻辑，并尽量用英语与小组成员进行交流。此外，笔者在日常议论文写作教学中还经常使用一些耳熟能详的广告图片，让学生分析这些广告想要表明的主张，以及根据和保证分别是什么。这些非文字材料的课堂教学效果有时要远远好于文字材料，不仅调动了学生的写作兴趣，也丰富了学生的生活体验。

非文字材料是设计活动时非常有效的教学资源。根据心理学家维果茨基（Vygotsky）的"最近发展区"理论，教学应该着眼于学生的最近发展区，也就是现有发展水平（指学生能独立完成问题解决）和潜在发展水平（指在成年人的指导下完成问题解决）之间的距离。[④] 非文字材料本身（比如图片）

---

① 中华人民共和国教育部.普通高中英语课程标准（2017 年版 2020 年修订）［M］.北京：人民教育出版社，2020：115–116.

② 程晓堂.课程改革背景下英语课程资源的开发和使用：问题与建议［J］.课程·教材·教法，2019（3）：96–101.

③ Treat L. Crime and Puzzlement: 24 Solve-Them-Yourself Picture Mysteries［M］. Jaffrey, NH: David R. Godine, 2003.

④ 尹贝."最近发展区"在第二语言习得研究中的影响与拓展［J］.淮南师范学院学报，2016（5）：59–63.

的性质决定了其意义可以引发多样化的解读。考虑到一个人的思维不能穷尽各种可能性，这时学生就需要借助伙伴或成年人的力量来完成任务。

因此，教师要做一个生活中的有心人，随时随地带着一种寻找资源的眼光来浏览日常报纸、杂志、网页上的多模态信息，将一些有趣的、可能对教学有用的资源及时保留下来，收录进自己的课程素材库，以便随时调用、更新、补充和分享。

二、高中英语议论文写作课程实施原则

在课程实施过程中，笔者遵循以下原则开展教学活动。

（一）课程内容有序递进，遵循认知规律

根据上篇所述，按照主张类型，议论文可分为事实型、价值型和政策型；按照论证方式，议论文可分为立论文和驳论文。因此，在实施高中英语议论文写作教学项目时，笔者按照事实型、价值型、政策型和驳论的顺序，设计了 15 个具体的写作教学案例。写作话题 1—4 为事实型议论文写作教学案例，写作话题 5—10 为价值型议论文写作教学案例，写作话题 11—14 为政策型议论文写作教学案例，写作话题 15 为驳论文写作教学案例。

在每个类型内部，写作话题安排也是层层递进、螺旋上升的。以价值型议论文的六个写作教学案例为例。写作话题 5 中，笔者通过择业述评这一话题，带领学生初次接触价值判断，并引出后果法和原则法，促进学生思考"好"和"坏"的价值标准。写作话题 6 中，笔者通过礼物选择这一话题，教会学生识别价值标准和选择对象之间的关系。写作话题 7 中，笔者借助校园生活中学生会换届的真实场景，让学生思考学生会主席的选拔标准，并依据价值标准进行人选推荐。写作话题 8 中，笔者鼓励学生将前几节课所学的有关价值型议论的相关知识应用于创业建议的新情境。写作话题 9 中，笔者借用教材课文 What Is a Great Book? 带领学生找出好书的判断标准，然后鼓励学生选取其中三条标准来推荐心目中的伟大著作。写作话题 10 中，笔者决定让学生自己尝试"价值标准"的写作，通过 Oliver Wants More 这篇课文，引出"Oliver 的行为是否属于'勇敢'范畴"这一议题，激发学生对"什么是勇气"这一价值标准进行思考，归纳出"勇气"的价值定义。这六个写作话题的安排，从价值判断到用给定标准进行选择，再到价值标准的写作，层层递进，为学生提供了充分的实践和内化的机会。

（二）概念学习基于情境，鼓励探究体验

《国务院办公厅关于新时代推进普通高中育人方式改革的指导意见》提出，教师要积极探索基于情境、问题导向的互动式、启发式、探究式、体验式等课堂教学。这15个教学案例构成的课程涉及许多有关议论文写作的概念知识教学，比如图尔敏论证模型的六要素（主张、根据、保证、支撑、限定、反驳条件）和三大议论修辞要素（理性诉求、人格诉求、情感诉求）。对于这些概念的教学，笔者采用了情境式学习和探究式学习方式。

情境学习理论认为，学习不仅仅是个体的意义建构过程，更是社会性、实践性的参与过程，知识具有情境性、实践性和协商性。[①] 而探究性学习指的是教师通过引发、促进、支持、指导学生的探究活动，来完成学科教学任务的一种教学思想、教学方法。[②] 两者的共同之处在于都以学生为中心，鼓励学生采取积极的学习策略，主动地获取和体验知识，而不是直接得到现成答案。在本课程中，笔者采用以上两种方式的结合来开展英语议论文写作中的概念教学。每一个写作话题都是一个贴近学生生活的独立情境，学生在教师的指导下自主开展知识概念建构，并思考概念之间的内在逻辑联系，从而形成对英语议论文写作全面、系统的理解。

以写作话题1为例，这是学生第一次接触图尔敏论证模型。为了让学生更好地理解该模型，笔者并没有直接给出相关概念，而是利用侦探漫画，创设了一个高中生比较感兴趣的探案情境。这幅漫画是关于玛丽房间被人闯入的案件，针对这幅漫画，笔者提出"闯入者进入玛丽房间是否为了图财？"这个问题并鼓励学生开展讨论。学生在分组讨论后给出判断，笔者随即引出主张的概念。接着笔者要求学生在漫画中找出证据证明自己的主张并说明原因，从而引出根据和保证的概念。通过这种探究式学习，学生以小组合作的形式发现问题、分析问题、解决问题，并在教师的指导下自主建构知识。此外，笔者并没有将模型的六要素在该案例中一次性教授完毕，而是在接下来的写作话题中，通过恰当的情境引出其他三个要素，并在后续的教学中不断通过探究性学习任务来巩固这些概念。

① 王薇. 指向问题解决能力发展的学习活动模型研究——基于情境学习理论的分析框架［J］. 教育学术月刊, 2020（6）: 88-95.
② 王升. 研究性学习的理论与实践［M］. 北京: 教育教学科学出版社, 2002.

再以写作话题 10 为例，这是一个价值标准写作话题，许多学生刚开始不知从何写起。为此，笔者首先将这一抽象话题进行解构。笔者认为，要写出"勇气"的定义，首先要明白这个概念的内涵，比如"勇气"是谁在怎样的状态下产生的怎样的品质，或这个概念的外延，比如"勇气"是否适用于"保镖为总统挡子弹"这样的情形，还有其对立概念，比如"鲁莽""厉害""胆子大""初生牛犊不怕虎"等。当然，笔者并没有将这些想法直接告诉学生，而是找到了若干个与"勇气"概念相关的事例，将抽象问题转化为具体情境，鼓励学生开展小组讨论，判断这些事例中的行为是否是有勇气的行为。最后，学生通过这些事例就能总结出"勇气"的定义。

因此，在写作教学中，如果涉及概念教学，教师自身需要先对写作话题进行深度解构，帮学生找到获取概念的最佳情境，从而把最重要、最核心的思维探究任务留给课堂上的学生，教师则充当探究性任务的设计者、组织者和支持者。同时，启发式提问也必不可少。学生在小组探究过程中常常会出现困难，这时教师要通过启发式提问有效地引导学生思考，而不是直接告诉学生答案。教师只有把思维的主动权还给学生，让学生的思维真正活跃起来，才能帮助学生切实领会概念的要义。

（三）活动联系现实生活，锻炼问题解决

议论文写作通常指向问题解决。前文提到，笔者在设计课程时创设了许多贴近学生生活的情境，其中很多都属于问题解决类。所谓问题式学习，是指通过联系生产生活中的现象设置问题情境，充分激发学生的学习动机和积极性，通过小组合作寻找解决真实世界问题的方案，让学生具备用批判的眼光去看待、分析问题的能力。[1]

笔者在课程实施的过程中，经常创设与写作话题相关的问题情境，或鼓励学生发现身边的问题，让他们意识到议论文写作在实际生活中的价值和意义。比如，在开展第三组政策型议论文教学时，笔者曾设想直接让学生分析一个社区中存在的问题或学生熟悉的社会问题，后来发现，如果一开始就让学生讨论全球变暖等影响人类生存的重大问题，部分阅读面不够

---

① Duch B J, Groh S E, Allen D E. The Power of Problem-based Learning: A Practical "How To" for Teaching Undergraduate Courses in Any Discipline［M］. Sterling, VA: Stylus Publishing, 2001.

广的学生可能完全无法参与讨论，也就是说，学生的课堂参与度取决于他们的知识储备。相反，笔者发现，学生对身边问题的感受度最高，也最容易全情投入并积极思考。因此，在设计写作话题 11（政策型议论文的第一个写作话题）时，笔者就鼓励学生寻找班级中存在的真实问题，期望他们从身边的问题入手，明白怎样的"政策"才是合理的。

在写作话题 11 的教学中，笔者首先让学生 4 人一组自行组队，讨论班级里存在的问题，并将意图探讨的问题交给笔者。学生们发现了许多真实问题，如"许多同学存在拖延症""自习课利用效率低""上课回答问题的积极性不够""许多同学存在考前焦虑问题"等。接下来，笔者引导学生设计调查问卷，并在班级内部进行发放、回收和统计。这样一来，学生们就能在课后自主开展调查，从而搜集大量的写作素材。在此过程中，学生们不仅发现，通过写作，他们有能力解决班级集体生活中真实存在的问题，从而收获了写作信心，还发现了政策型议论文写作的价值和意义。

（四）写作思维可视化，聚焦深度学习

许多教师认为，学生的思考过程就像一个"黑箱"。在课堂上，教师很难通过肉眼看出学生是否读懂或读懂了多少。大多数时候，教师只能通过设计各种问题链和产出活动来检测学生的学习进展。但对写作课来说，如果设计不当，教师的追问不一定能达到理想的效果。而如果通过产出活动，也就是等学生写出初稿后再指出其逻辑上的问题，教学又显得有些被动和滞后。因此，为了更好地帮助学生展现思考过程，教师需要设计合适的思维工具，即利用思维可视化的方法打开"黑箱"，促使学生在写作前展现其思维过程，方便教师及时介入。

思维可视化指的是通过图示技术呈现学习过程中的思考方法和思考路径。拉乔伊（Lajoie）认为，思维工具之所以有助于学习，其作用机理在于思维工具通过较为低层次的认知活动提供支持，以实现对认知负荷的分担，从而让学习者可以将认知资源留给更高层次的思维加工活动。[①]

在课程实施中，笔者特地设置了"搭建思维模型"和"撰写提纲"的环节。在这两个环节，教师带领学生利用图尔敏论证模型开展思考，并检验

---

① 赵国庆，杨宣洋，熊雅雯．论思维可视化工具教学应用的原则和着力点［J］．电化教育研究，2019（9）：59-66，82.

自己的思维是否符合逻辑。通过可视化的思维工具，教师可以在学生正式开始写作前及时指出其思维问题所在，促进学生反思自己的思考过程，从而为学生的思维加工提供更具体的元认知引导，帮助学生实现深度学习。

深度学习并不是指要把知识弄得很深奥，相反，深度学习是指学习者在理解学习的基础上，能够在众多思想间进行联系，并能够将已有的知识迁移到新的情境中，作出决策和解决问题的学习。[①] 思维可视化工具恰好能帮助学生找到众多思想之间的关联，并发现自己的思维误区，以便下次迁移到新情境时避免类似的错误。

因此，"思维可视化"是笔者课程实施的一个重要原则。借助图尔敏论证模型，笔者带领学生共同开展构思活动，将学生思维中可能出现的逻辑问题放在写前解决，通过合理的图示在板书中展现出来，以确保学生在充分理清自己的思路后再开始提笔写作。这也避免了教师在写作评价中的被动和滞后，提高了写作教学的效率。

（五）教学评一体化，倡导以终为始

《普通高中英语课程标准》指出，完整的教学活动包括教、学、评三个方面。在实际教学中，教师应处理好评价与教和学之间的关系，推动教、学、评一体化的实施。课堂评价活动应贯穿教学的全过程，为检测教学目标服务，以发现学生学习中的问题，并提供及时帮助和反馈，促进学生更有效地开展学习。教师要依据教学目标和评价标准有意识地监控学生在学习活动过程中的表现。在开展评价活动时，教师不仅要说明活动的内容和形式，还应给出活动要求和评价标准。评价标准也可以由师生共同协商确定，使学生在开展活动时有明确的目标，并能根据标准及时进行自评和互评。[②]

在本课程实施过程中，笔者在每节课上都会与学生共同生成评价清单，评价清单分为三个部分，从学生熟悉的"组织""内容"和"语言"展开。评价环节虽然出现在每个教学案例的最后，但事实上笔者会在教学过程中的每个环节和学生共同完成该评价清单。笔者通常会在黑板右侧专门划出一块区域，用于记录课堂评价清单的生成过程，也就是提示学生每

---

① 何玲，黎加厚. 促进学生深度学习 [J]. 现代教学，2005（5）：29-30.
② 中华人民共和国教育部. 普通高中英语课程标准（2017年版2020年修订）[M]. 北京：人民教育出版社，2020：77.

个环节需要注意的要点。这样一来,学生在每个步骤(比如"搭建思维模型")结束后就能知晓这个步骤的注意要点是什么,从而在写作时有意识地进行监控,同时可以将其作为初次写作和再次写作时自我修正和改进的依据,以终为始。

此外,评价清单若要达到应有的效果,必须表达清晰,具有可操作性。在以往的评价清单中,学生往往难以理解"中心明确""说理透彻""逻辑清晰"这类较为笼统的表述,教师往往也解释得含糊不清。究竟怎样的逻辑是清晰的逻辑,怎样的说理是透彻的说理呢?如今,借助图尔敏论证模型和三大修辞要素等英语议论文写作知识,评价清单的指向就能做到清晰明确。因此,教师在设计评价清单时,要特别注意各项条目的表述是否具有可操作性,换句话说,学生在对照这些条目之后是否能够清楚地知道可以从哪些方面去修改自己的习作。此外,教师可以提前进行自测,看自己能否根据评价清单中的条目给予学生切实可行的建议。

当然,在评价时,笔者不提倡完全按照评价清单上的顺序依次指出所有问题,而是应当根据每个学生的具体情况有选择性地进行重点反馈。学生不可能一次性解决内容、语言和结构上的所有问题,教师应当循序渐进地指出学生习作中的问题所在,不过多加重学生的认知负担。

最重要的是,学生互评永远不能代替教师评价,教师一定要在评价中发挥应有的作用。通过评价清单,学生或许能够看出习作在哪些方面存在问题,但具体应该怎样改,学生并不一定能明确把握,尤其是在语言方面,学生的修改很难超越自身的语言水平,这时就需要教师及时介入,给予切实可行的改进建议。

后记

　　本书的写作源于我多年来对高中生英语议论文写作教学的思考和探索。在高中英语新课程、新课标、新教材全面推进的大背景下，这样的思考变得更加具有必要性、方向性和前瞻性。语言是思维的体现，写作是对思维的检验，议论文写作尤其如此。

　　早在高中阶段，我就对议论文写作过程充满好奇，我的老师常常在评价习作时用到"中心不明确"或"逻辑不严密"这样的说法，但怎样的中心才是明确的，怎样的逻辑才是严密的呢？大学时，作为一名热爱英语表达的英语专业学生，我对英语演讲和辩论产生了兴趣，也参加过一些比赛，深刻体会到议论的力量。事实上，与他人沟通自己的观点既是一门艺术，也是一门科学。成为高中英语教师后，我发现许多学生存在和我当年一样的困惑，因此，我开始思考如何帮助学生构建严谨的思维，提高学生的英语议论文写作水平，并下定决心就此话题开展研究。

　　2016 年，我以"基于高阶思维能力培养的高中英语议论文写作课程设计的实践研究"为题，申请上海市青年教师课题。课题立项后，我明确了课题研究的路径，决定以高阶思维培养为切入点，借助图尔敏论证模型作为思维搭建框架，立足教材，结合学情，整体规划高中英语议论文写作项目布置的层次和程序，并制定详细的课程实施计划。经过一段时间的实践，我开发了一系列高中英语议论文写作课堂教学案例，分别围绕事实型、价值型和政策型议论文开展教学，积累了大量宝贵的实践经验。在课题结项和获奖后，我将成果整理出来，在之后几届学生中进行多轮教学实践，不断收集学生反馈，再进行调整和改进。

多年的实践证明，本套高中英语议论文写作课程设计操作性较强，在提高学生的思维能力方面效果较为显著。在研究过程中，我也阅读了大量文献，对英语议论文写作教学这一话题进行了持久、深入和系统性的思考，同时结合实践经验，得出了一些有价值的认识。为了与更多教师分享这些经验和认识，我决定将其整理出版，希望能为高中英语教师的议论文写作教学提供可借鉴的资源。

在课题研究以及本书编写过程中，我得到了许多人的关心和帮助。首先要感谢汤青老师，她的智慧引领解答了我诸多研究困惑，也正是她的鼓励坚定了我将实践成果撰写成书的决心。感谢区教研员杨瑞芳和何欣老师的悉心指导，使我的课题设计更加规范。感谢嘉定区教育学院"优青"培养计划和上海交通大学附属中学嘉定分校对我的栽培。还要感谢所有听过我公开课和研讨课的老师，你们的建议帮我找到了不足。最后，我由衷地感谢我在上海交通大学附属中学嘉定分校教过的所有学生，没有你们的积极参与和反馈，就没有这本书。特别鸣谢 2016 届的刘烨菲同学为本书提供了精美的图片。

我衷心期待这本书能够为高中英语教师提供一份有价值的参考，以及可借鉴的素材和资源。也希望读到这本书的学生朋友能够在写作中受益，成为优秀的沟通者和思考者。再次感谢所有帮助我的朋友们，是你们让这项研究充满意义。

尽管我在本书撰写过程中投入了大量心血，但仍不免存在一些不足之处，还请各位读者不吝指正。期待与更多英语教师一道为提高学生的英语学科核心素养而努力。

孙饴

2024 年 6 月

图书在版编目（CIP）数据

议论其实并不难：高中英语议论文写作教学研究 /
孙饴著. — 上海：上海教育出版社，2024.9. — ISBN
978-7-5720-2548-8

Ⅰ. G633.412

中国国家版本馆CIP数据核字第20248AT773号

责任编辑　周琛溢　茶文琼
封面设计　金一哲

议论其实并不难——高中英语议论文写作教学研究
孙　饴　著

出版发行　上海教育出版社有限公司
官　　网　www.seph.com.cn
地　　址　上海市闵行区号景路159弄C座
邮　　编　201101
印　　刷　上海龙腾印务有限公司
开　　本　700×1000　1/16　印张 20.75
字　　数　330 千字
版　　次　2024年9月第1版
印　　次　2024年9月第1次印刷
书　　号　ISBN 978-7-5720-2548-8/G·2244
定　　价　78.00 元

如发现质量问题，读者可向本社调换　电话：021-64373213